# Plato *or* Paul?

# Plato *or* Paul?

## The Origins of Western Homophobia

THEODORE W. JENNINGS, JR.

THE
PILGRIM
PRESS
Cleveland

The Pilgrim Press
700 Prospect Avenue
Cleveland, Ohio 44115-1100
thepilgrimpress.com

13  12  11  10      5  4  3  2

**Library of Congress Cataloging-in-Publication Data**
Jennings, Theodore W.
    Plato or Paul? : the origins of Western homophobia /
Theodore W. Jennings, Jr.
       p.  cm.
    Includes bibliographical references.
    ISBN 978-0-8298-1855-0 (alk. paper)
    1. Homophobia – History – to 1500.   I. Title.
Civilization, Classical.
261.8'3537660938 – dc22

                                    2009002891

Printed in the United States of America on acid-free paper

# Contents

## Part Three
## THE CASE OF PAUL

## Part Four
## CHRISTIAN HOMOPHOBIA

# Preface

The chief obstacle to overcoming homophobia in Western culture has been the alliance between homophobic discourse and the predominant forms of Christianity. So strong has this alliance become that many seem to suppose that Christian identity stands or falls with a commitment to homophobic discourse. Especially in the United States, politicians have even used traditional Christianity's alliance with homophobia to derail political discourse about war and peace, the economy, or health care by invoking the specter of a gay agenda, a gay lifestyle, or same-sex unions.

In previous work I have demonstrated that biblical narratives from both the Hebrew Bible and the Gospels accept and affirm same-sex relationships of many kinds. It is not that we are homophobic because of the Bible; rather, we read the Bible as we do because we are influenced by homophobia. But if the Bible is not the true source of Western and Christian homophobia, what then is the source? That is the question to which I turn in this study.

This project began as a seminar on the origins of homophobia that my then colleague at Chicago Theological Seminary, Tat Siong Benny Liew, and I taught in 1999. Since then, I have held this seminar twice more. It continues to evolve in response to what was discovered in earlier seminars and in relation to the interests and insights of the students.

Transforming some of this seminar work into a book was made possible by a grant from the Gill Foundation to the LGBTQ Religious Studies Center at the Chicago Theological Seminary for which I served as Research Fellow in the Fall of 2007. In addition to the students in the seminars and to Brian Carmany, who did some investigation of Greek sources, I must above all thank Adam Kotsko, whose work as research assistant on this and other projects has been indispensable. The grant from the Gill Foundation enabled him to organize my reading and research notes, to track down various sources and texts, to work on the bibliography and the index, all while being an extraordinarily productive scholar in his own right.

# Plato *or* Paul?

# Introduction

We are, I believe, confronted with two seemingly irreconcilable facts. The first is that Christianity has been the conveyer and enforcer of homophobia both within Western Christianity and thence into Western culture generally. On the other hand, careful work on biblical sources has demonstrated that there is very little biblical support for a rejection or condemnation of same-sex love and that indeed it may be that homoeroticism is an important element in the narrative texts of Judaism and of Christianity. But if the basic texts of these "religions of the Book" demonstrate for the most part an acceptance of, and even appreciation for, homoeroticism, then how does it happen that the religious traditions derivative from these texts and claiming them as authorization for their perspectives and practices come to propagate homophobia (and erotophobia generally)? The thesis that this book explores is that the origin of Western homophobia lies not in the biblical traditions of Judaism and Christianity but instead in the Greek and Hellenistic sources often assumed to have been accepting of same-sex eroticism.

Because this thesis runs against the grain of common opinion, it is necessary to provide some initial clarification. I first indicate how I use the notion of homophobia and illustrate this through two representative samples: official statements of the Vatican and opinions of the United States Supreme Court. I then indicate my reasons for saying that biblical traditions in and of themselves are not the basis for homophobia in the West. I then look ahead at the direction of this study.

## Homophobia as a Social Construct

For the purposes of this study I am concerned with homophobia as a characteristic of a social or cultural rejection and stigmatization of same-sex sexual practices.

1

Negatively this means that I will not be seeking to characterize psychological states or personal attitudes. Still less will I be seeking to maintain that homophobia is a pathology produced by a repressed "homosexual desire" on the part of individuals. That is, I am concerned with a social rather than a personal or psychological construct.

The objects of such a social construct, moreover, are sexual practices and associated characteristics of those who are thought to engage in such practices. The point of this is not to suppose that those who fall under the censure of cultural homophobia are, in modern terms, homosexuals. Thus, for example, in antiquity, including Christian antiquity, it was assumed that males would be tempted to desire sexual intimacy with at least certain other males (typically young and conventionally beautiful ones) not because they were "homosexual" but because they were male. What was problematic, if it was problematic, was not the desire (regarded as "normal") but the practice.

This starting point helps to avoid certain confusions that impede clarity in contemporary discussions of homophobia. There are some, for example, who may claim not to be homophobic because (a) they have no same-sex sexual desire and so are not "repressed" homosexuals or (b) they have nothing against homosexuals personally, but simply reject certain forms of sexual practice (love the sinner, hate the sin). Whatever the merits of these claims, they have nothing to do with the current study.

But if the object of the study is a social or cultural rejection and stigmatization of same-sex sexual practices, how are we to get at that social reality? This study limits itself to texts that enjoy a certain prestige within a social or cultural reality. Thus I will be concerned with texts that have come to have a certain influence on the development of Western homophobia or that demonstrate the influence of previous texts on that formation. Accordingly I will be concerned with certain texts of Plato and with texts that show the influence of those texts. The same will be true with respect to biblical texts. I am interested in discovering through later texts how these texts come to shape or to legitimate Western homophobia.

## Modern Homophobic Discourse

Although the erosion of the hegemony of official and social homo-phobic discourse characterizes contemporary public discourse, it is nonetheless the case that homophobia remains a widely influential cultural perspective. In order to get a sense of the character of this discourse today, it may be helpful to examine two sets of widely influential texts originating in "church" and "state" that articulate a homophobic perspective in ways that are, and are intended to be, deter-minative for the views of the social realities on behalf of which they speak.

In selecting texts that have a clearly Christian ambience one could choose the official pronouncements of nearly any major Christian group. Here I choose to look at documents from the Sacred Congrega-tion for the Doctrine of the Faith, which represents the official views of the Roman Catholic Church, by far the largest group of Christians on earth. In order to get at the homophobic discourse of a putatively "sec-ular" type I will turn to two influential decisions of the United States Supreme Court. It would of course be possible to turn to other polit-ically influential texts, for example, legislation that argues for what has been called "the Defense of Marriage," but these texts are typically derivative of the arguments advanced in the Supreme Court decisions and the Vatican documents. I thus focus on texts that shape opinions and attitudes in the public sphere rather than on the sometimes far more virulent examples of homophobic discourse articulated by the religious and political right wing.

### The Vatican

Although the most extended treatment of our issue in official Vatican documents is *On the Pastoral Care of Homosexual Persons* of 1986, it is helpful to see this in relation to an earlier statement from 1975, the *Declaration on Certain Questions Concerning Sexual Ethics*. This latter document addresses the cultural ferment occasioned by what has come to be called the "sexual revolution," which challenged reli-gious and cultural restrictions of sexual practice to the monogamous heterosexual conjugal pair.

The document makes a rather startling concession to modern sensibilities when it maintains that sexuality is fundamental to personhood. Any reader of the history of Western or specifically Christian thought would be struck by how far removed this view is from that of the philosophical views of the Greco-Roman world or the views of the theologians of the early church. This concession to modernity is, however, in tension with the insistence that both natural and revealed law are in harmony in insisting that sexuality aims and must aim at procreation. This claim has so often been repeated in Catholic tradition since Thomas Aquinas that it may seem to be the self-evident view of the Christian tradition as such. Yet as we shall see, this view has its origin not in the "revealed law" (that is, the Bible) but in the musings about nature of the Greek and Hellenistic philosophical world.

The notion that the natural law dictates that sex aim at procreation is the basis offered by this document for the warnings against the "unbridled exaltation of sex" expressed in fornication, homosexuality, and masturbation. The context of the sexual revolution helps explain the long treatment of "fornication" (especially since the modern proliferation of fornication was enabled by the dissemination of birth control). The brief mention of homosexuality seems to be motivated on the one hand by its association with sexual excess (fornication) and by its nonprocreative character. It is followed by a long and (from a contemporary perspective) exceedingly quaint discussion of the evils of masturbation, perhaps seen as the besetting sin of the celibate.

The subsequent document *On the Pastoral Care of Homosexual Persons* is the first Vatican document that is solely directed to the question of homosexuality. Its principal author was Cardinal Joseph Ratzinger, now Pope Benedict XVI.

This document presupposes the cohesion of "natural" and "revealed" law with respect to the condemnation of same-sex sexual practice, but it goes further in that it not only condemns these practices but also asserts that same-sex desire itself (attributed to "homosexual persons") is "a more or less strong tendency ordered toward an intrinsic moral evil [the practices]; and thus the inclination itself must be seen as an objective disorder." This statement may itself be regarded as a sort of backhanded concession to modernity in that it uses the category of "the homosexual" to identify those who feel a strong sexual attraction to persons of the same sex. In the discourses of antiquity, including Christian discourses, the attraction of males to other males was regarded as the common property of all males, rather than a particular (and particularly defective) class of males.

Unlike the previously cited document, this one goes to some lengths to buttress its argument concerning revelation with far greater attention to the specific biblical texts taken to be probative for the condemnation of homosexual practice (and by extension, homosexual persons). The creation stories of Genesis 1 and 2 are taken to establish the heteronormative and procreative perspective of Scripture generally, a perspective then buttressed by a citation of the proof texts usually cited within a homophobic perspective (no. 6).

First in line is the story of the punishment of Sodom, in which, the document claims, "there can be no doubt of the moral judgment made there against homosexual relations." As we shall see, it will take many centuries before this tale of attempted mob violation of vulnerable strangers comes to have any association with what the document calls homosexual relations. We have also the citation of sentences from Leviticus (18:22; 20:13), which do not enter into Christian homophobic discourse until the later Middle Ages. From the New Testament we have the citation of 1 Corinthians 6:9, which is said to contain the same doctrine as Leviticus (even though nineteenth-century translations of this text had placed the onus on the Vatican's bête noir of masturbation). The trump text is Paul's reference in Romans 1:18–32, especially 1:26–27, followed by 1 Timothy 1:10. None of this the writers of the document substantiate by attentive exegesis of the individual passages. Instead, the document contextualizes these standard homophobic proof texts in terms of its view that sex is for procreation (no. 7).

I should not leave the reading of this document without noticing one of its most alarming features. It deplores "crimes committed against homosexual persons" and then goes on to suggest that what causes this deplorable violence against homosexual persons is the insistence of these same persons that they should not be discriminated against (no. 9). That is, homosexuals becoming open about their inclinations themselves cause the violence against them! It is one of the most egregious examples of "blaming the victim" ever made in a public and official religious document.

This document is not intended for the private use of practicing Christians. It is meant as a public and political document that will serve as the basis for the leaders of the church entering into political discourse in order to "defend and promote family life" (nos. 8, 17). This political aim is even more explicit in the document *Considerations Regarding Proposals to Give Legal Recognition to Unions between Homosexual Persons* (2003), which applies the considerations of the previous two documents to the specific question of same-sex marriage or civil unions. Here also there is an explicit attempt to link this question to the Vatican teachings regarding abortion and birth control, which Catholic politicians are to oppose or resist, particularly any legislation opening society to these "evils." Failing that, they are to restrict permissive laws as far as possible.

While the document makes reference to the oft-cited Pauline texts (Romans 1:24–27; 1 Corinthians 6:10; 1 Timothy 1:10), it places greater stress on the Genesis creation accounts in order to connect more directly to its intention to offer a case that is grounded in natural law (thus Thomas Aquinas is cited twice here). Four considerations seem to be of greatest importance. The first is that same-sex unions lack the complementarity of male and female. The second is that they do not have procreation as an end, and procreation is deemed necessary for the "survival of the human race" (no. 7) and "the succession of generations" (no. 8). We shall see in the next two chapters that these perspectives derive from Platonic and Hellenistic sources.

A further concern has to do with the deleterious effects upon society (and the young) if same-sex unions were to make same-sex relations seem acceptable. Thus it would mean "approval of deviant behavior, with the consequence of making it a model in present-day society" (no. 11). Thus it is in the social interest to make same-sex relationships as hidden as possible. (We will encounter this trope in Plato.)

Finally, the document asserts that allowing same-sex couples to adopt children would "mean doing violence to these children" since it would deprive them of either a mother or a father. (This is a remarkable position, since it ignores the actual violence done to children in heterosexual homes and would seem to entail similarly condemning single-parent households.)

The statement of the Vatican seems to have in view the "crisis" occasioned by the European Union's move toward the recognition of same-sex partnerships. The Vatican position has not been very effective in Europe, where the recognition of same-sex unions has proceeded apace. But the Vatican has developed arguments that have proven effective in the political climate of the United States.

## The U.S. Supreme Court

So-called anti-sodomy laws were a regular feature of the landscape from the time of the British colonies until 1962, when such a statute was removed from the legal code of Illinois. Other states slowly followed suit, but in 1986, when the constitutionality of such laws was officially challenged before the Supreme Court, same-sex "sodomy" was still criminalized in the majority of states. The issue came before the Court in the case known as *Bower v. Hardwick*, where Bower was the prosecuting attorney in Georgia who charged Hardwick with a violation of the law, an alleged violation occurring in his home (in private) with a consenting adult male partner. On this occasion, the Court upheld the anti-sodomy statute. Seven years later the Court returned to the question in *Lawrence v. Texas*, this time to declare such statutes to be unconstitutional. The official homophobic discourse is to be found in the majority opinions of the first case and the minority (dissenting) opinions of the second case.

The majority opinion of Justice White in *Bower v. Hardwick* makes reference both to the law of nature (and procreation as the aim of sexual practice) and to the writings of Paul. In addition, we are told that the overthrow of laws against consensual sodomy would mean the overthrow of laws against adultery and incest. (The connection to incest is especially interesting.)

The concurring opinion of Chief Justice Warren Burger fully elaborates the bases for official homophobia in its reference to the Theodosian and Justinian codes (legal pronouncements of Christian emperors of the Roman Empire) as the evidence that these acts have been universally proscribed. We also have here reference to the Sodom story, Leviticus, Romans, and indeed Thomas Aquinas (on natural law) to strengthen the case for the statute's legitimacy as representing the universal Western tradition of millennia.

By the time of the opinion of *Lawrence v. Texas* only nine states still had laws proscribing same-sex (male) sodomy. The majority opinion notes that laws proscribing same-sex relations had their origin in the notion that sex is for procreation. To abandon that presupposition is to abandon the basis for the prohibition.

According to the dissenting opinion of Justice Antonin Scalia, the overturning of this law would make it impossible to enforce state laws "against bigamy, same-sex marriage, adult incest, prostitution, masturbation, adultery, fornication, bestiality, and obscenity." Scalia's comments may be the spark that ignites the movement to ban same-sex marriage. No such movement, however, has been detected to criminalize masturbation! The linkage to bestiality was especially popular among certain political and religious spokesmen outraged over the Court's decision. Incest seems to remain a popular association with (male) homosexual practice. (Note that the laws in question and the opinions articulated here do not suggest the criminalizing of female same-sex practices.)

The dissenting opinion of Justice Scalia has undoubtedly exercised considerable influence among those determined to turn back the tide of the acceptance of same-sex sexual practices. However, it has left to one side the references to Christian tradition and biblical authority. These arguments henceforth would become the property of more directly religious forms of homophobic discourse.

## The Bible and Modern Homophobia

The recent examples of homophobic discourse that we have examined rely upon the notion that the Bible is a primary source for and legitimation of both specifically Christian and also presumably secular legal stigmatization (as sin or as crime) of certain same-sex practices.

This is a view shared not only by those who subscribe to the stigmatization of these acts but also by those who vigorously oppose that stigmatization. Counter-homophobic arguments often agree that the Bible or biblical traditions are the source of homophobia and argue for a nonbiblical, prebiblical, or postbiblical approach to the questions regarding the approval of same-sex love and its associated practices. Thus for example, Eva Cantarella, in her impressive study of attitudes toward same-sex love in antiquity,[1] concludes by claiming that the idea that same-sex sexual practices were against nature was a distinctively Christian idea: "Christianity had introduced a new way of looking at sex, which came from the Hebrew tradition. It had introduced the principle of 'naturalness,' which was exclusive to heterosexual intercourse" (221). Thus the condemnation of male same-sex practices and the imposition of the death penalty for these on the part of late Christian emperors are regarded by Cantarella as simply an imposition of Christian morality (209). Similarly William Armstrong Percy, in his study of ancient Greek attitudes toward same-sex love in the form of pederasty,[2] concludes that the general acceptance and celebration of same-sex love in the ancient world was ended by Christianity: "Only with the triumph of Christianity, which produced the animadversions of St. Paul and repromulgated the prohibitions of Mosaic law against homosexuality, did the tradition of a thousand years finally give way" (192). These examples could easily be multiplied. They bespeak a widespread impression that governs the work of counter-homophobic writers as much as those who approvingly articulate an imagined homophobic tradition.

But are biblical texts really the source of Western or even Christian homophobia? There is growing reason to doubt this. The Supreme Court documents to which we have referred, for example, demonstrate a growing awareness that the story of Sodom, so long taken to license a condemnation of same-sex sexual practices is, in fact, not germane to that discussion at all. How does such a change happen? It happens through the sort of careful attention to biblical texts that characterized the work, for example, of Derrick Sherwin Bailey in 1955.[3] Indeed this work was cited in one homophobic opinion (Burger in *Bower v. Hardwick*) and in a subsequent opinion (Kennedy for the majority in

*Lawrence v. Texas*) declaring such an appropriation false. What happened in the meantime? Perhaps someone on the Court actually read the book! Even in this case there was a considerable time lag between the historical work of Bailey and the taking effect of that work. And of course, there are still to be found people who have not been affected by historical work of this kind.

A considerable body of work over the last fifty years has greatly reduced the amount of biblical material that can be regarded as in any way licensing homophobia. The work of Mark Jordan, for example, has shown the medieval roots of the Christian interpretation of the Sodom story as licensing homophobia.[4] The use of Leviticus in this regard appears to be even more recent.

On the other hand, there has also been a growing body of literature that suggests that biblical traditions, far from being hostile to same-sex love, actually seem to accept and even value same-sex relationships that may be sexually expressed. There is by now a rather long tradition of reading the story of David and Jonathan (and Saul) in this way.[5] I have attempted to show in my study of the Hebrew Bible that there is a great deal more in this literature than meets the homophobic or hetero-normative eye.[6] That is, there is a remarkable amount of narrative material in the literature of ancient Israel that takes same-sex attraction, same-sex relationships, and same-sex eroticism for granted and even makes it exemplary of the proper relation between the deity and "his" people. Thus if there are two verses of Leviticus that seem to condemn same-sex erotic practices, there are a great many narratives, including narratives produced in the prophetic literature, that take same-sex erotic relationships for granted.

Nor does this end with the Hebrew Bible. I have also shown that New Testament narratives (the Gospels) may be read as accepting same-sex relationships and even as suggesting that Jesus himself was engaged in such a relationship.[7] And I have sought to show that this reading, for example, of the Gospel of Matthew or John helps to make sense of the elements of the narrative as a whole. In neither the case of the Hebrew Bible nor that of the Christian Gospels do I claim that my reading is the only possible one, but rather that it is a reading that takes the narratives seriously and pays close attention to the texts in question. In the case of *Jesus and the Man He Loved*, I have also suggested that reading strategies in addition to the historical critical approach I have adopted also view that relationship in similar terms.[8]

But if Western Christian homophobia cannot be said to have originated in these texts, where does it come from? One possibility often mentioned is that it comes from Paul. In the current study I will consider this possibility. In that sense this work continues my work on biblical texts. But I will be arguing that the often cited texts from Paul do not by any means require a homophobic reading or appropriation. That is, I will suggest that a homophobic reading or appropriation must be supplied from elsewhere for it to become the "obvious" or "common sense" meaning of these texts. In this case, like the story of Sodom or the sentences of Leviticus, there must be a prior commitment to homophobia for the texts to be appropriated for homophobic purposes in subsequent Christian and Western discourse. Put differently, what Paul says doesn't cause Western or Christian homophobia; instead, (cultural) homophobia causes the texts of Paul to be read in a homophobic way. I am not imputing homophobia as a personal failing to those who read the texts in this way. I am again dealing with homophobia as a cultural or social reality, not a personal pathology. This is all the more evident here, since even those who are personally and professionally opposed to homophobia may nevertheless read biblical texts "homophobically," that is, read them through the lens of a preexisting tradition of homophobic reading or appropriation. This may even be true of scholars whose anti-homophobic credentials are impeccable, such as Robin Scroggs[9] or Bernadette Brooten.[10]

Of course, the point of this exercise is not to absolve biblical texts of any and all responsibility for the emergence of homophobia, but rather to ask how it came to make sense to appropriate just these texts in just this way. How does a tradition of interpretation come into being such that it could ultimately be made to seem that these texts produce the homophobia by which they are appropriated?

For this question to make sense, there must be some preexisting homophobic perspective that is itself the base for the homophobic reading of these texts. It is precisely this that the present study seeks to clarify.

In the commonsense reading of the history of this issue, it is supposed that Greek and Hellenistic culture were favorable to same-sex love, but that biblical perspectives managed somehow to overwhelm this openness to and celebration of same-sex love and replace it with its own uniquely homophobic perspective. What I will therefore be seeking to show is that it is Greek and Hellenistic intellectual culture that is itself the source of the homophobia that then appropriates biblical texts into its own preexisting and certainly nonbiblical form of homophobia.

## The Direction of the Study

The effective origin of Western homophobia, I maintain, is to be found in the very influential texts of Plato. This is no doubt ironic, for the texts of Plato have been regularly mined for discourses that affirm same-sex love, especially that between males. But at the end of his writing career, Plato argues in the *Laws* for the prohibition of same-sex love in terms that will come to shape all subsequent homophobic discourse. It is here that we will find it characterized as "against nature," that we will read that it is destructive of all virtue, that it is utterly shameful, that it should be made to seem so abominable that its practitioners should be unable to acknowledge its existence and should even be prepared to commit suicide rather than have anyone know that they are guilty of such an unspeakable shame. To be sure this is a side of Plato's work that is often ignored, at least in modern homophilic discourse. Thus it will be necessary to spend some time with texts of Plato to see how what may have been a rather accepting approach to same-sex love comes, through a series of texts, to be transformed into a "homophobic project" that will take many centuries to put into effect. We will also have to inquire whether Plato is completely alone in this view or if there are other, less radical but suggestive texts that may help us to situate Platonic homophobia within the context of fourth-century Greek perspectives and attitudes.

The next chapter will take up this question in terms of the effects of this perspective on first-century Hellenistic texts. I will look at three kinds of texts to ask how they carry forward this homophobic project:

the dialogues on love beginning with Plutarch, the Stoic philosophy of Musonius Rufus, and Hellenistic Judaism, especially in the work of Philo. In each case I ask how elements that surface in the texts of Plato are developed and appropriated in discourses that stigmatize at least some same-sex relationships and practices.

This will then serve as necessary background to take up the question of how Paul's texts, or rather those fragments of Paul's texts that are later used for homophobic purposes, may be understood. I seek to show that the homophobic reading of the texts is by no means required by the texts themselves and that other readings are not only possible but may even be far more plausible ways of getting at what the texts are saying. Moreover, it will be possible to see that Paul's texts are regularly incompatible with the homophobic perspectives of the Hellenistic intellectual culture (Jewish or pagan) that we have studied.

This will then lead to an investigation of how emergent forms of Christianity come to be influenced by certain homophobic perspectives. How does emergent Christianity come to have homophobia engrafted upon it? In the study of second-century texts it will become clear that this happens not by means of a citation of the Bible as such, but by way of the appropriation of Hellenistic perspectives that are themselves influenced by Plato. This will perhaps be most evident in the case of Clement. But I will also suggest that the second-century emergence of the cult of Antinous and the invidious comparison between this cult and Christianity provided added impetus to the appropriation of Hellenistic homophobic attitudes on the part of early Christian apologists, that is to say, those Christian intellectuals who sought to show that Christianity was not inferior to the intellectual traditions of the Hellenistic world.

The homophobic discourse of Christian writers at the end of the second century is in a very nascent form, still lacking many of the elements that will come to be associated with this tradition. In the following chapter I will attend to the ways in which certain biblical texts (whether concerning Sodom or derived from Paul) come to be integrated into this Hellenistic homophobia. As I will discuss, Philo suggested some possibility of reading Sodom homophobically in accordance with Hellenistic homophobia. The question is how, in the course of the next few centuries, that reading comes to have a place in Christian interpretation. How does Paul, especially the Paul of Romans, come gradually to be assimilated to the same Hellenistic and Platonic homophobic perspective?

Even at the end of this study, which will take us to the verge of what will be called the European "Dark Ages," it will still be evident that Christian homophobia is not yet at all like what will be considered self-evident as the typical Christian perspective by the end of the Middle Ages and even on into the modern period. Homophobia, far from being a natural concomitant of Christian perspectives, actually takes a very long time to be engrafted onto the body of Christianity. It is in this sense a "foreign element" that can therefore be removed without in any way affecting what is important about early or patristic Christianity.

Yet Christianity has been and is still the bearer and enforcer of homophobia in more recent Western history. It has not always been so, and thus need not still be so. Christian homophobia had a beginning; it must have an end.

# Part One

# Plato and Greece

I N CHAPTER I we look at several texts of Plato that provide a remarkable test case of the emergence of homophobia within the heart of
homophilic discourse. That is, the very texts that are typically cited
to affirm same-sex love are the ones in which we can also detect the
emergence of what will become a powerfully influential homophobic
discourse. After we examine these texts in some detail, we will seek
to locate them in relation to other texts from ancient Greece that may
also give us some insight into the plausibility of an emergent homophobia (Timarchus, Xenophon) and the social context that may also
contribute to the plausibility of this discourse.

In the reading of these texts from Plato, we may initially distinguish three sorts of attitudes toward same-sex love. First there are
those dialogues that seem to take same-sex love for granted and to
give to Socrates the role of something of an expert in and practitioner
of same-sex desire and love. These texts include *Charmides* and *Lysis*
and also many of the speeches in the *Symposium*. Then there are
those texts that, although taking for granted that men will fall in
love with youthful male beauty, will more or less strongly discourage
the physical or bodily (or as we might say, the sexual) expression of
this attraction and desire and instead deflect or sublimate this desire
toward a desire for some more abstract or universal good (or beauty).
The texts that come in for discussion here are the speech attributed
by Socrates in the *Symposium* to the woman sage Diotima and the
speeches on this subject attributed to Socrates in the *Phaedrus*. Finally
we will look at a text, the *Laws*, that offers a program for actually cre-
ating and disseminating homophobia. It is a program that seeks to
inculcate a loathing of same-sex sexuality and, in a certain way, to

15

criminalize that "love." It is this last text that will serve as a sort of template or program for the emergence of homophobic discourse in "pagan" philosophy and some first-century Hellenistic Jewish circles, which will ultimately be grafted into the body of emergent Alexandrian Christianity.

# – 1 –

# Affirmation

## Charmides

At the beginning of the *Charmides*, Plato has Socrates sharing the interest of the other men of his cohort in the beauty of youths. This beauty is displayed to the gaze of the men in the gymnasium, where men exercise in the nude ("gymnasium" itself meaning something like nude-itorium or place of nudity). Indeed the gymnasium will be regarded as the institution most responsible for the spread of pederasty into what will become the Hellenistic world. On this occasion Socrates says that he also is attracted to the beauty of the remarkable youth whose name is given to the dialogue itself. The proof of Socrates' attraction is an involuntary erection, a tribute to the boy's beauty, affirmed by the admiring stares of those around and of Socrates himself: "I was quite astonished at his beauty" (154c). We are then invited to imagine how much more beautiful is the naked body of the boy (154d). Then, in the rather demure translation of Jowett: "I caught sight of the inwards of his garment, and took the flame. Then I could no longer contain myself... for I felt I had been overcome by a sort of wild beast appetite" (155d–e). Allan Bloom notes concerning the crucial passage: "Plato gives us a Socrates who is ... a gossip and a lover, who even tells us — a unique admission among philosophers — of an erection he had when he glanced down into a boy's cloak."[1] We might, however, recall that it is the vagaries of the erection (or not) of the male member that will serve as the privileged symptom of the division of will from body that in turn serves to underwrite the doctrine of the fall for Augustine and medieval Augustinians.[2] The difference is that what is at stake here is an erection occasioned by the beauty of and sexual desire for another male. For centuries to come, even among Christian preachers and theologians it was taken to be self-evident that beautiful youths

17

were a source of enormous sexual attraction (and temptation) for all males.[3]

Now we might also pause here to remark that Socrates is regularly portrayed as a seducer of youths in the commonly understood pederastic sense. Indeed this is included in the charges brought against Socrates for which he will be sentenced to drink the lethal hemlock. In the dialogues Socrates will be depicted as an expert in pederasty and as one driven by the love of young (male) beauty who eagerly abets the love affairs of those similarly inclined. Some texts, like the comedy *Clouds*, written by Socrates' older colleague Aristophanes, will depict Socrates as giving rein to sexual desire and practice within this pederastic context. Others will insist that Socrates simply uses this same-sex desire as a springboard for purposes of intellectual companionship. Whether the latter is to be understood as an attempt on the part of his young friends to cover up Socrates' true character or the characterization of Aristophanes in an attempt to "smear" Socrates may be undecidable. Whatever Socrates' sexual practice in this regard, the participation in and support for same-sex desire is regularly attested in the texts.

## Lysis

The *Lysis* is one of the most charming Socratic dialogues that Plato has given us, and it is one of those dialogues (like *Charmides*) that uncovers ignorance about matters of common "knowledge." That is, it begins with the question of "what is X?" and proceeds to consider a number of conventional answers to that question, each of which in turn is exposed as inadequate. The result is not the revelation of the true definition but the disclosure of an achieved lucidity characterized by ignorance — knowing that one does not know. Since the form and direction of these dialogues correspond to Socrates' self-description in the *Apology*, they are most properly referred to as "Socratic," whereas the dialogues that aim at the discovery of some positive truth to be taught are more properly "Platonic," whether or not Socrates plays a major role. This is a distinction not always easy to apply.

The subject matter of *Lysis* is friendship and particularly a friendship structured by pederastic conventions, that is, the desire for a beautiful younger male (postpubescent but perhaps still "adolescent") on the part of an older but often still young adult male. The initial setting is the gymnasium and in particular the "locker room" or (un)dressing room [*apodyterium*] where friends are gathered to admire the beauty on display there. The presenting issue is the infatuation of one of Socrates' younger friends (Hippothales) with a boy of presumably astonishing physical beauty (Lysis), whose good looks are augmented by a delightful personality and good character. Hippothales' seduction of the boy is for various reasons not going as well as he would like, and Socrates offers to show him how best to seduce the boy. The proper seductive technique (Socrates passes for an expert in these matters) is not that of piling on stammering praise but rather a form of interrogation as instruction.

Socrates wants to know "who is the beautiful male one" [trans. by Jowett as "favorite among you"[4]] (204b). He further claims: "the gods have given me the power of understanding the [male] lover and the [male] beloved" (204c). Socrates offers to give Hippothales advice on "what a lover ought to say about his love, either to the youth himself, or to others." To this Hippothales agrees: Socrates explains his seductive strategy as follows: "This is the reason why the wiser lover does not praise his beloved until he has won him, because he is afraid of accidents. There is also another danger; the fair, when anyone praises or magnifies them, are filled with the spirit of pride and vainglory" (206a). Hippothales asks: "Will you tell me by what words or actions I may become endeared to my love?" (206c).

Socrates accordingly enters into discussion with the willing Lysis, who at one point will be so engaged by Socrates that he takes to whispering in Socrates' ear [211a], to the chagrin of the onlookers who want to know what is going on. The form of the discussion is that of proposing views of friendship to which Lysis agrees and then showing them to be fatally flawed. Socrates then says to Hippothales, who has retreated to the background, "This is the way, Hippothales, in which you should talk to your beloved, humbling and lowering him, and not as you do, puffing him up and spoiling him" (210e).

The chief perplexity concerning friendship in this dialogue has to do with the conflation of the lover/beloved structure with the friendship structure. The difficulty is that the language for love, whether the love of friendship or erotic love, is grammatically structured in a unidirectional and hierarchical way. One of the pair is the lover (or friend); the other is the beloved (or befriended). This is further complicated by the manifold character of desire that has a role in each of these ways of naming a relationship. If pederasty is the love of a lover (*erastes*) for a beloved (*eromenos*), then we may say that pederasty is an effect of grammar. The grammar does not allow for both to be the lover of the other. The central conundrum is thus expressed by Socrates: "Then which is the friend of which? Is the lover the friend of the beloved, whether he be loved in return, or hated; or is the beloved the friend; or is there no friendship at all on either side, unless they both love one another?" Lysis's friend Menexenus replies: "There would seem to be none [no friend] at all" (212c). After exploring the difficulties of mutuality Socrates maintains: "But if the lover is not a friend, nor the beloved a friend, nor both together, what are we to say? Whom are we to call friends to one another?" (213c).

While the dialogue explores a number of perplexities concerning the use of the language about love and friendship, it is the difficulty of understanding the relation between love (or desire) and friendship, of love as friendship and friendship as love, that seems to be central to the discussion. The dilemmas (or aporias, we might say) seem unresolvable. Thus Socrates concludes, as he, Lysis, and Hippothales go off together arm in arm, "Here is a jest; you two boys, and I, an old boy, who would fain be one of you, imagine ourselves to be friends, and we have not as yet been able to discover what is a friend!" (223b).

The dialogue thus takes the love of males for one another, a love rooted in physical or bodily desire, as the unquestioned presupposition for a discussion of friendship as a sort of ultimate value. Rather than casting aspersions on such love, it seeks, unsuccessfully, to give an account of it. Yet in the end it is the account, not the relationship, that seems impossible. The impossibility of giving an account of something of great value does not by any means serve to dismiss the value of that which is the subject of discussion (whether it be friendship or courage or justice, for example) but rather it encourages a wonder about what we might term the mystery of the commonplace, that is, the way that which matters most to us (necessarily?) eludes our comprehension.

## *Symposium*

The notion that erotic love and the love of friendship between males is of consummate value, at least for the elites of Athens, is also the background and the theme of another dialogue: the *Symposium*. This dialogue has a quite different form in that it consists of a series of set speeches at a drinking party on the theme of love, in particular the love of (male) lovers for their (male) beloveds. There is little of the interrogation that characterized the *Lysis*.

The scene is a dinner party for friends, many of whom are nursing hangovers from the previous night's celebration of the triumph of their host Agathon at winning the prize for the best drama. The medical doctor among them, Eryximachus, proposes that instead of overdrinking they engage in a competition of making speeches in praise of love. This will of course be for the most part the praise of same-sex love and of the particular style of pederastic love.

The first speech is that of Phaedrus, who affirms that Eros is a god, and indeed the mightiest and first among the gods (178b). He then turns to extol the effects of Eros, claiming that "I can hardly point to a greater good for someone to have from youth onward than a good lover, and for a lover a beloved" (178c). The proof of this benefit is that lover and beloved bring out the best in one another, for the sake of the other avoiding anything that would be an object of reproach (178e). This is exemplified in the way in which lovers encourage one another to be brave in battle. Thus the army composed of lovers would be the greatest and the society ruled by lovers would be the best (179b). Indeed at this point Phaedrus includes women lovers here as well, that is, women who because of love are willing even to die for their (male) beloveds (179b). One might be reminded here of the discourse of the Johannine Jesus at the Last Supper, which speaks of love as the willingness to lay down one's life for his friends (John 15:13). At this point we have the rather curious "correction" of tradition concerning the legendary love of Achilles and Patroclus in which Phaedrus contests the tradition received from Aeschylus that Patroclus was the beloved rather than the lover since "Achilles was surely the fairer of the two . . . and he was much younger, as Homer informs us, and had no beard" (180a). This dispute about who was lover and who beloved at least opens the possibility that in some relationships this may be undecidable, thereby casting into question the grammatical division of lover and beloved. Phaedrus maintains that as wonderful as the lover is, the reciprocation of love on the part of the beloved is the truly wonderful thing since it rightly honors the divine in the lover's love (180b).

We are then informed that there were some unmemorable speeches that followed, and we are hurried on to the speech of Pausanias, a general who is the lover of the host, Agathon. Pausanias's speech distinguishes two kinds of eros (and thus of pederasty). One he calls Pandemian, or common and the other he calls Uranian, which is noble and thoroughly masculine. The former includes male love for women, but the latter is exclusively oriented toward the beauty of the male. (Late nineteenth-century apologists for male same-sex relationships will call themselves Uranian, a term that curiously enough is also taken up by the society of Jungian analysts.) Indeed the Uranian lover is not attracted to mere adolescents but to young men who are sprouting a growth of beard (181d), for what is at stake here is the companionship of free men. (One imagines Pausanias casting a meaningful glance at his young adult beloved, the famous Agathon). This will then lead Pausanias not only to favor his own form of same-sex love but to actually propose criminalizing the more common form (181e, 182a). With friends of same-sex love like this, we might think, there is scarcely any need for homophobic enemies! One may be reminded of certain contemporary legislators who publicly favor criminalizing same-sex sexual practices while under some pretense or other indulging in them themselves. Their hypocrisy is, however, greater than that of Pausanias, who offers a public justification for his discrimination. Nevertheless the chilling face of something like homosexual homophobia here makes a ghostly appearance at the banquet.

Pausanias will continue to extol his own brand of same-sex love by pointing to the way it is inimical to tyranny. He suggests that this is the reason barbarians prohibit same-sex love and cites the example of

Aristogeiton and Harmodius who, for love of one another, overthrow the tyrant. Male same-sex love is made out to be the surest base of true democracy (in Pausanias' sense), a position that will be radicalized quite remarkably by Walt Whitman in the nineteenth century, but without the hypocrisy of Pausanias. He continues by affirming that "it is base to gratify one who is no good and to do so in a bad way; while it is noble to gratify the good and to do so in a noble way" (183d) and concludes that "for the sake of virtue alone is it wholly noble to grant one's favors" (185b). The self-serving character of Pausanias's speech nevertheless does suggest that the idea of same-sex love as engendering lifelong attachments among adult males was not as foreign to Athenian society as is commonly thought.

In any case the speech doesn't exactly end. Rather when Pausanias pauses for breath, the listeners pass the torch quickly to another who may be less long-winded. Since Aristophanes is temporarily afflicted with hiccups the doctor Eryximachus takes up the theme. As befits his profession, we get quite a lot about biology and cosmology, which may seem rather beside the point except that he finally comes to a fairly commonsense position that overturns the sententiousness of Pausanias. He supposes that, medically speaking, it is probably not such a bad thing to indulge the lesser or common sort of erotic desire: "decent human beings must be gratified, as well as those who are not yet decent so that they might become more decent; and the love of the decent must be preserved. And this love is the beautiful one, the Uranian. . . . But the Pandemian one is Polyhymnia's, which must . . . be applied cautiously in order that it might harvest its own pleasure but not instill any intemperance" (187d–e). The good doctor then is not taken in by the binary proposed by Pausanias and seems to recommend a more commonsense approach to human desire and its gratification, a sort of "healthy-mindedness" in relation to sexual indulgence.

This digression into medicinal perspectives has given time for Aristophanes to recover. Although Aristophanes in one of his plays had caricatured Socrates' addiction to the love of boys, he here launches into one of the most interesting, if odd, justifications for same-sex love.

The basic idea is that humans were originally two-in-one but were separated by the gods and fated to search for their other half. This distraction would perhaps prevent them from again challenging the divine. The original double beings were male-male, female-female, or male-female. This suggests that humans are (in modern terms) by nature gay, lesbian, or heterosexual, a position at some variance to the presumed "bisexual" character of much same-sex love among the ancient Greeks, where the men typically married and had children as their social duty (and perhaps erotic interests) required, but also found in the love of youths a primary social preoccupation whether in the gymnasium or, as here, in the symposium. We might also note that the heterosexual types are not only those who seek marriage in the conventional sense but also adulterers and adulteresses (191e). Aristophanes offers this legend as a way of accounting for the hold that eros has over all human beings; eros is a yearning for completion by the beloved who is indeed one's "better half." What is at stake here is not exactly sexual satisfaction but the more fundamental completion that finding one's true complement can bring (192c). While we might not find the ideal in this life, nevertheless eros leads us to seek a satisfying relation with another person, and this is indeed a blessing of the gods (193b–c). With a sort of oblique grin at the notorious couple Pausanias and Agathon, the speech ends.

Agathon, the beloved and celebrated, takes up the theme in such a way as to "correct" some of what Phaedrus said: Agathon claims that Eros is the youngest and loveliest of the gods. Agathon then goes on to praise the benefits of Eros as the source of all that is lovely and delightful, gentle, and becoming. We do not hear of boldness and manliness as we did in Phaedrus or Pausanias but rather a kind of luxuriating indulgence, comparable to flowers and fragrance. To be sure, Agathon will gesture toward temperance and justice as fostered by Eros, but in general as a consequence of the agreeable and peaceable nature that he has prescribed for love. The tough general has found his other half not in one like himself but in one who is pliant and sings the praises of gentleness and sweetness.

The texts that we have been examining take the relationship of lover-beloved for granted and indeed affirm and celebrate this form of love. Moreover, as we have seen, some of the features of the *Symposium* actually seem to extend in remarkable ways the conventional

pederastic model from that of the love of a (young) adult for his adolescent beloved (a relationship that is necessarily temporary since the
flower of desirable youth soon fades). Supposing that the beloved may
be consumed with desire for the lover, that relationships of desire and
delight may actually endure for a lifetime, and supposing that this love
may even undermine the one-way structure of older lover and younger
beloved either because they are of the same generation (Aristophanes)
or (in terms of the discussion of Achilles and Patroclus) because it
is undecidable who is the lover and who the beloved. What may be
glimpsed here is not only the affirmation of conventional pederastic
forms of same-sex love but a wider spectrum of same-sex loves.

In any case these speeches and the other texts with which we began
not only to seem take male same-sex love for granted; they also seem
to affirm and celebrate it, if not for its own sake than at least for
some benefits that it provides — benefits that are often thought to be
of importance not only for the lovers themselves but for the society
of which they are a part. At the same time, we may detect a certain uneasiness at the difficulty of reconciling erotic infatuation with
friendship and erotic friendship with its sexual expression. To be sure
here this is taken for granted (even if in the case of Pausanias it is
restricted to an elite), but the complexities of love conceived in this
way may lead to an attempt to escape some of the difficulties through
a sort of sublimation, spiritualization, or process of abstraction from
the imperious and perhaps inconvenient insistence of the body itself.

# – 2 –

# Sublimation

In contrast to this broad acceptance and even celebration of same-sex love, we also find here in the *Symposium*, along with the *Phaedrus* and some other associated texts, a discourse that, while rooted in the self-evidence of male same-sex desire and attraction, points to the ways in which the physical (sexual) dimension of that love should be transcended in order to direct this desire to other, more philosophic ends: the contemplation of the good, the true, and the beautiful. Each of the discourses we examine has Socrates as their presumed speaker.

## *Phaedrus*

Rather than immediately turning to the speech in the *Symposium* that articulates a version of this position, we may look first at the *Phaedrus*, a dialogue that has been long admired for its depiction of the character of the person as a divided or struggling self, struggling for the mastery that will give it the chance for blissful immortality. Yet instead of beginning directly with the famous speech that articulates that position in the *Phaedrus* it may be helpful to turn to the Socratic speech that precedes it and to which it is meant to be contrasted. The earlier speech is occasioned by the report of the lovely youth Phaedrus of a speech by a famous orator, Lysias, to whom the youth is much attracted. The speech of Lysias praises the man who is not a lover of youths, that is, one who is not driven by homoerotic passion. After Phaedrus has read a transcript of the speech, Socrates is moved, perhaps by some muse, to make a speech with a similar orientation, which he does with head covered as if he were a prophet or an oracle (237a). Indeed Socrates pauses in the midst of this speech to ask Phaedrus whether he is inspired (perhaps by the nymphs that inhabit the river next to which they are lying on the ground together) (238c).

26

Socrates begins his initial discourse with a rather sly undermining of the integrity of Lysias's speech: Socrates begins to tell a story: "Once upon a time there was a fair boy, or more properly speaking, a youth; he was very fair and had a great many lovers; and there was one special cunning one, who had persuaded the youth that he did not love him, but he really loved him all the same" (237b). Of course this may also serve to undercut the content of the speech of Socrates himself insofar as it takes a position similar to that of Lysias: the praise of the nonlover as opposed to the pederast.

The brunt of this speech is that it is possible to distinguish two kinds of men, those who are governed by desire for the good, the other governed by desire for youths: "let us first of all agree in defining the nature and power of love. . . . Everyone sees that love is a desire, and we know also that non-lovers desire the beautiful and the good. . . . There are two guiding and ruling principles which lead us whither they will; one is the natural desire of pleasure, the other is an acquired opinion which is in search of the best" (237d).

What is at stake here is desire, a yearning for that which is in a certain way beyond or outside the self. This yearning will govern all the texts that we will consider. Note that at this stage the love of pleasure (and thus of youths) is termed "natural," while the love of the best is termed "an acquired opinion." At this stage at least the love of pleasure and thus homoerotic attachment to the beloved is in accordance with nature.

However, the speech intends to praise not a natural inclination to pleasure but an acquired taste for the good. "When opinion conquers . . . , the conquering principle is called temperance; but when desire, which is devoid of reason, rules in us and drags us to pleasure, that power of misrule is called excess" (237e–238a). The next move is to connect this excess to love (again the love of youths): "I had better say further that the irrational desire which overcomes the tendency of opinion towards right, and is led away to the enjoyment of beauty, and especially of personal beauty, by the desires which are her kindred — that desire, I say, the conqueror and leader of the rest, and waxing strong from having this very power, is called the power of love" (238b–c).

The speech then proceeds to cast aspersions on love precisely as the love of youths. He maintains that the lover is positively harmful to the beloved in trying to keep him inferior so that the lover may be the master. And so the lover will desire a youth who is delicate rather than strong (239c) and will further weaken him by seeking to separate him from anyone (including family and friends) who might interfere with the lover's domination and possession of the youth (240a). Although friendship aims at equality, the lover seeks that which is quite unequal in that he seeks sexual pleasure from the youth, who for his part can find none in the appearance of the lover: "similarity begets friendship. . . . Now the lover is not only unlike his beloved, but he forces himself upon him. For he is older" (240c). "But what pleasure or consolation can the beloved be receiving all this time? Must he not feel the extremity of disgust when he looks at an old withered face [O'Connor proposes the amended translation: "an older face and no longer in its prime"] and the remainder to match, which even in a description is not agreeable, and quite detestable when you are forced into daily contact with them" (240d–e). The contrast between the desirable beauty of the young and the relative ugliness of the older lover will be a regular trope of anti-pederastic discourse in the Hellenistic period. The speech concludes with the tagline: "As wolves love lambs so lovers love their beloveds" (241d). Of course if we recall the suspicion directed against a similar discourse at the beginning of this speech, we may wonder whether Socrates is himself something of a wolf in sheep's clothing.

Although the point of view of this speech is consonant with the position that Plato will adopt in the *Laws*, it is here immediately retracted by Socrates as an impious denigration of the gods, for love (Eros) is a god (242d–e). Accordingly Socrates will now offer a different speech not covered like a prophet, but with open face like a man of reason. It is this speech that invokes the famous simile of the soul as a charioteer who manages two horses of different nature and temperament.

The frame of this discourse is the immortality of the soul, whose true home is, like that of the gods, a celestial realm in which the soul is nourished by "the sight of truth. . . . During the revolution she beholds justice, temperance, and knowledge absolute, not in the form of generation or of relation, which men call existence, but knowledge absolute in existence absolute" (247d).

However, the human soul is one that fails to soar in this realm of knowledge but sinks lower and lower to eventually take the human form weighed down by a body of earthen frame. Depending upon the recollection of knowledge and virtue this soul is embodied in accordance with various classes or castes of human beings:

> The soul which has seen most of truth shall come to the birth as a philosopher, or artist, musician, or lover; that which has seen truth in the second degree shall be a righteous king or warrior or lord; the soul which is of the third class shall be a politician, or economist, or trader; the fourth shall be a lover of gymnastic toils, or a physician; the fifth a prophet or hierophant; to the sixth a poet or imitator will be appropriate; to the seventh the life of an artisan or husbandman; to the eighth that of a sophist or demagogue; to the ninth that of a tyrant — all these are states of probation, in which he who lives righteously improves, and he who lives unrighteously deteriorates his lot. (248d–e)

The idea then is that of the transmigration of souls either from higher to lower estate or the reverse, depending on the virtuousness of the life that is led in a given "incarnation." (There is no place assigned here for the majority of the Athenian population, the slaves, who are in this respect outcasts.) The goal of course is through a cycle of births and rebirths to attain again to the capacity to soar into the celestial realm. One cannot but be struck by the many parallels between this framing "myth" and the perspectives familiar from the religious and intellectual traditions of India. (We shall return to this later.)

It is the human soul, the incarnate soul, who is now to be described as a sort of charioteer with two horses, one of which tends toward the heavens and the other toward the earth. At first this may seem to closely follow the depiction of the previous speech. The difference here is that love (and this means homoerotic love) will be assigned the honorable position as that which serves the aim of the charioteer in returning toward the celestial home. In this way Socrates' new thesis, that "the madness of love is the greatest of heaven's blessings" (245b), will be verified. Socrates will maintain: "only the soul of a philosopher, guileless and true, or the soul of a lover [of youths], who is not without philosophy, may acquire wings in the third recurring period of a thousand years; and if they choose this life three times in succession, then they have their wings given them" (249a). Thus homoeroticism, so long as it is not without philosophy, may be a means of ascent rather than descent in these cycles of life. How is that to be explained?

Of all the "forms" (goodness, justice, and truth, for example) the one that is most easily seen is beauty. Of course beauty may inspire wanton lust (the example here seems to be primarily heterosexual: "rushing on to enjoy and beget" [249d] even though it is called pleasure "in violation of nature" [250e]). But more fundamentally one may be struck by the divine beauty of the beloved in such a way that the recently initiated person "is amazed when he sees anyone having a god-like face or form, which is the expression or imitation of divine beauty.... Then looking upon the face of his beloved as of a god he reverences him" (251a) "as he receives the effluence of beauty through the eyes, the wing moistens and he warms ... the lower end [O'Connor suggests "stalk"] of the wing begins to swell and grow from the root upwards, extending under the whole soul — for once the whole was winged" (251b) "and when looking at the beauty of youth she receives the sensible warm traction of particles which flow towards her, therefore called attraction (*himeros*)" (251c). "And wherever she thinks that she will behold the beautiful one, thither in her desire she runs" (251e). This "is the reason why the soul of the lover never forsakes his beautiful one" (252a). "And this state, my dear imaginary youth, is by men called love."

What are we to make of this remarkable description of love? The eroticism is blatant, for the being smitten by a beautiful face and body, the moistening and swelling of the "stalk" (the erection that follows), the desire to pursue the object of this psychophysical attraction, all show the state of the lover as psychosexual desire. The point, however, is not to indulge the sexual appetite, at least not at first. Thus when the lover is beginning to be enamored of the beloved, "the obedient steed, then as always under the government of shame, refrains himself from leaping on the beloved"; not so with the bad horse, who tries to convince the driver and the other horse, in contemporary terms, to "hit that" (254a). "They at first indignantly oppose him and will not be urged on to do terrible and unlawful deeds; but at last, when there is no end of evil, they yield" (254a–b). On this account the better part of the soul holds back from the sexual expression that the worse part insists upon immediately. Restraint may, however, at some point be overwhelmed by desire and in a curious anticipation of the (in)famous advice of Saint Paul, that it is better to marry than to be aflame with desire (1 Corinthians 7:36), the better part concedes at least some sexual consummation. Insofar as this consummation is not immediate and remains rare, then no great damage seems to be done. Indeed the beloved turns more and more to the lover in spite of the opinions of those who hold the relationship to be shameful. The beloved, who has been served in this way, "if in former days he has blushed to his own passion and turned away his lover, because his youthful companions or others slanderously told him that he would be disgraced, now as years advance, at the appointed age and time is led to receive him into communion" (255a).

Moreover, when he has received him into communion and intimacy, then the beloved is amazed at the good will of the lover" (255b). The beloved "approaches and embraces him, in gymnastic exercises and at other times of meeting. Then does the fountain of that stream, which Zeus when he was in love with Ganymede called desire, overflow upon the lover" (255a–b) and fill the soul of the beloved also with love (255d). Indeed the growing and still virtuous love between lover and beloved comes to the point that "he wants to see him, touch him, kiss, embrace him [O'Connor suggests: "go to bed with him"] and afterward his desire is accomplished" (255e). "When they are side by side [in bed?], he is not in a state in which he can refuse the lover anything, if he asks him, while his fellow steed and the charioteer oppose him with shame and reason. Yet they are constrained by modesty and temperance from often indulging this desire having once enjoyed they continue to enjoy, yet rarely because they have not the approval of the whole soul" (256c). Sexual practice then seems to have a certain therapeutic effect as a compromise (or mean) between the two horses by which the charioteer retains a wise control. As a consequence, after this lifelong companionship has ended: "At last they pass out of the body, unwinged, but eager to soar, and thus obtain no mean reward of love and madness, ... happy companions in their pilgrimage, and when the time comes at which they receive their wings they have the same plumage because of their love" (256d).

Although this speech sets out with a dichotomy between passion and virtue, body and intellect, it takes a different route than the first in that it supposes first that the love of the lovely lad, and his in return, may become a path toward the aspiration for and eventual attainment of the good. Moreover this is true even if, from time to time, and in the context of growing friendship and orientation toward the good, it happens that the lesser passion is indulged. In this discourse indeed it seems almost inevitable that it should be, but with due modesty and perhaps pangs of morning-after remorse so that the friends may continue in their pursuit together of the good. The tie thus cemented in this life seems even to be promised a certain immortality as they come at length to receive the same colored plumage in token of their love. Sexual expression of the relationship, though understandable and perhaps inevitable, should be delayed as long as possible and gotten over as quickly as possible so that the quest for truth and goodness may be the basic or fundamental content of the relationship.

Now in a certain way this speech echoes some of the ideas that we find in the early speeches in the *Symposium*, although it also has a rather more refined and judicious character than the speeches of, for example, Pausanias or Agathon.

But this is not the speech that Socrates will offer in the *Symposium*. Instead we will get a related speech, but one less accommodating of sexual passion, represented not as the view of Socrates but that of a mantic or prophetic woman: Diotima.

## *Symposium* Again (Diotima)

It is surprising that Plato should introduce into this male gathering the perspective represented as being that of a woman, just as it is also remarkable that we should have the speech indirectly, that is, as reported by Socrates. For in this way it is not entirely certain that the perspective offered here can be taken to be the position of Socrates, even if he thinks it well worth sharing in this all-male drinking party. That the speech is a reported speech reminds us that this entire dialogue is set up as being reported at second or third hand, and at a great distance of time. The narrator (Appolodorus) was only a child when the symposium took place and has heard of it from another, Aristodemus. Thus, rather than simply narrating the discussions, Plato interposes two other mediators: first Aristodemus and then Appolodorus. With the speech of Socrates we get a further mediation (Socrates recalling Diotima) and a further distance in time. One possible function of this elaborate form of narration may be to preserve a certain deniability: the views offered here are not necessarily those of the persons to whom they are attributed.

The discourse attributed to Diotima is characterized by at least three images or metaphors that will be mined for insight into the character and value of love. The first will develop the idea that love (as desire) is not a god but is the child of need or lack, which, however, is or may be attracted to the good. This will regard love as the hybrid offspring of the divine and the all too human. The second metaphor deployed is that of reproduction, making and getting to be pregnant, and giving birth as oriented toward immortality. The third metaphor is that of an ascent from the particular to the general, from the physical to the spiritual, from the concrete to the most abstract, as the proper orientation of human aspiration toward the beautiful and so the good. While there is here no straightforward attack upon the love of youths as in the first speech of Socrates in the *Phaedrus*, there is also no clear allowance for its enduring value nor for its physical expression as in the main speech of Socrates in the *Phaedrus*. That speech, we recall, began with the reminder that Eros is a god, a position that had been articulated in the *Symposium* by a rather flowery speech from Agathon, and it is by bringing that position into question that the Diotima discourse begins.

This first part of the discourse will distinguish between that which love loves (the good, the beautiful, etc.) and love itself, which is a lack of what it desires. This is set in motion with the tale of a poor woman (poverty itself, or *penia*) who enters the home of a rich man (*poros*, or plenitude) and seduces him (203b). The child of this presumably illicit seduction is Eros, who is neither a god (like *poros*) nor simply human but will be an intermediary between the divine and the human, transmitting the desires (prayers) of the human to the divine and the mandates and blessings of the divine to the human (202e). It is as well a "mean" between the mortal and the immortal (202d). As to love or Eros itself, he is always in want or in poverty, lacking what is essential. Indeed it can even be said (in a way like the speech of Lysias or the first of Socrates in the *Phaedrus*) that Eros is not only not lovely but "he is always plotting against the fair and the good" (203d).

This then is applied to the situation of the philosopher who is, as the name suggests, the lover of wisdom. Like Eros itself the philosopher is characterized by lack or poverty yet also by a desire for the good and beautiful. No god could be a philosopher, for the gods possess wisdom and thus cannot be desirous of it (203e–204a). The philosopher is thus also in a certain way in the middle between folly and wisdom.

Having thus set up a sort of description of the nature of Eros, Diotima's discourse turns to depict the act of eros as aiming at a certain procreation. The image here is of the heterosexual desire that aims at procreation, generation, or bringing to birth: "I mean to say, that all men are bringing to birth [O'Connor suggests: "conceiving and impregnating"] in their bodies and in their souls. There is a certain age, at which human nature is desirous of procreation, and this procreation must be in beauty and not in deformity; and this is the mystery of man and woman [O'Connor suggests: "The intercourse between man and woman is a parturition, or birth"], which is a divine thing, for conception and generation are a principle of immortality in the mortal creature" (206c). "Beauty, then, is the destiny or goddess of parturition who presides at births" (206d).

The upshot of this is that the object of desire is not beauty as such but rather that which is enabled by beauty: impregnation, birth, or reproduction. Thus Diotima remarks: "For love, Socrates, is not, as you imagine, the love of the beautiful only. [Rather, it is] the love of generation and birth in beauty" (206e).

The bridge from this depiction of the reproductive aim of desire to the question of the philosophic eros comes by suggesting that the reason humans desire reproduction is to ensure for themselves a sort of immortality; that is, to generate that which will survive their own death and will bear their name and fortune forward beyond their own death. Thus Socrates asks why birth: "Because to the mortal, birth is a sort of eternity and immortality." This is even extended from the human to the animal: "the mortal nature is seeking as far as is possible to be everlasting and immortal; and this is only to be attained by generation, because the new is always left in the place of the old" (207d).

From this it is relatively easy to turn from the quest for immortality (or at least the survival of mortality) to the attraction for that which does not perish, namely, justice, wisdom, and so on. The philosopher then is one who is himself impregnated with that which orients toward the immortal. There is here a certain autoeroticism that seeks to make oneself pregnant with virtue or whatever else may be said to be immortal or to confer immortality.

It is here that we finally get the appearance of the pederastic pair that has provided the theme of the prior discourses on love. (One can imagine the stirring with impatience of the male companions at the intrusion of so much heterosexual metaphor — spoken in imitation of the woman's voice — into their praise of love as the love of youths. At last now we seem to be getting back to familiar territory.) Given what we have heard about love from Diotima, what are we to make of the love of youths?

We may imagine that the lover is one who has the thirst for beauty already impregnating his soul. He then finds a beautiful beloved who awakens the desire to give birth to that which is immortal. Thus this person seeks beauty, and when he finds a beloved, "they are bound together by a far nearer tie and have a closer friendship than those who beget mortal children" (209c). This invidious comparison of the love of youths with the lesser form of procreative immortality may at last strike a responsive chord in the partners to this drinking party.

The place of rebooting this discussion will again be the attraction to beautiful bodies (a starting point as well for the *Charmides*, which begins with the glimpse of the beauty of Charmides' body or genitals and the resulting erection attributed to Socrates). However, we "take off" from this attraction to one especially attractive body to a consideration of the other beautiful bodies and thence to that which all beautiful bodies have in common or indeed to the beautifulness of bodies generally (210b). From this Socrates/Diotima will proceed to consider that the true beauty resides not in the body but in the soul, so that however little the body may seem beautiful it still is the bearer of a (potentially) beautiful soul (210b–c). From this abstraction from one beautiful body to all, and thence to the soul, we are invited to contemplate the beauty of human laws and institutions and so estimate the body's beauty as a slight affair (210c). From this we go on to the beauty of all forms of knowledge until we glimpse the vast "sea of beauty." Thus one is encouraged to seek to contemplate "beauty only, absolute, separate, simple, and everlasting.... He who under the influence of true love [or, rather, "correct pederasty" as the Greek has it] rising upward from these begins to see that beauty, is not far from the end" (211b). The whole movement then from falling in love with a particular body to the contemplation of beauty as such means that any particular beauty is but a springboard for the journey toward beauty in general: "use the beauties of earth as steps along which he mounts upwards for the sake of that other beauty" (211c). Indeed, from the vantage point thus gained one will regard beauty itself as vastly superior even to the beauty of particular boys or youths [*paides* and *neaniskos*].

Now if we were to step back from this discourse and to ask about its basic sense we might want to protest that eros is properly directed not to the general but to the particular, whether of friendship or of erotic attraction or what have you. Or we might wonder at the implicit praise of promiscuity in that one proceeds from the infatuation with one body to the two and thence to many and ultimately to all. The love of a particular youth becomes, perhaps like the youth himself, a disposable catalyst for the ascent to true beauty, no sooner encountered than discarded. For it is the general or universal that is more valuable than the individual or particular.

This is in some contrast to the thrust of at least some of the other speeches about love that have supposed that the particular is not disposable. Think for instance of the undying loyalty of lovers to one another expounded in the speeches of Phaedrus or Pausanias, or the grounding in an odd sort of creation narrative in the speech of Aristophanes of the eternal quest for one's "other half."

And yet the discourse of Diotima does agree with aspects of other speeches here in that it allows that pederasty, the love of youths and of youthful beauty, has an aim outside itself, whether that aim be the inculcation of courage or virtue or in this case the philosophic contemplation of the beautiful as such.

But unlike those other speeches this one implicitly regards the beloved as ultimately dispensable. What matters is the solitary quest of the lover of wisdom for wisdom. Thus there is nothing here of the joining of the lover and beloved in common quest as in the *Phaedrus*. Ultimately the erotic attachment to the other is transcended in the autoerotic attachment to one's own immortality. Thus the justification here for correct love of boys and youths seems ultimately to leave the boys in the lurch. They are discarded as one ascends to the philosophic ideal.

## Alcibiades

In a certain respect this "leaving the beloved in the lurch" is enacted in the narration of the protest of the beautiful and beloved youth who bursts into the symposium in the person of a drunken Alcibiades. This is certainly one of the most dramatic moments in Plato's dialogues. Along with the entrance of Alcibiades we have the introduction of copious quantities of wine to "loosen up" the rather sober proceedings of the evening, setting up a drinking bout that will last till dawn and leave all but Socrates incapacitated. In addition, the discourse of Alcibiades will be offset by teasing banter between him and Socrates that suggests the erotic jealousy of Alcibiades occasioned by the unfaithfulness of his "lover" Socrates, who is seated on the same couch as the handsome and still youthful Agathon. Socrates seeks protection from Alcibiades' jealous rage while Alcibiades seeks sympathy for his position as the jilted beloved. It is all in all a rather delightful mime of the dynamics that might be imagined to play out between lovers.

Although the praise of Eros had been the theme of previous speeches, Agathon changes the terms of the evening's entertainment to be that of the praise of one another, presumably related insofar as they are lovers and beloveds. The actual content, however, is the rather rueful praise of Alcibiades' lover, Socrates. While there is much here about the ways in which Socrates is a worthy lover in the conventional senses suggested by Phaedrus and Pausanias (he is brave, temperate, and so on), what drives the speech is the complaint that while Socrates manages to inflame the love of his beloved, he refuses to requite this love in ways that would please the beloved.

This first involves something of a reversal of roles since the much older Socrates is cast as a lover of beautiful young men (and a rather promiscuous lover as well). Here, though, it is Alcibiades the beloved who is obsessed with getting Socrates into bed. Alcibiades thus recounts how he first tried the coy approach of the conventional beloved, making himself available. Then he sought to stimulate more physical responses by nude wrestling at the gym and then arranged to be alone at home for supper with him. None of these ruses work. Finally Alcibiades does maneuver Socrates into spending the night in his bed covered by the same cloak. Alas, the irresistible charm and beauty of Alcibiades are all too easily resisted by the object of infatuation.

The lover has become the object rather than the subject of passion, and the beloved has become the shameless pursuer rather than the innocent quarry. To his chagrin Alcibiades discovers that Socrates, who had seemed to be attracted to Alcibiades' beautiful body, is instead only interested in his mind. Of course for Alcibiades this is a sort of "come-on" that in some circles would lead Socrates to be accused of being a "cock-tease." He seduces and then leaves the seduced in the lurch. The aim of such behavior, we might suppose, is to improve the character of Alcibiades. There is good reason to suppose that it may have the opposite effect or that it is at least ineffective in that respect. Instead, what it does is make Socrates out to be something of a paragon (or to be so in the eyes of Plato, perhaps). The lover makes use of the beloved youth to polish his own reputation for virtue, or so the cynic might conclude.

The drama of Alcibiades serves then to represent the protest of those whose lovers follow the advice of Diotima and use and then discard the amorous attachments to beautiful lads, and ultimately the lads themselves.

Thus, however, jarring the change it will nonetheless be not unimaginable for Plato ultimately to conclude that the love of youths should be dispensed with altogether. It is to that position that we will next turn.

# – 3 –

# Rejection: The *Laws*

One of the principal preoccupations of Plato is with the forms of social order by which free men may best organize their life in common. While this is a theme in many of Plato's dialogues (and we have just heard in Diotima's reported discourse that the love of youths ascends to the contemplation of laws and institutions), it is the explicit subject matter of three of Plato's most extended dialogues or treatises (for the dialogue form seems increasingly dispensable): the *Republic*, the *Statesman*, and the *Laws*. It is the last of these that may well be the last work that Plato wrote and that comes near the end of his life. In it the figure of Socrates recedes entirely from view, and his place as the wise man is taken by the anonymous Athenian who is in a sort of conversation with a fellow traveler from Crete and one from Sparta, two other societies that have been founded by particular lawgivers. They are also societies that have valorized male (and perhaps, in the case of Sparta, also female) same-sex love, especially that which takes the form or structure of a certain kind of pederasty.

The theme throughout the discussion is the constitution of a just society that will also and thereby form just citizens. Like all such discussions of the just society in this cultural world, the focus is on the ordering of society for and by free men. What is left out of account entirely is the base of the social order, the institution of slavery. In these slavocracies the concern for justice leaves out of account the lot of the majority of the population who are the slaves, upon whose labor the leisure of the citizens to form their common life is based.

The fragment of this discussion that will interest us comes in the midst of a discussion of the common life of the citizens, in which it is argued that these citizens should have all things in common in a way that mirrors the institutions of Sparta. Here, for example, all meals were taken together and the ownership of private property as well as private space was reduced to an absolute minimum so that the common good might be always foremost. It is admitted that it will be difficult to persuade people accustomed to seek their own advantage to agree to such an arrangement, and much time is spent thinking out ways to persuade folk that this is ultimately in their best interest as members of a social fabric.

It is in this context that we then get what may appear as a digression into the question of same-sex love. The goal of the conversation will be to seek ways to get men to agree to prohibit same-sex love, to make it an object of shame, indeed to make of it an unthinkable crime. This will be the starting point then of a Platonic homophobia.

Two speeches that we have considered may be regarded as precursors of the one we are to read. The one is the speech of Pausanias, who was quite willing to outlaw the gratification of same-sex love as commonly thought of and practiced (the Pandemian). But here there will be no valorization of a higher form of same-sex love that ought to be sexually expressed. Rather, same-sex love as such will be prohibited. In general we may also say that the point of view taken here is not too far distant from that expressed by Socrates' first speech in the *Phaedrus*, in which he denies the significance of same-sex love. Socrates, as we recall, had himself disowned this perspective as both irrational and impious. Yet ironically it is the position to be taken up here by the Athenian. Socrates has been banished from this dialogue altogether and perhaps not without reason. But one can easily imagine the protests of his ghost as the argument unfolds.

The subject of same-sex love and sexual practice is first introduced in book 1 of the *Laws* and then discussed at greater length in book 8. The starting point for the discussion will be an agreement to engage in frank discussion of the merits as well as the flaws of the constituted civil order in their respective societies (Crete, Sparta, and Athens [634d]).

The initial treatment will simply open the subject for discussion. The theme is broached by way of reference to the practices of common meals and of common exercise in gymnasia. These institutions are regarded as beneficial to the state in that they promote a strong sense and practice of the common or social good. But they may also have their drawbacks (636b). It is in this connection, and specifically with respect to the gymnasium, that we turn to the question of same-sex attraction. This connection derives from the fact that the gymnasium is the place where men exercise together in the nude and thus where the display of naked youthful beauty can be appreciated by older admirers. We have earlier seen Socrates hanging out at the gym (and in the "locker room") with precisely this pleasure in view (*Charmides, Lysis*). The Athenian has the following observation: "This institution [the gymnasium] when of old standing, is thought to have corrupted the pleasures of love [*aphrodisia*] which are natural [*kata phusein*] not to men only but also natural to beasts. For this your states are held primarily responsible, and along with all others that especially encourage the use of gymnasia" (636c).

The gymnasium, then, as the privileged site for the incitement of homoerotic desire and attachment is emphasized. A few decades later Alexander's conquest will spread Greek culture and institutions throughout a world that will then be called Hellenistic. And this diffusion will prominently include the establishment of gymnasia throughout the Mediterranean world with their attendant pleasures and dangers. Thus Plutarch, writing in the first century C.E., will again maintain that it is through this institution that same-sex love and pederasty or the love of youths in particular has been spread throughout that world.[1]

We may pause here to note that the elites of Jerusalem (Jason et al.) are said to have invited the Seleucid Hellenistic emperor to establish a gymnasium in Jerusalem around 170 B.C.E. From the standpoint of the author of Maccabees this is a betrayal of the religio-cultural identity of the holy city (1 Maccabees 1:12–15; 2 Maccabees 4:7–17). We are further informed that exercising in the nude together leads the lads of Jerusalem to seek to cover the marks of circumcision, marks that mar their naked beauty from the perspective of a Greek ideal. It is not sufficiently noted that we have here the introduction of something like institutionalized pederasty into the heart of Jerusalem. Nor is it sufficiently noted that this institution continues after the Maccabean wars into the time of Jesus, with a gymnasium within sight of the temple itself.

The attitude taken by the Athenian with respect to this institution is one that the unwary might have attributed not to Greek but to Jewish sensibilities. For he speaks of the gymnasium with its incitement of male same-sex love as having "corrupted the pleasures of love." These pleasures (the reference to Aphrodite here particularly focuses attention on the pleasures of the sexual expression of attraction), he suggests, are in a certain respect natural [kata physein], insofar as human and animal are inclined to them. But that the gymnasium corrupts these pleasures, what exactly does this mean? "And whether one makes the observation in earnest or in jest, one certainly should not fail to observe that when male [arrenon] unites [koinonian] with female for procreation the pleasure experienced is held to be due to nature [kata phusein], but contrary to nature [para physein] when male mates with male or female with female, and that those first guilty of such enormities were impelled by their slavery to pleasure" (636c).

Here a distinction is introduced that will be decisive for the development of homophobic discourse: that between according to nature [kata physein] and contrary to nature [para physein]. Same-sex practices are squarely on the side of that which is "contrary to nature."

We note further that this is said equally with respect to women and men. That is, female same-sex practice is treated in the same way as male same-sex practice. Both are equally "contrary to nature." We have encountered this parallel between male and female same-sex attraction (and practice) before, in Aristophanes' speech, but there the perspective proffered was that these attractions are "natural" in the sense that they proceed from the original nature of the persons involved (even if the women in that case were strangely referred to as courtesans or prostitutes). In this case, however, the equivalence may be motivated by the way in Sparta (and perhaps in the poetry of Sappho) the structure of female same-sex love was basically similar to the pederastic model so taken for granted in the earlier dialogues of Plato.

The terminology employed to characterize male (and by extension female) same-sex love is neither the terminology for love nor that of the pederastic structure. It is simply the intercourse [koinonian] of male with male.[2] Plato seems to be placing as much distance as possible between the position he is suggesting here and any idea of friendship or love. It is the mere sexual gratification of desire that is focused on here, shorn of any possible higher value. The motivation for the valorizing of such same-sex practices is simply the "slavery to pleasure." Here it seems that there is a sort of normal degree of pleasure (that leading to cross-sex unions) and a more exaggerated "slavery to" or indulgence in pleasure that occasions same-sex sexual practices. Does this mean that same-sex practices are more pleasurable than cross-sex practices?

In any case the speaker has begun by suspending his characterization between seriousness and jest. It will be the task of further discussion to take away the possibility of regarding this perspective as a joke.

Before leaving this preliminary introduction of the theme of antipathy to same-sex desire and practice we may also note the way in which the society of Crete is assigned the blame for the origin and spread of this practice. Crete is of importance here because it is the society from which supposedly many of the most important Greek institutions are derived, since it was the first city-state to have emerged from the so-called Greek Dark Ages. The institution that is especially in view here is the approval of male same-sex love (and of course the gymnasium). What the Athenian says is, "And we all accuse the Cretans of concocting the story about Ganymede. Because it was the belief that they derived their laws from Zeus [Dios], they added on this story [mythos] about Zeus [Dios] in order that they might be following his example in enjoying this pleasure as well" (636d).

The legend or mythos referred to here is one that has Zeus especially smitten by the beauty of a lovely shepherd lad named Ganymede. In order to satisfy his infatuation Zeus turns himself into an eagle (a raptor), swoops down upon the lad, and carries him away from any who might interfere with Zeus's satisfaction of his pleasure. The lad then becomes Zeus's boy toy, charged with the task of being his cup-bearer and so with being at his side in the feasts and drinking parties of the gods. Zeus as the chief of the gods stands for god as such, which is why Plato's Greek text does not give him his "personal name" but simply calls him God (Dios). Zeus's marriage to Hera (the protectoress of heterosexual marriage) does not prevent him from being an equal opportunity seducer or, as the Ganymede story suggests, rapist (the word rape being taken from raptor, the form assumed by Zeus in order to kidnap the lovely boy to satisfy his own lust.)

I dally a bit over this story because it will be so critical for the subsequent history of same-sex love. The term "Ganymede" and its transformation into "catamite" will over time become synonymous with the object of male same-sex desire, whether as young prostitute or as favored boy toy. Eventually he will make his appearance in the translation of a certain Pauline text to which we will later turn. The reference to same-sex love is suspended in book 1 in order to take up the question of banishing drinking parties (*symposia*) in accordance with Spartan legislation (the Athenian opts for moderation instead) and the institution of taking all meals together in a common mess hall, also of Spartan provenance.

In book 8 of the *Laws*, after agreeing to the desirability of these Spartan institutions (in spite of the common meal being in some sense "unnatural" [*para physein?*]) and before taking up the question of the place of athletic contests in the formation of citizens of the state, we return to the question of same-sex love. What is now in view is the abolition of male same-sex eroticism generally. (There seems here to be no interest in legislating against female same-sex love.)

Here there is reference to Sparta in the days before its great lawgiver, Laius, had institutionalized pederasty (perhaps on the model of Crete[3]): "Were one to follow the guidance of nature and adopt the law of the old days before Laius — I mean, to pronounce it wrong that male should have to do carnally [*koinonein . . . aphrodision* = sharing pleasure] with youthful male *as with female* — and to fetch his evidence from the life of the animals, pointing out that male does not touch male in this way because the action is unnatural, his contention would surely be a telling one, yet it would be quite at variance with the practice of your societies" (836c).[4]

We have once again the introduction of the idea of nature and the suggestion that the love of youths is unnatural. Here we revert to the more traditional vocabulary of pederasty. But the perspective here is that pederasty involves sex with youths "as with female," a turn of phrase that is associated with the supposed prohibition of same-sex practice in Leviticus.[5]

The supposition that the indulgence in these pleasures is contrary to nature encounters the difficulty that this would be at odds with the common sense of the societies of Crete and Sparta (curiously the Athenian does not mention Athens). The reference to animals occurs again as a presumed pattern for what is natural, but this is initially agreed to be unconvincing.

The question then is how to make a condemnation of male same-sex practices more convincing. Here the Athenian proposes first an argument about virtue and gender. He argues that the male who indulges his desire for youths is one who is intemperate (desire for youths is an indulgence in excessive pleasure). Moreover, he can even be said to be cowardly because he retreats in the face of his own passions or surrenders to them. The lover or seducer then is "unmanly," and the beloved too is unmanly in that he is placed in the position of the female. This then is Plato's rejoinder to the perspectives attributed to Phaedrus (and Pausanias) in the *Symposium:* "Will it lead to the growth of the temper of valor in the soul of the seduced? Or the growth of a temperate character in his seducer?" (836d). "That is surely more than any man can believe. Surely the very opposite is the truth. Everyone must censure the unmanliness of the one party, who surrenders to his lusts because he is too weak to offer resistance, and reproach the other — the impersonator of the female — with his likeness to his model" (836e).

Never mind that it would seem that nearly everyone (in this cultural world) would in fact believe (or want to believe) that courage and temperance are the outcome of same-sex love. Plato is willing to turn this conventional wisdom on its head. Here we have Plato approximating the position that had been rejected by Socrates in the *Phaedrus* as insane and impious! Two sorts of unmanliness or feminization are here suggested: one for the seducer, the other for the seduced. In the development of homophobia it is the latter that will most typically carry the connotation of "effeminate."

In order to counter further the association of same-sex love with "manliness" and the defenses of same-sex love that ensue, Plato now first attempts to distinguish friendship from love or desire (eros). The intersection of these had made for some of the difficulties in the argument of the *Lysis*, as we saw. So Plato now seeks to rigorously distinguish them. Friendship is the association of like with like and thus of equals, whereas eros involves inequality (the lover and the beloved). These are now cast not as complementary terms but as pure opposites (also ignoring that *fileo* partakes of a similar grammatical asymmetry). We now have the binary — either friendship or eros — that, moreover, is treated as the difference between the same (friendship) and the opposed (eros). The question then arises whether it is possible to have a certain "mixed economy" in which eros leads to or expresses friendship. This had been the suggestion not only of Pausanias regarding Uranian same-sex relationships but also of Socrates' second speech in the *Phaedrus*. Plato will now maintain that it is not only the Pandemian sort of same-sex relation that is to be condemned or ruled out but also the Uranian (and so perhaps the Socratic as well).

But this seems very difficult given the honor in which this mixed economy was held in all Greek societies. How then will it be possible, in the face of common sense and strong attraction, to get people (males of course) to agree that instead of being honorable the indulgence in or even recognition of this desire is shameful, repugnant, unthinkable?

Here the Athenian thinks he glimpses the possibility of a solution: "Even today, as you know, lawless as most men are, they are very effectually deterred from cohabitation with the fair, and not against their own will either, but with their full and entire consent," that is, "persons who have a fair sister or brother." The law against this is "unwritten" (838a). The idea of having sex with one's sibling doesn't even enter one's mind. This is because "all such lusts are extinguished by a mere phrase," to wit: "The saying that they are all unhallowed, abominations to God, deeds of black shame" (838b–c).[6] Everyone believes the same thing on this matter, so that "from our very cradles, [we] are constantly hearing the same report of them from all quarters" (838c). Megillus agrees: "Common fame is indeed a wonderfully potent force, provided only no single soul dares to entertain a sentiment contrary to the established usage" (838d). The Athenian concludes that this is the strategy that the lawmaker should use with respect to same-sex attraction: "He has merely to get the sanction of a common fame which is universal — embraces bond and free, woman and children, and every section of society alike — and he will without more ado have secured the best of guarantees for his law" (838d–e).

Here we clearly have the presentation of a rather full-fledged homophobic program. For the idea is to make same-sex love to be universally condemned in much the same way as incest is universally condemned. The association of same-sex love with taboos as deep as that of incest depends here not on Leviticus but on Plato's fantasy of a society with a uniform opinion. Indeed the idea is to make any other opinion simply unthinkable (who would think to defend the rights of the incest practitioner?). Same-sex love is to be regarded as despised by the gods and as utterly shameful.

The efficacy of this common opinion is so marked that "those who do this inflict death upon themselves willingly as punishment for their sins [hamartias]" [838c]. The contemporary reader cannot but be chillingly reminded of the efficacy of Plato's homophobic program. Movies and novels that depicted same-sex love in the last century quite often ended with either the suicide of the infamous lovers or at least with their death as the only possible ending for an impossible and shameful practice. And even today it is still the case that adolescents who are or think they might be gay or lesbian take their own lives in disproportionate numbers. What Plato desired has come to pass.

What will make the law that prohibits same-sex love work is precisely the inculcation of a universal opinion on the model of that which effectively restrains incest. Now this is in a certain way ingenious since obviously the opinion concerning, for example, adultery is far less effective than that concerning incest and this has in part to do with the radical interiorization of fear and repugnance and shame at the very idea of the violation. Plato has clearly got hold of the right analogy for his homophobic program. But the question, as Megillus notices, is still how to get from here (acceptance or valorization of same-sex love) to there (the dominion of homophobia).

What Plato offers here is an iteration of the arguments previously encountered albeit with a few additional twists that will become standard fare for the development of homophobic discourse. One that will have a curious history is the comparison of sexual practice with the sowing of seed, in which the Athenian says: "I said I knew of a device for establishing this law of restricting procreative intercourse to its natural function by abstention from congress with our own sex, with its deliberate murder of the race and its wasting of the seed of life on a stony and rocky soil, where it will never take root and bear its natural fruit, and equal abstention from any female field whence you would desire no harvest" (838e–839a).

I mention this analogy of sowing on rocky soil first because it will be taken up by Philo as a trope for male same-sex (anal) intercourse. Its appearance there will be an indication of the influence of this text on later developments of homophobia. The analogy will also make a curious appearance in one of the best-known parables of Jesus (of the sower) which commentators have universally failed to see as having any connection with sexual practices (Mark 4:1–9).

With this reformulation of the task we then get suggestions that will lead toward the desired goal. This will involve once again an argument from nature. The law must teach people that "it is not for them to behave worse than birds and many other creatures which flock together in large bodies — these animals practice continence until marriage" (840d). "Surely you, we shall say, ought to be better than the beasts."

Of course, the road to achieving cultural unanimity about this is arduous. Indeed the Athenian agrees: "Possibly however, some young bystander, rash and of super abundant virility, on hearing of the passing of this law, would denounce us for making foolish and impossible rules" (840b). Thus the argument from nature still does not seem convincing. (We may also note that same-sex passion here is attributed to an excess rather than a deficiency of virility.) Plato must revert to the "victory over passion" argument: "shall our boys be unable to hold out in order to win a much nobler victory [than an athletic competition] — that which is the noblest of all victories, as we shall tell them from their childhood's days, charming them into belief, we hope, by tales [*mythoi*] and sentences and songs" (840c).

The "twist" here is the invention of a sort of popular culture that will inculcate a loathing of same-sex practices and a positive desire for conquering of this (and other) desires. Of course much of this will have to do with the reinterpretation of well-known *mythoi*, or stories, and we will have striking evidence of this in the Platonically informed reinterpretation of the story of Sodom by Philo and others.

We are still a long way from inducing this common opinion and so the abolition of the desire itself. In the meantime the aim may be to make it shameful, if not to engage in the practice, then to let it be known that one does. Thus same-sex practice must be shrouded in secrecy: "it must be the ordinance of custom and unwritten usage that secrecy in such matters is a point of honor, and the discovery of the act, though not necessarily its mere commission, discreditable" (841b).

We have here the Platonic invention of the closet! The closet exists here so that the emergence of a common opinion about the shamefulness of such practices will never be disturbed by the appearance of counterexamples. (We have seen that the Vatican document opposing same-sex unions opposes them in part because they breech this conspiracy of silence.)

In summary, then, we get: godly fear, desire for honor, and the development of a love of beauty that is spiritual and not physical. But this is not quite enough. For Plato also desires that the force of law be brought to bear on any who are discovered to have engaged in this outrageous behavior and that they lose their rights as citizens (841e).

Before turning to the question of how to account for the appearance of this homophobic project at the end of a body of literature so often invoked to celebrate or at least justify same-sex love, it is important to note just how pertinent this project is for thinking about what has subsequently happened in the development of Western homophobia. The place of the argument about what is natural or against nature will become essential to homophobic discourse. Even though Plato expressed some doubt about how convincing it would be, it has succeeded in becoming a standard trope of that discourse. The suggestion about inventing stories and songs to reinforce homophobia certainly accords well with the ways in which popular culture, including religious culture, has inculcated homophobia. The closeting of same-sex love so as to make it "the love that dare not speak its name" certainly had great success at the height of homophobic hegemony. As Plato suggested, the resources of religion have been brought to bear so as to make same-sex love seem an abomination. Those who do indulge in these appetites are branded as effeminate, as less than manly. And the impossibility of combining same-sex love with any sort of human fulfillment or happiness has resulted, as Plato apparently hoped, in the increased incidence of suicide among those so "afflicted."

Of course not all that we encounter here has continued to characterize the development of homophobia. Same-sex love has more often been associated with a deficiency than with an excess, as Plato several times suggests. The salience of terms like "honor" and "shame" has been replaced with that of "guilt" and "righteousness." The project has in odd ways been Christianized as Christianity has had homophobia grafted onto it. That, however, will be the theme of later chapters.

Before leaving the Classical Greek culture for which Plato will come to be a primary representative for Christian authors, we should ask how Plato's perspective may be like or unlike texts that also may take a somewhat jaundiced view of same-sex relations. In order to do this we will look at two texts that may come from the period of the *Laws* or later: Xenophon's *Symposium* and the indictment of Timarkhos. We will conclude with some reflections on the possible causes of the emergence of Greek homophobia.

# – 4 –

# Other Greeks

## Xenophon's *Symposium*

The ambivalence that we have noticed in Plato's dialogues regarding pederasty finds interesting, if condensed, expression in Xenophon's *Symposium*.[1] The discussion of love is framed by the infatuation of a certain Callias with a beautiful lad named Autolycus. In fact we are told of the astonishing beauty of the lad in terms not unlike those used of Charmides in Plato's dialogue of the same name: "In the first place, his good looks drew everyone's attention to him, as surely as a light draws all eyes towards it in the dark; and secondly, there was not a man there whose feelings were not moved at the sight of him. Some became more silent, and the behavior of others underwent a sort of transformation. Possession by a god always seems to have a remarkable effect" (228). After some by-play occasioned by the remarkable beauty of another boy, the dancer brought in to entertain the guests at the house party at the home of Callias's father, Hipponicus, and in a situation at first reminiscent of that of *Lysis*, Socrates advertises his skills as a pimp or perhaps match-maker (238). Thus the aim of what follows will be for Autolycus to become enamored in turn of Callias and in that way to become the beloved of his older (but still youthful) would-be lover. This will appear to be successful, as at the end we will be informed that Autolycus "kept his eyes focused on Callias" (265).

In addition we are informed of the love affair between two other members of the party, Critobulus and Clinias, and are told that Socrates acts like he is tired of hearing about Clinias and asks why Critobulus wants to see Clinias so often when he obviously has his appearance memorized; apparently this fixation has been going on for a long time, which Socrates indicates by reference to hair growth (243).

52

This appears to indicate a longstanding attachment. Its erotic expression is discreetly alluded to by Socrates, who claims that Critobulus "has even kissed Clinias, and nothing is a fiercer inducement to love than that. It's an insatiable thing, and it produces a kind of delicious anticipation. That's why I say that anyone who wants to be able to behave responsibly ought to refrain from kissing the young and attractive" (244). Is this to be taken ironically, or does it presage something more critical?

If the outer frame of the discussion seems to take for granted a nonchalant attitude toward the love affairs of men with youths that had appeared to characterize some of Plato's earlier dialogues, the discussion that serves as the main course of this symposium moves toward the perspective given expression in the *Laws.* Later it becomes clear that the physical expression of love is something to be actively discouraged.

To this end we are first told of the disagreeable inequality that must characterize any physical expression of love between a lover and his beloved:

> Must not those whose affection is mutual look at each other with pleasure and converse in amity; must they not trust and be trusted, be considerate to each other, share pleasure in their successes and sorrow if anything goes wrong.... It's this sort of conduct that maintains people's mutual devotion to their friendship and their enjoyment of it even into old age.
>
> As for the lover whose attachment is physical, why should the boy return his affection? Because he assigns to himself the gratification of his desires, leaving the boy to the extremity of shame? Or because the favor that he is eager to exact cuts the favorite off completely from his family and friends? (260).
>
> Again, is one who sells his youthful beauty for money any more likely to love the purchaser than one who trades in the market? Certainly, the fact that he is young and his partner is not, or that he is beautiful and his partner is so no longer, or that he is not in love and his partner is — this will not stir his affection. A boy does not even share the man's enjoyment of sexual intercourse as a

woman does: he is a sober person watching one drunk with sexual excitement. In view of all this, it is no wonder if he even develops contempt for his love...the shameless form of intercourse has led before now to many atrocious deeds. (260–61)

In the first place we see here the contrast between friendship and erotic attachment, which the *Laws* opposes outright. Then we see the divergence between the lover's and the beloved's interest in the physical or sexual expression of their attraction in ways that are reminiscent of Socrates' first (and subsequently retracted) speech in the *Phaedrus*, a position taken up again, as we saw, in the *Laws*. This contrast between the pleasure of the lover and the lack of pleasure of the lad will become a staple of certain forms of homophobic discourse in this and the following Hellenistic era.

It is in this connection that we are informed of the shame that must attach to the gratification of sexual desire. In fact Socrates has ominously just referred to sexual gratification of pederastic eros as a "shameless form of intercourse" and moreover one that leads men to commit atrocities.

It appears that one of the difficulties in this position is the by now well established tale of Zeus and Ganymede, a tale that had been cited as a precedent for the lover's love of youths. In the *Laws* the Athenian had maintained that the tale was an invention of the Cretans. But here we are treated to a reinterpretation of the story that will seek to make it count not for, but against, the gratification of sexuality. Thus it is maintained here that "Ganymede too was carried off by Zeus to Olympus on account not of his body but of his mind" (262).

In addition to finding a way to cope with the example of Zeus and Ganymede, it is also necessary to deal with the apparently widespread view that same-sex love produces virtue in the lovers. We must separate the example that Phaedrus cited in Plato's *Symposium* of Achilles and Patroclus from serving as a precedent for the physical expression of same-sex love:

Homer has made Achilles exact his famous vengeance for Patroclus not because Patroclus was his lover, but because he was

a friend and was killed. Also, Orestes and Pylades, and The-
seus and Pirithous, and many others among the greatest heroes
are celebrated in song for having jointly performed the greatest
and noblest exploits, not because they slept together, but out of
mutual admiration. (262)

Now of course this is an exercise in hermeneutical bravado. It
asserts: yes they were lovers, but they didn't have sex. How do we
know that they didn't have sex? Because they were admirable, and
admirable people don't have sex in these relationships. The argument
is quite circular in form. To be sure the opposite argument may also be
circular: it is not shameful to have sex, because these admirable men
had sex with one another. How do we know that they had sex with
one another? Because they were lovers and that is what lovers do. In
the nature of the case the evidence for or against sexual expression is
indirect.

Having staked out a way of trying to reinterpret many of the
exemplars taken to legitimate the sexual expression of same-sex love,
Xenophon turns to deal with the more contemporary perspective of
the good soldier Pausanias in Plato's *Symposium*. We may recall that
while Pausanias had been willing to outlaw the Pandemian, or common, forms of same-sex love, he had maintained that the Uranian
form, which encouraged valor among the lovers, should be celebrated.
What we get is as follows:

And yet Pausanias, the lover of Agathon the poet, in his defense
of those who wallow in debauchery [referring to the *Symposium*,
according to the note] has said that an army composed of boys
and their lovers would be braver than any other, because he
said he thought that they would be most ashamed to desert one
another — a remarkable statement, that those who make a habit
of disregarding censure and acting shamefully towards each other
should be most ashamed of doing something shameful! (263)

Now if, as seems plausible, this is a reference to the speeches in
the *Symposium*, then Xenophon has actually conflated two different
speeches: the one by Phaedrus (which actually does refer to warriors)

and the one by Pausanius. In both speeches the question of honor and shame plays an important role, and in both there is the assertion that the love of lovers leads to honorable behavior, although Pausanias restricts this to the Uranian love, one that he claims permits the beloved's gratifying the desires of the lover. (We may also recall that Eryximachus, the doctor, rejoined that there was no harm in gratifying the desires of the lover even in what might appear to be the Pandemian sort of same-sex attraction.)

The rejoinder to all of this that Xenophon places in the mouth of Socrates is basically a counterassertion to be taken, one supposes, on faith: since it is shameful, it cannot produce honor. Now this is the position that Plato, as we have seen, put in the mouth of the Athenian in the *Laws.*

The position that we get in Xenophon's memoir of Socrates seems to be that same-sex love can be good so long as it never has sexual expression. This is rather more extreme than the position that Plato gives us in Socrates' second speech in the *Phaedrus,* where occasional sexual expression is no big deal. It seems to aim at a perspective like that of Diotima, but instead of edifying suppositions about the vision of the beautiful as such, it brings to bear the shaming tactics contemplated in the *Laws.* To this end it even suggests how a certain interpretive strategy may be employed not only to render harmless stories and assertions that had been used to approve same-sex love but to turn them to good advantage in the project of rendering same-sex love a cause of universal reproach. The position is, however, still some distance from that of Plato's *Laws.* There is here no appeal to nature, nor to the horrors of incest. Nor do we have the attempt to make same-sex love unspeakable. Pederasty is still quite loquacious, the desire still quite palpable. But it is deflected away from "physical" expression.

In the end the dialogue may even attempt a bit of reprogramming of same-sex love into heterosexual desire. The dancing boy who had been the object of rapt admiration earlier in the dialogue (and who apparently sleeps in bed with his Syracusan patron every night) stages a play in which he kisses one of the also lovely dancing girls. This amorous display has the result that, "When the guests eventually saw them in each other's arms and going off as if to bed, the bachelors swore that they would get married, and the married men mounted their horses and rode away to their own wives with the same end in view" (266).

The attempt to inculcate heterosexual desire through the media, even among those who are attracted to same-sex love, will have a long history, although not attended by the universal success for which this morality play seems to hope.

## Aiskhines v. Timarkhos

The indictment of Timarkhos in an Athenian trial in about 346 B.C.E. provides us with another glimpse into the emergence of Greek homophobia. The document that survives serves as the frame for K. J. Dover's influential study of homosexuality in Greece.[2] The text comes from about the time of Plato's death and so perhaps after the dissemination of the *Laws*. There is little to suggest that Plato's views in that text have yet taken hold in Athenian society, even though there is plenty of evidence of a marked uneasiness about at least some same-sex relations. I will not here reproduce Dover's magisterial work on this text but rather seek to identify through the text some of the motivations that would help to explain the emergence of Greek homophobia.

The situation is rather fraught with political consequence. If by the time of the writing of Plato's *Symposium* Athens had suffered the blow of losing its hegemony to the Spartans, this is now followed by events that presage the domination of all of Greece by Macedonia, now under the kingship of Philip and soon to be ruled by his all-conquering son, Alexander. In order to escape the devastation of Athens at the hand of Philip, who had taken much of the outlying territory remaining to Athens, a peace treaty had been made by a group including Demosthenes. However the latter had second thoughts, perhaps because the treaty seemed to others and perhaps to himself as a sell-out of Athenian interests. Accordingly he enlists Timarkhos to accuse the other ambassadors of selling out the country to foreign domination. In response Aiskhines countersues the plaintiff, maintaining that Timarkhos has sold his own body and so is in no position to accuse others of selling their country.

The subtext for the discussion of the vagaries of same-sex love then is the question of the integrity of the social body, which is under threat and suffering considerable humiliation. Somebody will have to pay to purge the social body of its shame.

Against this backdrop the brunt of Aiskhines' indictment of Timarkhos is that the latter is little better than a common prostitute and so has no right to speak in the assembly of free men, still less to bring charges against others. Indeed, Aiskhines maintains that Athenian law prohibits anyone who has sold his sexual favors from speaking in the assembly or undertaking any other public role (ambassador, priest, etc.). Not only is taking such a role prohibited, but if one does undertake such a role this offense is punishable by death. The logic here appears to be that if one sells one's own body then one cannot be trusted not to sell out one's own country or the public interest.

Aiskhines then attempts to substantiate the claim that Timarkhos has in fact given his sexual favors in return for something like remuneration and that he had done so repeatedly. The trick is determining what counts as remuneration. For, after all, pretty boys in Athens could expect to be showered with gifts by their (would-be) lovers — at least wined and dined. And in the case of Timarkhos, he had actually lived with one of these lovers in a public way and (since this would not itself be a problem it seems) had profited thereby in terms of having a noticeably affluent lifestyle. (This is all very tricky according to Dover's reading, since Aiskhines wants to indict Timarkhos without damaging the reputation of the presumed former lover, Misgolas.)

Now if Dover's reading of the text is correct (and I have no grounds for disputing it), then it would seem that same-sex love is not yet a source of shame in itself. But what is at stake is the possibility of indicting the beloved boy (or ex-beloved) as one who sells or has sold his (sexual) favors for gain to one or more of his lovers. This could be something of a slippery slope. How to distinguish the normal benefits received by a youth who is being courted from a certain sort of prostitution broadly enough defined? We can see the difficulty if we were to apply the same question to heterosexual courtship and even, as Engels seems to have noticed, to marriage itself. If there is financial benefit (dinner, a ring, a house), is there "prostitution"? Only, one supposes, if there is no sexual practice can the charge of prostitution be wholly avoided.

Aiskhines wants, however, to make sure that no one will suspect that he is indicting ordinary pederastic attachments. Perhaps he feels that if he came close to this he would lose his case with the body of Athenian free males whose opinion he is seeking to influence. Accordingly, he quite cheerfully admits not only to having pursued boyfriends but to have become jealous and quarrelsome with rivals and, moreover, to have written erotic poetry to boys (though, of course, not offering them coarse inducement to respond favorably to his appeals).

There is one point at which it may appear that the position of Aiskhines approaches the discussion in the *Laws* of what is "natural" and so of suggesting that the activity of Timarkhos is against nature. He asserts that Timarkhos has "outraged himself contrary to nature" (Dover 60). This is further connected to the charge that Timarkhos "has committed a woman's transgressions" (ibid.). Moreover Timarkhos is said to have acted shamefully: he is "guilty of the most shameful practices."

The text suggests that Timarkhos is guilty of crimes (against nature) that women commit in accordance with their nature. One way of reading this is the misogynist one that supposes that women are naturally prostitutes but that men by nature are...well, different. Another is that women are by nature promiscuous but men are so only "against nature." Finally there is the possibility that Timarkhos actually enjoyed being (or sought to be) penetrated as is natural for a woman but not for a man. Something like the last seems to be to be most probable: Timarkhos sought out men to penetrate him, most likely to gain some advantage convertible into lifestyle enhancement, that is, cash.

In this reading what is against nature is not the desire, nor the practice of the lover. The problem is the desire of the beloved to gratify the sexual desires of the lover. The motive is specified as financial gain, presumably so as not to offend the views of his male listeners.

Yet this denigration of the passive partner leads to a seeming contra-diction: after all, surely many of the men involved hoped that their desires would be gratified by their beloveds — not, of course, because of financial gain but because of . . . love.

What are we to make of this text with respect to our question of the origins of homophobia?

In the first place this text will obviously have little or no impact on the emergence of homophobia — certainly nothing comparable to the texts of Plato.

Second, this text does show us that it is possible to mobilize certain anxieties endemic to the pederastic model of same-sex love in order to shame and, as it turns out, condemn and exclude persons who are perceived to be a threat on other grounds.

Third, this sets up the question of how same-sex love will come to be associated both with promiscuity and with prostitution. Both of these associations manage to cast the blame upon the "passive" or younger partner in the same-sex relationship. There is as well the beginning of an association with femininity, albeit in terms that have misogynistic presuppositions as their background. (So, for example, it might be supposed that women are more likely to be in some sense prostitutes or promiscuous, so men who are willing "bottoms" in these relationships may be associated with the feminine in these respects.)

We have also seen how the anxieties that may typically be associated with same-sex love on the pederastic model may be exacerbated by the analogy to the threat of external cultural penetration or political domination. It is this last, I believe, that will do most to explain how it is that certain emergent forms of homophobic discourse come to have such plausibility in the world that the Alexandrian conquest will bequeath to us.

# – 5 –

# Why Homophobia?

Before leaving our discussion of Plato and the invention of what I have termed the homophobic project, it may be useful to see whether it is possible to account for this turn from a general acceptance and even celebration of pederasty to the attempt to discredit it. We will consider three possibly interacting hypotheses that together might help to account for this rather sudden turn, a turn that will have far-reaching implications for the development of Western homophobia.

Since this fundamental transformation can be traced in the work of a single philosopher (and one who will be the single most influential of philosophers for many centuries to come), it is tempting to try to account for this transformation in biographical and perhaps psychological terms. What is it that happens to Plato himself that produces such a transformation in his attitudes toward same-sex love? Is this the product of an aging process in which the appreciation for erotic adventures gives way first to an attempt to compensate for the disappearance of erotic opportunities by means of philosophical consolation (sublimation) and thence to an attempt to extirpate the very source of disappointment? Since we have love poetry ascribed to Plato that celebrates his love for Astral and Dion, does this mean that Plato once was in love and then through the death of his beloved was driven in grief to deny that love which had caused so much pain? Does Plato come to see that the Uranian love espoused by Pausanias has been overrun by the Pandemian so that the former has become but a pipe dream and that therefore there is nothing to be done but to extirpate the love so far as possible, as Pausanias had suggested?

These are all intriguing possibilities, but we have little to go on in terms of Plato's own personal biography that would enable us to reconstruct with any confidence what immediate events in his life might have occasioned this transformation. Of course it is by no means unknown that persons who enjoyed erotic relationships in their youth come later to distance themselves from all erotic attachments in later life. In antiquity, for example, we have the example of Augustine, whose *Confessions* suggest just such a trajectory. And no doubt many readers of this text will recognize from among their acquaintances something of this type of withdrawal from and denial of prior experience in this realm, whether in "heterosexual" or same-sex relationships. Sometimes this happens as a result of grief, sometimes as a result of terrible disappointment and even betrayal in love, sometimes for no discernible reason save a general diminution of erotic energy or withdrawal from life's vicissitudes. And of course for modern people there has also been the incentive of seeking the safety of social approval within a generally homophobic context. Some of these factors may have entered into the change in Plato's perspective, but we simply do not know enough of his biography to determine with any confidence which if any of these contributed to his turn toward the development of a homophobic project.

A second hypothesis would have to do with the ascendency of new (to Plato) or newly persuasive cultural or intellectual currents that have the effect of persuading Plato that his former openness to same-sex love may have been an intellectual error, one that can be corrected only by an attempt to discredit those forms of eroticism now seen to be in error. But what cultural/intellectual trends might have produced such an effect?

Later Christian writers are eager to demonstrate the agreement between Plato and Moses. Eusebius, for instance, in his *Demonstratio Evangelica*,[1] expends considerable effort showing the supposed parallels between the two thinkers, including agreement on very abstract philosophical topics. A few even suppose that Plato was influenced by the Bible in general and by Moses in particular. For example, Justin Martyr detects the influence of Moses on Plato's *Timaeus*, in which he also finds a doctrine of the cross.[2]

Leaving aside the question of Moses, what of biblical literature generally? I have shown in another book that the literature of ancient Israel is generally accepting of same-sex love; in fact that there is rather more variety of homoeroticism in that literature than is found in Greek literature. Only at a very late date do we get the famous, yet isolated, proscriptions of Leviticus.

There is a strong likelihood that the Holiness Code, within which we find the prohibitions, does not predate Plato. Even if the Holiness Code, and thus the prohibition of certain male-male sex acts, had been formulated and promulgated in some fashion by this time, nothing else in the *Laws* gives evidence of influence from Leviticus. And of course Plato does not call for the death penalty as does Leviticus 20. In addition to the problem that we do not know of any Greek translation of the Torah prior to the Septuagint (more than a century after Plato), there is, as we have seen, no terminology in common between Leviticus and the expressions used by Plato that seems to come closest to the perspective of Leviticus.

What of Persian influence? We know that the *Vendidad* contains prohibitions reminiscent of Leviticus. But again there is the difficulty of knowing just when such prohibitions might have been formulated. Moreover, the general outlook of the *Vendidad*, with its concern about demon possession and pollution, seems uncongenial to the outlook of Plato, whether early or late. There may well be some relation between the *Vendidad* prohibitions and the Leviticus prohibitions, since the latter may have been redacted (at the earliest) into what is now Leviticus during the time of Ezra (a contemporary of Plato's) while Judea was under the suzerainty of Persia. But it is also quite possible that the Holiness Code dates from the Hellenistic period, that is, after Alexander had conquered Persia.

The quest for Persian influence, then, seems nearly as much a dead end as the quest for biblical influence. It even seems from Herodotus that influential and elite circles in Persia (the only ones who were likely to have had much influence upon the aristocratic Plato) had come under the spell of pederasty themselves.[3]

The one cultural-intellectual tradition that does seem to have been at work in Plato's actual discussions of same-sex love is that of India. In discussing the *Phaedrus* we noticed that his notion of the transmigration of souls (a view that also appears elsewhere in his work) was one that seemed to bear the mark of Hindu influence, as does the caste-like division of souls to which he also refers. Even in the *Republic*

Plato had seemed to take it for granted that persons were really of quite different types and the divisions there may also have some similarity to that of influential Hindu perspectives. Of course slaves don't come into the picture for Plato, something also true for the Hindu structures that relegated the casteless to perpetual and hereditary exclusion and servitude. Nor would Plato be alone among Greek philosophers in having adopted perspectives from India. Pythagoras quite notably had earlier been influenced by ideas from India.

This is also an ongoing cultural influence that may have been accelerated by Alexander's conquest of parts of India, which for a time were on their way to being integrated into Hellenistic culture. Indeed, several Christian patristic authors seem to have knowledge of these cultural perspectives. One who is strongly influenced by Plato, Clement of Alexandria, makes explicit reference to these traditions,[4] and the adventurous speculations of his successor, Origen, show strong attraction to some of these ideas.

The difficulty, however, comes in identifying particularly homophobic texts or traditions from India that may have influenced Plato or indeed other developments in the homophobic project that he seems to have introduced into Western consciousness. Until much more is known about this, an Indian origin for this project will remain highly speculative.

A third hypothesis looks neither to idiosyncratic developments in Plato's experience, nor to vaguely identifiable intellectual influences from other cultures, but to developments more clearly determined by events in Greece itself, events that shook the confidence of Athenians in their own institutions and traditions. This is the likeliest source of at least a partial explanation.

Pederasty had been in flower from about 530 B.C.E. (decades after the conquest of Judah by the Babylonian Empire and about the same time as the conquest of Babylon by Cyrus the Great of Persia) until sometime near the end of the fifth century (before 400 B.C.E.) — thus for just over a century. Of course, it was the century of the Greek miracle as well: Socrates, Euripides, Sophocles, Thucydides, Aristophanes, and so on.

Toward the end of this period (431–404), Athens and Sparta were engaged in a struggle for hegemony over the city states of Greece and their colonies in Asia Minor. The struggle ended with the ascendancy of Sparta in 404 B.C.E. It was only five years later that Socrates was convicted of corrupting the youth of Athens and required to drink the hemlock. At that time Plato was still a young aristocrat, one of those who had presumably been corrupted. He left Athens for a number of years, returning in 387 to found his Academy and to write until his death in 347. The last years of Plato's life were characterized by another power struggle, this time with Macedonia to the north, a struggle that ended with the humiliating terms dictated by Philip of Macedon (Alexander's father) in 346, the terms of which occasioned the lawsuit against Timarkhos.

If we transpose Plato's career into the key of this larger socio-political landscape, we can see that he is at work during a period of successive humiliations inflicted upon Athenian greatness. If his earliest dialogues deal with a time when Athens had not yet succumbed to Spartan hegemony, then his latest dialogues come from a time when Athens (along with Sparta) is subjected to the further humiliations of defeat at the hands of the upstart Macedonians.

The effects of this double humiliation can be read not only in the writings of Plato. Eva Cantarella notes that the glorification of pederasty was suffering noticeable effects as well. She notes that the turn away from pederasty results from a social crisis (64) and continues:

Love inscriptions [dealing with pederastic love] on Attic vases ...disappear at the same time as the Peloponnesian war. This was the same time in which Xenophon was writing, and Aristophanes, in the theatre, was aiming the shafts of his irony at homosexuals... the years when, as Thucydides says, the morality of the city had undergone an absolute upheaval... pederasty had degenerated into vice.... The Peloponnesian war had decimated the city's youth: it was vitally important for Athens that new families should be set up, and that they should produce many sons for the fatherland. Hence, perhaps, the newfound interest in women, also evident in painting and sculpture, which at this time present images of women which are more sensual and, in particular, less androgynous. (64–65)

If we view them in this light we might conjecture that the early dialogues of Plato express a sort of nostalgia for the more innocent days in which pederastic relationships were the seedbed of virtue and, in the case of Socrates, of intelligence. This then moves toward a critique of ordinary pederasty in the speech of Pausanias in the *Symposium* and the rejection expressed in Socrates' first speech in the *Phaedrus*, but this is placed in tension with an attempt to radically idealize the pederastic relationship in the second speech of the *Phaedrus* and especially in the speech attributed to Diotima in the *Symposium*. Finally Plato gives in to what we might term the "rejectionist front," not only acquiescing to the critique of pederasty anticipated earlier (and presumably growing in strength in Athens generally) but going much further in the *Laws* to develop a thoroughgoing critique that seems to go much further than anything yet expressed in the Greek culture of the time. That is, once Plato adopts the critique of pederasty he characteristically thinks through this critique in a far more consistent and radical way than lesser thinkers.

Plato's critique, to the extent that it was influenced by sociopolitical events, would have been similarly overtaken by events with the ascendancy of Greek culture ironically brought about by Philip of Macedonia's son Alexander. For it was his conquest of the "world" that would lead to the dissemination of Greek language and cultural institutions — including the gymnasium, the symposium, and the valorization of male same-sex relations of a pederastic model — throughout the new Hellenistic world.

One explanation for the rise of homophobia then would be the perceived threat to the social body construed as a masculine body. Thus social domination or penetration could be represented also as heightened anxiety concerning the threat of the domination, penetration, or feminization of the male body. Male same-sex relationships would then be a casualty of this heightened anxiety.

Of course this is only a hypothesis. But it is one that we can take into account as we trace the emergence of Christian homophobia in later chapters.

As for Plato, for now we can simply wonder about the relative strength of these three possible factors: the personal issues, the influence of other cultures, and the social anxiety contributed by Athenian humiliation. Of course such factors will not to account wholly for Plato since, whether in idealization or in rejection, Plato's thought is always more rigorous, more consistent, and more daring than that of his contemporaries. Even with respect to the homophobic project that we have noticed, it will be centuries before this project is fully actualized in the Western civilization that is marked (for better and for worse) by his genius.

# Part Two

# Hellenistic Discourse

I N THE CASE OF PLATO we have seen the emergence of a homophobic project in the heart of a culture and a body of literature that also had been hospitable to the discourse approving and celebrating same-sex love. The task to which we now turn is to discover the effects of that discourse in subsequent Hellenistic thought. Is the late position of Plato simply idiosyncratic or does this homophobic project gather momentum in the brave new world inaugurated by Alexander's conquest and the diffusion of Greek language, culture, and institutions through the Mediterranean world?

In order to have a sense of what happens to Plato's homophobic project we will examine three sorts of texts that stem from three different parts of this civilization but that are roughly contemporaneous both with one another and with emerging Christianities. It will obviously be impractical to attempt to survey all Hellenistic literature for traces of the emergence and development of homophobic discourse. But by restricting ourselves to these three sorts of texts from this period we will have a way to understand the intellectual context within which Christianity emerged and the homophobic discourse that will become a part of that intellectual heritage.

The first text to which we will turn is Plutarch's *Dialogue on Love*, a text that takes up the question of eros, which had been the theme of the symposia of Plato and Xenophon. Plutarch was an extraordinarily prolific writer, whose indebtedness to Plato he regularly acknowledges. The *Dialogue on Love* attests to this indebtedness and in turn influences imitations in the Hellenistic world to which we will also give some attention: the dialogues of Achilles Tatius and of Pseudo-Lucian. The dialogues on love generally explore the relative merits of same-sex and of cross-sex (or as we would say, heterosexual) love and so are also sources of homophilic discourse.

The second text to which we will attend is that of Musonius Rufus, a Stoic thinker writing in the environs of Rome although in Greek. His indebtedness to Plato again is explicit, and he develops some of the homophobic themes in important new directions. He is an acknowledged source for the appropriation of homophobic themes into the Christian tradition, as is Maximus of Tyre, whose text on Socratic love will also come in for some attention.

Finally we will deal with texts of Hellenistic Judaism, especially texts of Philo, which both acknowledge the influence of Plato and come to have influence in emergent Christianity, especially that form of Christianity that emerges in Philo's own sphere of influence, the Hellenistic city of Alexandria. We will also examine briefly texts that supplement our view of first-century Hellenistic Judaism, those of Josephus and of Pseudo-Phocylides.

These three kinds of discourse from the first century but from different ends of the Hellenistic world will demonstrate the effectiveness of the homophobic project initiated in the work of Plato.

# – 6 –

# The Arguments on Love

## Plutarch's *Dialogue on Love*

In first-century Greece, Plutarch (45–120 C.E.) wrote an extraordinary body of work. He is perhaps best known for his *Lives of Famous Men*, a series of paired biographies, which is one of the main sources for our knowledge of the ancient world. He also wrote prolifically on themes that we might loosely characterize as "ethics" (the generic term applied to this literature is *Moralia*) in which he conducts what was then the chief business of philosophy: reflection on the good life, or what makes life good (as opposed, for example, to what we might term speculative or metaphysical questions). Within this body of literature, he produced a dialogue on love that would serve as a pattern for similar works in the Hellenistic world.

A discussion about love among friends will obviously owe something to the dialogues of Plato that deal with this theme. There are elements of form as well as of content that are reminiscent of the *Symposium*, already one of Plato's most famous dialogues. For example, for Plutarch and his imitators discussions of love will be remembered conversations that are set up as having occurred long ago, and perhaps far away. That is, there is the gesture of distance or distantiation, which recalls the rather odd second- or third-hand character of the *Symposium* of Plato.

But if in the case of Plato the discussion of love has primary, even exclusive, reference to male same-sex love of the pederastic form, the dialogue or argument to which we now turn is set up as a debate on the relative merits of two kinds of eros or love, that between males and that between male and female. One can scarcely imagine Plato composing speeches in favor of heterosexual marital bliss, but this will be one characteristic of the dialogues in question. We might detect here the influence of Xenophon, whose own *Symposium*, while mostly dealing with same-sex love among males, ends with an incitement to marriage and to the practice of its sexual pleasures.

Because of the attempt to give each side of this debate its say, these dialogues will not themselves be strictly homophobic in overall character. Indeed, they are often read as evidence of the continuing approval of same-sex love, whether in opposition to cross-sex love or as a necessary or desirable supplement. Here I will attend to these texts in order to see to what extent the argument for heterosexual love also takes the form of an argument against same-sex love and to see whether in this context we can find traces of the development of Plato's homophobic project.

The *Dialogue on Love* is presented as a conversation that took place prior to the birth of the putative narrator, Autobulus, Plutarch's son.[1] The latter has, therefore, indirect knowledge of the discussion that he reports. It is presented as if occurring in another time and another place (Helicon) on the occasion of a visit by Plutarch and his bride to a shrine to present an offering aimed at somehow resolving a dispute between their in-laws. The frame is thus heterosexual partnership set over against the socio-legal structure of institutional family values. Not surprisingly, the upshot of the discussion of love will be a praise of cross-sex love as intimate partnership rather than pederasty on the one hand or familial and procreative duty on the other.

The immediate occasion of the discussion, or rather dispute, that concerns us is that a lovely boy, still a minor (749e), is the object of the determined love of an older (though still young) and wealthy widow, Ismenodora.[2] The lad's friends are mostly opposed to this match. Two of these friends come to Plutarch and his companions to resolve their dispute: Pisias, who is the male lover of the youth, and Authemion, who actually favors the match with the widow. Plutarch's friends take up their respective causes, with Protogenes representing the side of the love of youths and Daphnaeus representing the love of women. This section of the "dialogue" has the combatants not so much defending their own amorous proclivities as attacking those of the other. Thus Protogenes will attack the love of women by giving vent to misogyny, while Daphnaeus will attack the pederastic alternative. It is therefore the discourse of the latter that is of most interest to us.

Love for women is characterized by Protogenes as effeminate and as yielding too easily to pleasure, while the love of youths is ordered toward virtuous and manly friendship. Accordingly "there is only one genuine love, the love of boys" (751a). The Greek word used is *ephebe* and should be understood as referring to someone in their late teens. The unrestrained attack upon women and the lover of women provokes a similarly strong attack upon same-sex love in its pederastic form from Daphnaeus.

It is in Daphnaeus's discourse that we encounter the clear effects of Plato's homophobic project, though the position staked out here is not as clear-cut as Plato's. Daphnaeus admits at least a superficial similarity between the love of youths and the love of women: "if union contrary to nature [*para physein*] with males does not destroy or curtail a lover's tenderness, it stands to reason that the love between men and women being normal and natural will conduce to friendship" (751c–d). On the one hand these loves are comparable, while on the other they are divided by the "natural." Their comparability will be suggested again: "excitement about boys [*paidas*] and women is one and the same thing: Love" (751f). Yet it continues to be characterized as "contrary to nature." It is this appellation that the seeker derives from Plato: "But to consort with males (whether without consent, in which case it involves violence and brigandage; or if with consent, there is still weakness [*malakia*] and effeminacy [*thalutati*] on the part of those who, contrary to nature, allow themselves, in Plato's words 'to be covered and mounted like cattle') . . ." (751d–e). The paraphrase of Plato may refer to *Phaedrus* (250e), but if it does, the animal reference there is to cross-sex love that aims at procreation, which is then conflated with boy love as "contrary to nature" in the immediate sense of that nature shared with animals. Indeed, Daphnaeus will maintain that this procreative instinct is one that "co-operates to win immortality for the human race by kindling afresh through new generations our being, prone as it is to extinction" (752a). We may recall that this had been touched on by Diotima's speech in the *Symposium*, only to be discarded in favor of a greater immortality to be won through contemplation of the beautiful as such. Plutarch has less interest in speculative immortality, however, being concerned with a more "practical" point of view. He will indeed suggest that the only measure of a woman's proper age for marriage has to do with her capacity to bear children (754c). This whole discussion is mediated to the reader through the narration of the immediate bearer of Plutarch's imagined immortality, his son. Early Christian discourse will not take up this form of the "defense of marriage" and of procreation since it will entertain an immortality that it will suppose to be closer to that envisaged by Diotima. Only following the Reformation would a defense of marriage on these terms (citing Genesis 1 and 2) become a central part of Christian homophobic discourse.

What we learn from this fragment of the dialogue, then, is that Plato is cited to affirm the view that same-sex love is contrary to nature and that it is effeminate, at least in the case of the youth who takes the place of a woman in sexual congress. We are not yet at a place where it is possible to identify same-sex love as unthinkable and unspeakable. Indeed, Plutarch will praise the pederastic form of love, the role of lovers with handsome young men as he will say (758b), and in this he seems not far from the position adopted by Socrates in the *Phaedrus*, which he seems to cite (758d), and goes on to echo some of the themes that we have encountered in the speeches of Phaedrus and Pausanias in the *Symposium* in praise of love in its pederastic form (760–62). This is then combined with the affirmation of the love of beautiful persons that conduces to the love of beauty, an argument that seems to owe more to Socrates in the *Phaedrus* than to Diotima in the *Symposium*. Finally, however, Plutarch will bring this all back to a praise of conjugal love between man and woman, a theme, as we have noticed, that did not commend itself to Plato.

Thus the discussion, having given vent to some of Plato's homophobic tropes, settles for the conclusion that a more moderate boy love (especially the sublimated sort) is fine but the love of women is far better (and more "natural").

## Achilles Tatius

In the course of a remarkable novel of adventure and romance, which may have been written not long after the dialogue of Plutarch, we find another discussion of the relative merits of the love of youths and the love of women.[3] In this case the spokespersons are good friends who stage their discussion for the sea captain who is taking them a further step on their journey to recover Leucippe, the girlfriend of Clitophon, from her captors. It is Clitophon who speaks for love of women while Menelaus will speak for the love of youths, a love to which Clitophon is sympathetic if for no other reason than the grief of his friend Clinias, whose boyfriend had died tragically in the earlier pages of the novel, a tragedy mirrored in the tale of Menelaus. The discussion will therefore have none of the invective that was present in the early pages of Plutarch's debate. (We might, however, be given some pause at the way that same-sex love seems here to have a tragic death as its consequence rather than "they lived happily ever after," which will ultimately characterize the love of Leucippe and Clitophon. In both cases the death of the beloved youth implicates the guilt as well as the grief of the male lover.)

The main further contribution of this little dialogue to homophobic discourse is the interpretation it offers of the story of Zeus and Ganymede. We may recall that this tale had been cited, according to Plato, as precedent for the love of youths, a love disseminated from Crete, the birthplace of Ganymede. Plato dismisses the tale as one simply concocted by the Cretans and one that defames the god. Xenophon had offered instead a moralizing (and implausible) reflection on the tale as one indicating a less physical and more "spiritual" love. Clitophon, responding to a more traditional reading of the tale offered by Menelaus, offers an interpretation that will more closely parallel the interpretation that will be offered (as we shall see) by Christian readers of the story: "I am even sorry for him [that is, Ganymede] in the manner of his assumption — a savage bird swooped down upon him, and when he had been seized by it he was placed in an ignominious position, looking like one crucified [estauromeno]. Can one imagine a viler sight than a youth hanging from a beast's talons?" (2.37). A tale that had been told to justify same-sex love as "divine" is here reimagined as one that characterizes at least that episode as violence and violation. This will become the standard early Christian reading of the story.[4]

## (Pseudo-)Lucian: The Affairs of the Heart

This rather extended and sometimes ribald discussion of the relative merits of the love of youths and the love of women, its editor suggests, comes from the early fourth century C.E. and thus later than the two dialogues we have been considering.[5] The debate and action is framed by the perspective of Theomnestus, who is an enthusiastic lover of both youths and women and who will ultimately affirm that they are both fine even if the edge goes to the love of youths (perhaps in imitation and reversal of Plutarch).

The internal debate, however, remembered by Lycynos, Theomnestus's admiring friend, is between Charicles the (homophobic) lover of women and Callicratidas the (misogynistic) lover of youths. Humor is added to the debate by the fact that the proponent of the enduring love of youths is himself a stodgy and bluff masculine type who, however, keeps only pretty beardless youths in his home, while the lover of women is a rather feminine Corinthian who wears makeup and keeps a bevy of dancing girls in his home. The discourses accordingly undercut both one another and themselves.

What is of interest to us, however, is the evidence we deduce from the talk of Charicles concerning the forms of homophobic discourse as this has developed in the popular literature of the early Christian era.

Charicles initiates the debate with reference to a sort of "Mother Nature" who "allowed males as their peculiar privilege to ejaculate semen, and made females to be a vessel as it were for the reception of seed . . . that each should retain its own nature and that neither should the female grow unnaturally [para physin] masculine nor the male unbecomingly soft [malakizesthai]" (19). This is linked to the mechanism for the perpetuation of the human race as we might expect (without forgetting that the speaker is one depicted as using cosmetics and otherwise characterized as effeminate). It is only in a later age of decadence, he maintains, that transgressing the laws of nature, males looked at "the male as though at a female after using violence like a tyrant or else shameless persuasion" (20). The use of a male as a female echoes a trope we first encountered in the Laws and is reenforced by the use of a simile we also first encountered in the Laws, that of sowing seed on barren rocks as the way of describing male anal intercourse: "sowing their seed, to quote the proverb, on barren rocks they bought a little pleasure at the cost of great disgrace" (20). (The readers have been treated to the aftermath of a more literal sowing of seed on barren rock in the recounting of the damage done to a statue of Aphrodite by a male adherent of the love of women who had inflicted damage and stain upon the buttocks of the statue, with which he had attempted intercourse.)

The theme of the emasculation or feminization of the boy toy is expounded at some length. And, we are told, "certainly among animals, incapable of debasing anything through depravity of disposition the laws of nature, are preserved undefiled" (22). This had been the first attempt of the Athenian to discredit pederasty, albeit one in which he did not seem to have much confidence. The ease with which Callicratidas will overturn it by maintaining that animals also have no use either for friendship or philosophy shows that Plato may have been right not to put all his homophobic eggs in the basket of animal behavior.

In an enlargement upon this argument, which will be echoed also in Hellenistic Judaism, he maintains, "if each and every man should choose to emulate such conduct the human race would come to a complete end" (22). Of course both Callicratidas and Theomnestus will agree that procreation is necessary to the human race, though Callicratidas might qualify it as a necessary evil. But again necessity is not exactly an argument for virtue and Plato's view does not seem to have expected much more of heterosexual attraction than compliance with natural (and social) necessity.

There is more rather inventive material, including an attack upon those who, allegedly emulating Socrates, defend the love of youths in the name of virtue. While this would undercut most of what we have in the Platonic dialogues, it is consistent with the view of the old Plato in the *Law*s that would banish the love of youths altogether. On the other hand we are later told by an approving Theomnestus that Socrates did in fact have sex with Alcibiades (54)![6]

Of course it is not possible to do justice to the delightful and sometimes intricate character of these debates about the relative merits of the love of youths and the love of women. We have only been able to give a certain amount of attention to the ways in which the defenders of the love of women make use of homophobic arguments to discredit the other side of the debate (as in turn that side ventures into blatant misogyny). The culture within which such debates were read and enjoyed could not have been seriously homophobic since the side of the lover of boys is always given rather full hearing. Nor could it have been entirely innocent of homophobia or of the staple arguments used to discredit pederastic forms of same-sex love. We have by no means reached the point that Plato desired, in which same-sex love would dare not speak its name.

However, we have seen that several of the ways to discredit same-sex love that Plato deploys in the *Laws* do seem to have penetrated popular culture. There is often explicit reference to him and invocation of his authority in the discourses that seek to discredit same-sex love. Certain notions seem to be gaining currency from Plato: the argument from nature, the question of effeminacy, even the "proverb" of sowing seed on rocky soil. These discourses are, however, playful in tone and as such will not significantly influence the rather serious church fathers who will increasingly adopt the Platonic homophobic project as their own. Of greater influence in this regard will be the work of Musonius Rufus, to which we now turn.

# – 7 –

# Stoic Homophobia

From one point of view it is by no means obvious that Stoicism should have become one of the sources for a transmission of some homophobic elements of Platonic philosophy. The putative founder of Stoicism, Zeno, had the reputation of being himself a lover of youths. Moreover, well into the early Christian era, Stoic philosophers were apparently regarded as continuing that tradition and even of using philosophical talk for the purposes of seducing youths and boys. This is one of the sallies of Charicles in the Pseudo-Lucian text we have just read. And we have additional work attributed to Lucian that points to the hypocrisy of Stoics in talk of virtue and philosophy as a cover for their pursuit of pederasty.[1] Is this simply a form of satiric character assassination or were the Stoics in the Hellenistic period simply following along the path marked out by Zeno or by the Socrates of the early dialogues of Plato?

## Musonius Rufus

In any case the Stoic philosopher most cited by early Christian apologists seems to be Musonius Rufus, whose views on sex and marriage will, in modified form, be adopted by many early Christian thinkers, most notably the Alexandrians, whom we will discuss in a later chapter. Although little is known of Musonius Rufus's biography, it appears that he was born about 30 C.E. and may have survived until the end of the first century, living and teaching primarily in Rome and its environs. His work may originally have had the form of dialogues and may have exhibited considerable Socratic irony. Yet what has come down to us are apparently summaries of the gist of these dialogues in the form of a series of short essays on various topics compiled by his student Lucius.[2]

Musonius does provide an antecedent for the rejection of same-sex love and particularly its pederastic form but within an ideological context that will become definitive for Christianity: that sex is for procreation and not for pleasure. It is because of this context rather than on account of the degree of his opposition to pederasty that Musonius will influence the development of Christian homophobia. That is, it is the view of sexuality generally that will become the decisive framework within which Christian homophobia develops.

In order to get at that framework, however, it is important first to indicate how Musonius understands and presents the task or meaning of philosophy. For Musonius, philosophy is about instructing people in how to live the good life. He will even write that "being good is the same as being a philosopher" (107). Lutz characterizes his view as supposing that "the primary aim of philosophy is the care of the soul in order that the qualities of prudence, temperance, justice, and courage may be perfected in it" (27). This summary seems correct, save that there is little talk of the "soul," but rather something more like the self, the person, the human being as such. So what we will encounter here is a sort of self-help manual or instruction guide for those who seek to be good. Thus insofar as the virtues of justice and courage and prudence are at stake here, and they are, it is not with the abstract or ultimate essence or form of these virtues that Musonius is at all concerned (as in the dialogues of Plato, or the investigations of Aristotle) but with the practical matter of training in ways that enable one to acquire them and to persevere in them. Philosophy consists in "thinking out man's duty and meditating upon it" (107). Philosophy thus is "training in nobility of character and nothing else" (49). Even less than Plutarch is Musonius interested in the Platonic quest for the contemplation of the good or the true or the beautiful, but rather in what it means to be good or just, and to be so habitually. The hope of Musonius seems to be that if one will adopt the point of view that he recommends and then practice this with constant vigilance and effort as if in training for an athletic contest, one will achieve one's aim. "Whatever precepts enjoined upon him he is persuaded are true, these he must follow out in his daily life. For only in this way will philosophy be of profit to anyone, if to sound teaching he adds conduct in harmony with it" (37). Nor does Musonius offer the reader much in the way of incentive to desire to be or become good. He supposes that this is in fact what his hearers want and proposes to show them how to achieve their aim. This is related to his supposition that "the human being is born with an inclination toward virtue. And this indeed is strong evidence of the presence of good in our nature" (37).

In order to achieve this aim there are essentially two basic principles that may seem to be in some tension with one another. One is to avoid pleasure, and the other is to live in accordance with nature. The text actually begins with the first, "the proposition that pleasure is not a good" (33). The argument for this is odd, an oddity that may result from Lucius's "tin ear" for irony. The argument is this: "At first sight we do not recognize it as true, since in fact pleasure appeals to us as a good. But starting from the generally accepted premise that every good is desirable and adding to it a second equally accepted that some pleasures are not desirable, we succeed in proving that pleasure is not a good" (33). Now for this to work we must suppose that what people desire is the good and we have seen that he does affirm this. That some pleasures are not desirable he will exhort us to believe by showing that in the long run they not only conflict with what is good for us but also with something like long-term happiness or at least equanimity. Yet instead of concluding from this that *some* pleasures are not good he insists that pleasure as such is not good; in fact that pleasure is in general and as a rule positively harmful and bad. This leads him to insist upon a strenuous, Spartan, or near-ascetic style of life that will regard every indulgence or even comfort with the gravest suspicion. It is in this connection that he will deploy one of his favorite epithets, that of *malakia*, to characterize the pampered lifestyle adopted by the rich and unphilosophical. While some have translated this term as effeminate in contexts in which we have already encountered it (in the dialogues on love for example), that cannot but be a misleading way of translating the term here, since Musonius will maintain, rather at length, the strict moral equality of males and females. Rather, it means soft in the sense of luxurious and self-indulgent. Thus young men who have had a Spartan upbringing will have an easier time in learning philosophy than those who have been reared in luxury. For a similar reason he will recommend the life of a farmer rather than a city dweller to those who seek to become philosophical. In any case it is by abstinence from pleasure that we learn the self-control necessary for the cultivation of the good character (55).

At times overlapping with this principle of the avoidance of pleasure and at times in some tension with it is his advice to live in accordance with nature. Musonius claims that the best method is to live "in accordance with nature" (107, 111). This he supposes is in accord with the first principle since "Neither man nor horse nor dog nor cow were created for pleasure" (109). He will maintain indeed that our more natural diet is vegetarian. In any case "when food is performing its real function it does not produce pleasure for man" (119). In some cases the animals provide us with illustrations of the natural in Musonius's sense as when he points to the courage of animals (59). On other occasions the limits of an appeal to the good character of the animal kingdom appear as when he speaks of humans who become greedy like swine or dogs rather than men. Or when he asserts that "to return evil for evil is the act not of a human being but of a wild beast" (89).

In one very important respect Musonius will depart from the way in which an appeal to nature had commonly been made by insisting that male and female are to be viewed as completely equal as regards all that pertains to philosophy. In the third and fourth essay of these reflections Musonius insists that it easy to see that "there is not one set of virtues for a man and for a woman." Both must have understanding, justice, chastity, avoidance of adultery, self-control, courage. He supposes therefore that both sons and daughters should be taught philosophy. To be sure he makes allowances for what he takes to be differences between men and women and sometimes seems to be saying that philosophy will enable a woman to be "content with her lot" (43), which may seem like an overlarge concession to convention. Later he will suggest that while it may be true that men's bodies are stronger than women's and that thus "tasks should be assigned which are suited to the nature of each," he does admit that "occasionally, however, some men might more fittingly handle certain lighter tasks and what is generally considered woman's work, and again, women

might do heavier tasks which seem more appropriate to men whenever conditions of strength, need, or circumstance warranted." Thus
all human duties are common and so "none is necessarily appointed for
either one exclusively" (47). While such a perspective certainly under-
cuts the misogyny that we encounter in some defenses of pederasty,
it also may overcome some of the gender dualism that is at work in
some of the defenses of the love of women as well.

This discussion of gender, however, prepares us for Musonius's discussion of sex and marriage, a discussion that will be influential in
Christian circles. Basically the views he will put forward are that sexual pleasure is not a good, that sex is in accord with nature when it
aims at procreation, that the good of marriage is companionship first
in the begetting and raising of children and then in whatever else pertains to life. By the end of the second century, these views, held by
Tertullian and Clement of Alexandria, will largely have been adopted
wholesale into Christian moral discourse. But it is in Clement that the
homophobic consequence will be most strictly drawn.

The following quotation is illustrative of Musonius's way of bringing
together these themes:

> For to what other purpose did the creator of mankind first divide
> our human race into two sexes, male and female, then implant
> in each a strong desire for association and union with the other,
> instilling in both a powerful longing each for the other, the male
> for the female and the female for the male? Is it not then plain
> that he wished the two to be united and live together, and by their
> joint efforts to devise a way of life in common, and to produce
> and rear children together, so that the race might never die? (93)

We have seen something similar in the dialogues of Plutarch and
Pseudo-Lucian, but there it was a sort of mother nature rather than
a father god who designed sexual difference and desire with a view
toward marriage and procreation. This last is emphasized at various
points: "Gods watch over marriage, for the purpose of procreation, and
those gods belong more properly to marriage than anywhere else" (95).

In some cases this procreative activity seems to be consistent with
sexual pleasure, as when he affirms that the true place of Aphrodite

is in marriage (95), but in another essay he will be said to affirm that "men who are not wantons or immoral are bound to consider sexual intercourse justified only when it occurs in marriage and is indulged in for the purpose of begetting children, since that is lawful, but unjust and unlawful when it is mere pleasure-seeking, even in marriage" (87). And he will maintain that the chief physical criterion for marriage should be a body "not wanting in strength to bear or beget children" (91).

Alongside this emphasis upon procreation, however, and perhaps in some tension with it is the ideal of companionship as the chief end of marriage. Thus all marriages must have "above all perfect companionship and mutual love of husband and wife, both in health and in sickness and under all conditions, since it was with desire for this as well as for having children that both entered upon marriage." Those who fail to attain to this ideal marriage eventually either separate or "they remain together and suffer what is worse than loneliness" (89).

The view of marriage as having as much to do with companionship as with procreation has much in common with Plutarch's view. Indeed, we may say that here marriage is taking on the form of the friendship ethos so regularly associated with same-sex love.

Before leaving this, however, we must underline the absolute value of procreation for Musonius. The emphasis upon the duty to procreate may have something to do with the imperial policy inaugurated by Augustus even before Musonius was born, which sought to require Roman citizens to marry and bear children. This decree appears to have met with enough resistance to require the imposition of significant tax penalties on those who did not comply.[3] Over the period of the empire Rome faced the threat of depopulation due to war and plague as well as resistance to marriage. Accordingly Musonius claims that marital procreation is a duty to the race and to the nation since it is only by this means that humanity is continued and the city populated. Thus, "whoever destroys human marriage destroys the home, the city, and the whole human race. For it would not last if there were no procreation of children and there would be no just and lawful procreation of children without marriage" (93). Indeed, it may be this sort of argument that will persuade Christians otherwise disposed to do without marriage altogether to adopt a more moderate stance, if only not to seem to flout imperial policy in this regard. But, as we shall see in Philo, this will also be used not only to maintain that marriage is necessary but that all nonprocreative sex is a betrayal of the human race, even genocide.

Musonius's version of homophobic discourse is far more muted than that, however. Indeed, if it were not for the way in which his general ethical perspective became so influential for Christians, his bare reference to same-sex love would not really be significant for our discussion. It is, however, precisely within the framework that we have been outlining that Musonius refers to same-sex love in ways that will portend trouble ahead. He refers in his discussion "On sexual indulgence" to the sexual mores of the wealthy and luxurious who therefore seek loves that are not only lawful but unlawful as well, "not men alone but also women." In our discussion of the histories of Rome in the chapter on Paul, we see that this may indeed refer to any number of evils. Musonius goes on to say that men "invent shameful intimacies, all of which constitute a grave indictment of manhood." Given the conditions in Rome that we will explore in the next chapter we could well imagine he is speaking of incest, for example, but Musonius adds that all forms of sexual intimacy that are outside marriage and that even within marriage do not aim at procreation are "unjust and unlawful." Although adultery seems for him to be the highest crime he will add: "and no more lawful are those of men with men, because it is a monstrous thing and contrary to nature" (87).

Now to be sure Musonius does not evince any particular animus toward this particular form of sexual outlawry (as he conceives it); he seems equally, or more, opposed not only to adultery but to prostitution, consorting with courtesans, having sex with maidservants, and general fornication. In fact he has more to say about the unlawful forms of heterosexual intercourse than the bare mention of same-sex relations. In this way it would be unfair to class his views as especially homophobic. However, it is the coming together of the denunciation of pleasure and the insistence that nature allows sex only for procreation that will provide a decisive context for homophobic views to flourish,

even if the fully grown plant of homophobia may seem wildly disproportionate to Musonius's own actually expressed views. The tropes of
nature, of monstrosity, of soft indulgence, and of the (possibly related)
violation of manhood, will not only echo themes that we encountered
in Plato but also begin to take on a life of their own as (male) same-sex
love becomes a privileged target of sexual opprobrium.

## Maximus of Tyre

Writing a century after Musonius, Maximus of Tyre, another philosopher believed to have influenced Christian thought, devotes four of
his forty philosophical orations to the question of "Socratic Love."[4]
The difficulty that Maximus addresses is that Socrates on the one
hand appears as a lover of beautiful lads while on the other is one who
seems committed to virtue. He intends to clear Socrates of the charge
that he corrupted youths in any "sexual" sense while defending his
quest for virtue and wisdom. His purpose is served by adopting a variation of the speech of Pausanias in the *Symposium* that distinguishes
the Uranian love of youths from the Pandemian, with the difference
that even in the case of the former Uranian love he will seem to deny
the appropriateness of sexual practice. Thus he will claim that "men
have taken a twofold phenomenon, one form of which is a companion
of virtue, while the other is a companion of Vice, and given to it the
single name of love (eros)" (18.3).

In the course of making this argument Maximus will also engage in
a hermeneutical move to ascribe to the exemplars of same-sex love a
chastity that precludes sexual expression. This is clear, for example, in
his reading of Achilles and Patroclus in Homer (18.8). He goes further,
however, in rereading the history of Crete and Sparta as exemplary of
nonsexual same-sex love. Thus "it is a matter of shame for a Cretan
boy to be without a lover, but equally it is a matter of shame for a Cretan youth to lay hands upon his boyfriend" (20.8). And this also goes
for Sparta: "A Spartiate may love a Spartan boy, but he loves him only
like a beautiful statue" (20.8). Thus, while even Plato in the *Laws* could
take Crete and Sparta to task for the promulgation of same-sex love,

Maximus offers a bolder revisionist history in aid of a homophobic project.

Maximus takes for granted the attraction of men to beautiful male youths. Indeed he extends this to include the example of Sappho with respect to a woman's desire for beautiful young women (18.9). Yet he cautions against the one that is attracted to superficial beauty and seeks pleasure while the other love is attracted through outer beauty to the beauty within and seeks only virtue (19.2–4): "One of them is maddened by the goad of pleasure, the other is in love with beauty" (19.4).

Accordingly, Maximus will represent the desire for pleasure as one that is manifestly excessive ("a violently excessive love is a shameful thing to hear about," 20.5). It is this desire that he says strains "after physical pleasure and burns to mingle body with body, clinging to an embrace that is neither seemly nor lawful nor even truly loving" (20.5). With respect to love of male and female, however, he will describe this as follows: "The opposite kind of love, which from innate desire forms legitimate liaisons exclusively with generative partners, for the purposes of the propagation of its kind, and confines itself to the female, is the ordinance of the gods of Marriage, Clan, and Birth. It holds sway over the entire animal kingdom." In this reflection Maximus seems indebted to the arguments of Plato in the *Laws* as he also is, rather tellingly, in his reference to same-sex love as "sowing on rocks" (20.9).[5]

The notion that youthful beauty exercises a powerful attraction for others of the same sex continues to be taken for granted by Christian authors in the patristic period. At the same time, ideas underlined by Maximus concerning the propagative intention of nature and come to play a decisive if subsidiary role in the emergence of Christian homophobic discourse. The development of this theme as well as that of the importance of a non- or even anti-homosexual reinterpretation of "canonical" texts and stories will be especially undertaken by Philo of Alexandria.

# – 8 –

# Hellenistic Judaism
# and the Hermeneutic
# of Homophobia

It is a commonplace that Christianity inherits not only from Athens but also from Jerusalem, not only from philosophy but also from the Bible. However, the variety of Judaism from which it learned most concerning homophobia is a style of thinking that had very little influence on emergent Judaism itself and, moreover, is the Jewish style of thought in the Hellenistic world most indebted to Plato. Indeed, as we shall see, it is even possible that Musonius was influenced by the most notable practitioner of Platonic Hellenistic Jewish discourse, Philo of Alexandria. It is not Jerusalem and Athens but Athens and Alexandria that will be decisive in the emergence of Christian homophobia.

For more than three centuries before the time of Paul, Judaism had been engaged in a protracted effort to come to terms with Hellenism. This may have begun as early as the Persian period as Persia, after conquering Babylon, had attempted to deal with the growing rivalry of Hellenic culture. The Hellenic states fought a series of wars that were ultimately successful in thwarting the Persian efforts at conquest (500–480 B.C.E.). The penetration of Hellenic culture into Persian culture is signaled by the suggestion of Herodotus that the Persian elites had learned the temptations and joys of pederasty during this period, a time when the Judeans were only beginning to emerge, with Persian sponsorship, from the Babylonian captivity. This sponsorship included the sending of Nehemiah to Judah around 420 B.C.E. In the aftermath of the subsequent mission of Ezra (also at Persian behest) after 358 B.C.E., it appears that the recodification of Israelite law was undertaken, a recodification that produced the Holiness Code, within which we find the proscriptions of certain forms of same-sex sexual practice. This may well come after Plato's *Laws*. (Plato died in 347.)

In the aftermath of Alexander's conquest of the eastern and southern Mediterranean (around 320 B.C.E.), the urgency of coming to terms with Greek culture and ideas became especially acute. Judaism was already well established as a diaspora not only in Babylon and Persia but also in Egypt, where it had been present at least since the time of Jeremiah (Jeremiah 43, 44).

Alexander established the city of Alexandria in Egypt, which was to become in many ways the cultural capital of Hellenistic civilization. The most dramatic instance of the mutual engagement of Judaism and Hellenism was the appearance of the Septuagint, the Greek version of the Scriptures of Israel, produced at the behest of the Ptolemaic emperor of Egypt (285–250 B.C.E.). This became the standard edition of the Bible for most of Judaism, including not only the diaspora but also Palestine, which was no less subject to Hellenistic rule and culture. This is the version of the Bible that is cited by all early Christian writers (including all the documents that will much later be called "the New Testament"). Only after the Roman–Jewish wars that resulted in the destruction of the Jerusalem Temple was a standard version in Hebrew of the Jewish Scriptures produced (the "Masoretic" text), resulting in the not inconsiderable irony that the oldest text tradition of these writings (the "Hebrew Bible") is in Greek, rather than Hebrew.

In the time following the Alexandrian conquest there was the production of a great many texts within the context of Hellenistic Judaism, many of which are to be found in the Apocrypha as well as in Pseudepigrapha related to the "Old Testament." In addition there are texts within the "Hebrew Bible" that were written during the time of intensive engagement with Hellenistic culture and rule. The book of Daniel most likely comes from the second century B.C.E., dealing, as it seems to do, with the crisis provoked by the Seleucid policy of cultural hegemony under Antiochus Epiphanes a century and a half after the Alexandrian conquest. Esther as well may reflect issues relating to this period, and the parallels with the story of Joseph in Genesis may even suggest that it too belongs to the Hellenistic period. This has led some scholars to suggest that all the "Hebrew Bible" was heavily edited or produced during the Hellenistic period.[1] Whether or not we give any credence to that suggestion, we should understand that there is a good bit of evidence, both canonical and extra-canonical, of the many creative attempts of Judaism to come to terms with Hellenistic ideas and culture during this period.

The question of the extent to which Hellenistic culture should be accommodated or resisted is well illustrated in 1 and 2 Maccabees, in particular with respect to the question of the introduction of a gymnasium into Jerusalem. We have already noted that according to Plato and others this institution was the primary carrier of pederastic same-sex customs. What is evident from the introduction to both accounts of the Maccabean revolt against the Hellenistic imperial policies of Antiochus Epiphanes is that there were many who favored this hellenization as well as others who opposed it. What is intriguing about the representatives of Hellenistic Judaism that we will be reading is how they find ways to oppose same-sex love on Hellenistic grounds, that is, by way of the appropriation of views from Plato.

What will ultimately be at stake in these discussions is the attempt to show that Jewish culture is not inferior to Greek culture, that Judaic polity (as represented by "Moses") is not inferior to Roman polity, and so on. What will emerge then is an alliance between Hellenistic Judaism and Greek philosophical traditions, traditions that will be understood to represent the best of Greek language and culture. The critique of polytheism and the emphasis on moral or ethical consciousness will provide the essential point of contact for these developments. In the course of emphasizing the moral significance of Hellenistic culture, a tradition of *paideia* or education had developed in Hellenistic circles that allowed for the reinterpretation of Greek classics (Homer, above all) so as to render them exemplary of the moral values appropriate to the education of the young in ways that cohered with the aspirations of philosophical culture.[2] Hellenistic Judaism adopted many of these same hermeneutical strategies to offer "allegorical" interpretations of its own traditions, a process from which in its turn Christianity also had much to learn.[3]

When we come to deal with Philo (as well as Josephus and Pseudo-Phocylides), we are dealing with texts that reflect a long and sophisticated tradition of Hellenistic Judaism, and, especially in the case of Philo, a Hellenistic Judaism steeped in the philosophical traditions of Greece. While post–second temple Judaism will subsequently turn away from the project of thinkers like Philo in order to develop a Talmudic and rabbinic form of life and culture, the contribution of Philo and others will be preserved in Christianity, which directly inherits from his work and accomplishments. The Alexandrian Christian thinkers will take over many of his insights and transmit them to the emerging Christian intellectual culture that they will do so much to shape.

## Philo

Due to his remarkable productivity and intellectual acumen as well as his location in Alexandria, the intellectual capital of the Hellenistic world, Philo would have a significant influence, if not on later Judaism, then on Christian and even pagan authors. Lutz suggests points at which the language of Philo (30 B.C.E.–50 C.E.) may have influenced the younger Musonius Rufus (30 C.E.–100 C.E.) working in Rome![4] Philo himself came from a wealthy and influential family, and his nephew later became procurator of Judea and, as an apostate from Judaism, prefect of all Egypt.

Philo's contribution to our theme comes in the form of his use of the allegorical hermeneutical process to assimilate biblical materials to the Platonic philosophical project. His approach was to seek a middle way between those who argued for an entirely allegorical approach that would dispense with the application of the literal meaning of the texts to contemporary Jews and those who held out for a merely literal interpretation and application. Philo's characteristic approach will be to seek to conserve the literal sense as a guide for Jews while adapting an allegorical interpretation to bring the texts into line with Platonic philosophical perspectives.

This approach is especially evident in his interpretation of the "special laws" of Israel and his reading of Genesis. The aspects of this work that are most important for our purposes are his approach to the Leviticus texts that seem to proscribe certain forms of same-sex sexual practice, and his approach to the Genesis narrative concerning the crimes of Sodom and the cities of the plain. The challenge for later Christian authors, as we will see, will be to adopt some of what he says about same-sex practices without relying directly upon the biblical texts that he is interpreting. It will be centuries before his interpretation of the Sodom story becomes a staple of Christian exegesis and many more centuries before Christian authors will be able to directly appropriate the Levitical texts as authoritative for their views. It will be easier to adopt his philosophically informed views of same-sex love than to adopt the specific texts to which he refers as determinative for Christian ethical reflection.

We turn first to what Philo writes in connection with the texts from Leviticus. The context is Philo's interpretation of "special laws" (those peculiar to Israel) that deal with sexuality.[5] In this discussion Philo displays a special avidity for the death penalty, perhaps under the influence of Leviticus 20, even for sexual offenses for which no such penalty is prescribed in "Mosaic" legislation. Thus he interprets the text of Deuteronomy 24:4 (concerning a man taking back a wife who had left him) as if it prescribed the death penalty, as he does also in the case of a prostitute in the interpretation of Deuteronomy 23:17.

In addition Philo deals with the case of sex with a menstruating woman, a theme that does figure in Leviticus. Here he uses a metaphor for sexual relations of sowing seed (which we have encountered in Plato) with the interesting explanation that having sex with a menstruating woman is like sowing seed "in ponds or mountain streams instead of the plains" (3.33). One of the marks of Christian sexual discourse is that it is not tempted by the Levitical or Philonic abnegation of sexual activity with menstruating women. Indeed Levitical taboos concerning menstruation or contamination by corpses are consistently resisted. The part played in this by recollections of Jesus' ministry whether with the menstruating woman in Mark 5:25–34 or with apparent corpses may have made the preservation of these taboos impossible.

Philo's talk of menstruating women as ponds or rivers in which seed is wasted may occasion an addition to Levitical (and other Mosaic) legislation concerning knowingly having sex with a barren woman, which he likens to sowing seed on a "hard and stony land" (3.34). He suggests that these should be counted as "the impious adversaries of God" who "stand confessed as the enemies of nature" (3.36).

It may be the reference to nature that then leads Philo to consider the case of pederasty. Having already used the trope of sowing seed on rocky ground for sex with barren women, Philo must use different rhetorical moves to discredit same-sex sexual practice. In another context I have argued that the Levitical prohibition has its starting point in the condemnation of the male who desires to be penetrated as a woman (the "lyings of a woman"),[6] and this is precisely the way in which Philo treats the Levitical prohibition, spending most of his ink describing the passive partner (and one he takes to be playing the part of the woman) and dealing with the active partner almost as an afterthought. Philo's rhetoric here is quite heated: "Mark how conspicuously they braid and adorn the hair of their heads, and how they scrub and paint their faces with cosmetics and pigments and the like, and smother themselves with fragrant unguents" (3.37). He concludes: "These persons are rightly judged worthy of death by those who obey the law, which ordains that the man-woman (androgunon) who debases the sterling coin of nature should die unavenged, suffered not to live a day or even an hour, as a disgrace to himself, his native land, and the whole human race" (3.38). This rhetoric seems wildly "over the top" compared to the laconic Levitical sentence: "shall be put to death." Certainly much more than an interpretation or even defense of the law seems to be at work here.

Only after this do we get to the "active" or older party to a pederastic relationship who he says "is subject to the same penalty" (3.39), basically for encouraging or abetting the behavior of one who defies gender absolutes. Thus Philo returns immediately to the specter of these "hybrids of man and woman," and here we get a sense for some at least of what may motivate his alarming rhetoric. It is that these "hybrids" (males who in one way or another, or to one degree or another) have privileged places in the festivals of the cities and nations. Here he mentions especially the rites of Demeter, whose male acolytes, the galli, mutilated their own genitals under the influence of a religious frenzy, and thus become sacred to the goddess (3.40). Ironically, these men whom Philo condemns as enemies of nature are themselves the most avid adepts of the goddess of nature: Demeter. Philo suggests that if these were condemned as public enemies this would serve as a deterrent to those who for whatever reason seek to play the woman's part (3.42). It is clearly this betrayal of male gender identity that must bear the brunt of Philo's rhetorical rage, even if it seems to take him far beyond what may have been contemplated in the Levitical legislation. But he has some sound precedent at least in the way in which Plato has taken aim in the *Laws* against those males who choose the passive part. And we recall that this opprobrium is exaggerated in subsequent texts influenced by Plato. Nevertheless the outrage directed against what in modern parlance would be called transsexuals is an attempt to deal with a situation far different from that which was contemplated by Plato since Greek pederastic rhetoric generally insisted that pederasty enhanced rather than threatened masculine gender identity. The literal de-masculinizing of the beloved has been carried much further, at least in the view of Philo, and thus he views pederasty as being on a continuum whose far (and all too blatant) pole is the exhibition of trans-gendered adepts of Demeter. In the Roman context his concern is not without some foundation for in spite of exaggerated concern about masculinity (or perhaps because of it), the castrated worshipers of Demeter will eventually include in their number the emperor Elagabalus. As we shall see, this transgendering of the male will also be the apparent target of the homophobic legislation of Christian emperors several centuries later.[7] It is a bitter irony indeed that an emperor famous for the revival of an old fashioned form of pederasty, Hadrian, is so opposed to "male genital mutilation" that he will launch the final Roman war against Judah, a war that will have the consequence of destroying Jerusalem itself. For Hadrian regarded circumcision itself as a crime against masculine bodily integrity.

Leviticus does deal with same-sex sexual practice as well as sex with menstruating women and also with the question of sexual practices with animals. Philo takes off on bestiality as well despite his social location in urban Alexandria, thereby developing a stereotype that will link bestiality with male same-sex sexual practices. (We may recall that in the aftermath of the supreme court decision legalizing "consensual sodomy," there were many who raised the specter of our society being treated to a wave of unrestrained bestiality, leaving one to wonder whether there was an imminent threat to the well-being of urban pets to which the SPCA ought to be alerted.)

What is interesting here, however, is that Philo suggests that this and other sorts of sexual outrage are the product of "wine-bibbing and the other pleasures of the belly and the parts below it" (3.43). This serves as his segue from a more traditional to a homophobic reading of the story of Sodom.

The rather disproportionate attention, at least to a modern reader, to the apparent pleasures of sex with beasts enables Philo to at least make an apologetic for Mosaic law concerning cross-breeding of animals (including that which produces mules). Moses' legislation, he maintains, is a wise provision to prevent persons from engaging in that other form of cross-breeding involving humans and animals that can only result in the birth of monsters. It is here that Philo will again invoke the idea of that which is "against nature," a trope that seems to link all nonprocreative forms of sexuality but especially bestiality and pederasty.

Accordingly, we can say that so far, at least, Philo's treatment of same-sex relations bears the mark of some of Plato's concerns and even language (sowing seed). Like Plato, Philo is concerned with sexuality that opposes or contravenes "nature" and with a sexuality that undermines the male ideal of separation from all that is "womanly."

I have noted Philo's interest in the death penalty. This may be to defend the Judaic death penalty for offenses not similarly punished under Roman law (although Roman law was hardly bashful about applying the death penalty). And we will see something similar in the case of Josephus. Yet it is one of the ironies of history that there is no record of Judaism ever imposing the death penalty for same-sex sexuality.[8] However, once Christianity finds itself in a position to directly cite Leviticus as warrant for its own homophobia (something that will not happen until the late medieval or early modern period), then Christianity will enthusiastically execute "sodomites and catamites." And in a terrible irony the execution of all passive or effeminate same-sex practitioners for which Philo calls will be carried out most ruthlessly by the same Nazi regime that sought to exterminate the Jewish people.

## Sodom

Philo also appears to be responsible for the introduction of a homophobic reading of the story in Genesis concerning the crimes of Sodom. So entrenched has this reading become in the history of homophobia that it is important to note that it was by no means obvious to earlier readers of this text. Accordingly, it may be helpful to review some of the earlier biblical and Hellenistic Jewish texts that deal with this story in order to underscore the innovation that Philo introduces. This need be no more than a relatively brief survey since the material has been so ably covered in the monograph by J. A. Loader.[9]

Several of the prophets make reference to Sodom in the course of a denunciation of the sins or crimes of Israel and/or the empires. The opening chapter of the book of Isaiah, which serves as a sort of prologue to the work as a whole, compares the punishment of Judah to that of Sodom and Gomorrah. Those cities had apparently become a byword for utter destruction. Judah's case is somewhat different: "If the Lord of hosts had not left us a few survivors, we should have been like Sodom and become like Gomorrah" (Isaiah 1:10). But then Israel is addressed as Sodom and Gomorrah (11:10) in order to lead into a rejection of Israel's cultic worship of God and to urge Israel instead to "cease to do evil, learn to do good; seek justice, correct oppression; defend the fatherless, plead for the widow" (1:16–17). Given the parallel that these oracles set up between Sodom and Judah it appears that the punishment of both is directed against their injustice, an injustice that is especially evident in the treatment of the most vulnerable: orphans and widows.

In Jeremiah the parallel has to do with the behavior of Judean prophets who instead of warning oppressive rulers, collaborate in adultery, whether literal or, more likely, of the metaphorical sort that involves worshiping other gods alongside YHWH (23:14). The threat of devastating punishment (like that of Sodom) is also directed at Edom and then the Babylonian Empire itself, which has destroyed Judah

(49:18; 50:40). If we are to judge by the more or less contemporary oracle of Zephaniah, the cause of the divine wrath is the arrogance of the powerful (Zephaniah 2:9).

It is from the prophet Ezekiel, however, that we get the fullest picture of the grounds for YHWH's catastrophic punishments: Sodom is said to be a sister to Jerusalem and her punishment anticipates that directed against Jerusalem, save that the crimes of Jerusalem are even greater than those of Sodom. And what were the crimes of Sodom? The prophet answers: "She and her daughters had pride, surfeit of food, and prosperous ease but did not aid the poor and needy" (Ezekiel 16:49). As we shall see, it is the combination of arrogance and avarice that will set the tone for the subsequent depictions of the crime of Sodom.

In the *Testaments of the Twelve Patriarchs*, a composite work that attributes discourses to the twelve sons of Jacob and that dates from the middle of the second century B.C.E., there are a number of references to Sodom. The *Testament of Levi* makes reference to sexual sins but no mention of same-sex practice: "polluting married women, deflowering virgins of Jerusalem, having intercourse with whores and adulterous women and taking heathen girls!" (4:6; Loader, 81). All references to sexual crimes of Sodom are to what we would term heterosexuality. The same is true of the reference in the *Testament of Benjamin* where the reference is to "wanton deeds with women" (Loader, 82). In the *Testament of Naphtali* (3:4) there is reference to the "order of nature," a repetition of a prophetic theme of unjust enrichment and a reference to the way gentiles or pagans change the order of nature in following idols. Here there is no mention of sexual transgression at all, still less of male same-sex practices. A reference to the "Union of Watchers" Loader interprets as an allusion to same-sex practices, but the reference seems more naturally to be understood as an assault upon the divine, a recollection that the object of the crime of Sodom was an assault upon the divine messengers of God. This notion also appears in Jude 7, which some English translations have suggested deals with same-sex practices. But this is exactly the opposite of what Jude actually says, since he accuses the people of Sodom and Gomorrah of going after *alien* flesh (*sarkos heteras*) rather than the same or similar flesh, and his entire argument is about violation of the representatives of God.

In the Apocrypha, Jesus Ben Sira refers to the sin of Sodom as pride or arrogance (hubris; 16:7–10). The Wisdom of Solomon (a text roughly contemporary with Philo) refers to the violence of the people of Sodom and to their violation of the bedrock ethic of hospitality. It is this that will also dominate subsequent rabbinic literature, where the predominant theme is arrogance, avarice, and violence that expresses itself in the violation of the poor and of defenseless strangers.

Philo makes reference to the story of Sodom at least three times but the most extensive is in his treatise on Abraham, whom Philo interprets (allegorically) as a paragon of philosophic virtue. Although his main interest in the discussion of the story of Sodom and the cities of the plain is an allegory concerning the mind and the senses, it is in keeping with his approach that he first indicates something of the literal sense of the story and it is here that we find the seeds of homophobic exegesis.

Philo is certainly in touch with the general consensus in Jewish literature that the presenting evil of Sodom has to do with a general corruption stemming from wealth. Thus, he writes of "innumerable iniquities such as arise from gluttony and lewdness" (133) and continues: "The inhabitants owed this extreme license to the never-failing lavishness of their sources of wealth" (134). In this connection he cites Menander to the effect that "the chief beginning of evils is goods in excess" (134). Philo is not content, however, with what seems to have been a tradition of ascribing mere heterosexual lust to the Sodomites, but goes on to implicate them in same-sex lust as well: "They threw off from their necks the law of nature [phuseous nomos] and applied themselves to deep drinking of strong liquor and dainty feeding and forbidden forms of intercourse. Not only in their mad lust for women did they violate the marriages of their neighbors but also men mounted males without respect for the sex-nature, which the active partner shares with the passive" (135). Thus we have a progression from strong drink and gourmandizing, to adultery and then to same-sex sexual practices. All of these seem to run counter to the laws of nature which may be understood as much in terms of moderation as in terms of "law" in some more juridical sense. At this point Philo is taking over the view that same-sex lust is a hyperbolic form of cross-sex lust — a question of excess, then, rather than deficiency. Not surprisingly, given what we have read of his discussion of the Levitical prohibition, he then segues into the extremer forms of feminization: "they accustomed those who were by nature men to play the part of women" (136), through which "they saddled them with the formidable curse of a female disease" (136). Here we move toward a different discourse that treats same-sex relations as a lack, rather than an excess, of a certain masculinity. He then turns to the catastrophic fantasy that had also appeared in his reflections on Leviticus: "Had Greeks and barbarians joined together in affecting such unions, city after city would have become a desert, as though depopulated by a pestilential sickness" (136).

This supposition that same-sex unions (which in some discourses has been understood to be compatible with, or even a hyperbolization of, heterosexual desire) would end in the utter ruin of the human race and so was justly punished with the devastation of the cities of the plain is what Philo concludes "is the natural and obvious rendering of the story as suited for the multitude" (147).

This is not, however, where Philo will choose to put the emphasis in his reading of the account. Rather this becomes the jumping off point for an allegory of the five senses (that correspond in certain ways to the five cities of the plain, one of which was spared destruction) in order to maintain that sight rather than the other senses is the one most suited to philosophy, in the course of which he will be able to enlist Plato (from the *Timaeus*) on his side. In another text, *The Confusion of Tongues*, Philo will develop another related allegorical interpretation of the story of Sodom in which he will write of the assault of the senses upon "those Sacred and holy thoughts which were its guests, its guardians and sentinels."

A similar movement from literal to allegorical can be seen in Philo's *Questions and Answers on Genesis*, a text extant in the form of an Armenian translation of a lost Greek original. After seemingly suggesting an etymological perspective referring to blindness or sterility

(31), Philo again maintains that the literal meaning refers to pederasty: "servile, lawless and unseemly pederasty" (the note says: "unseemly and male pederasty" (37), or again, "The literal text very clearly shows that the Sodomites were pederasts" (38). And once again he offers a more philosophical meaning as indicating the soul or mind beset by the passions.

It would be a mistake, I believe, to suppose that Philo has developed his contribution to homophobic exegesis primarily under the influence of an imagined Jewish tradition. We have seen that the traditional understanding of the Sodom story has no interest in suggesting that it had to do with same-sex sexuality. Rather Philo must be understood within the context of making the sacred writings of his people a proper object of philosophical study and reflection. The allegorical interpretation, which is where he places the greatest stress, attempts to offer a reading compatible with certain philosophical and indeed Platonic discourses. The same may also be said of his literal reading, in which he aligns the text with themes already well developed in philosophical, and especially Platonic, thought concerning the ill effects of pederasty. Thus the themes of immoderation, of demasculinizing, of the contravention of nature, even the threat of depopulation all have a philosophical rather than a biblical ancestry. Philo's "contribution" is to show that these texts that seem at first so alien are making the same point as has been made in the pagan philosophical tradition. This will eventually make it possible for others, including Christian intellectuals, to read the story of Sodom as homophobic, similarly intending to align biblical traditions with the prestige of philosophical discourses, including especially those that may be cited in support of what I have termed Plato's homophobic project.

## Josephus

If Philo is the first to suggest such an interpretation of the Sodom story, does he stand alone in this among Hellenistic Jews? It seems not. For Josephus, who appears later on the intellectual scene (37–100/120 C.E.), will also make a contribution to this hermeneutical approach.

Josephus had been a part of the defense of Jerusalem against the Roman army in the war of 66–70. He later decided that resistance was a bad miscalculation and went over to the Roman side, and he was eventually made a citizen of Rome. He wrote two books about the war as well as a book introducing Jewish history and tradition to a pagan audience (*Jewish Antiquities*) and a philosophical defense of Judaism addressed to a pagan who had disparaged the ancient faith (*To Apion*).

Before looking at the texts that address the question of same-sex relations, it is intriguing to read his odd account of transvestite Galileans during the Roman siege of Jerusalem:

> The citizens thus found Simon without the walls a greater terror than the Romans, and the Zealots within more oppressive than either; while among the later for mischievous ingenuity and audacity none surpassed the Galilean contingent, for it was they who promoted John to power, and he from the position of authority which they had won for him requited them by allowing everyone to do whatever he desired. With an insatiable lust for loot, they ransacked the houses of the wealthy; the murder of men and the violation of women was their sport; they caroused on their spoils, with blood to wash them down, and from mere satiety unscrupulously indulged in effeminate practices, plaiting their hair and attiring themselves in women's apparel, drenching themselves with perfumes and painting their eyelids to enhance their beauty. And not only did they imitate the dress, but also the passions [or experiences] of women, devising in their excess of lasciviousness unlawful pleasure and wallowing as in a brothel in the city, which they polluted from end to end with their foul deeds. Yet while they wore women's faces, their hands were murderous, and approaching with mincing steps they would suddenly become warriors and whipping out their swords from under their dyed mantles transfix whomsoever they met. (*Jewish War,* 4.556–63)

While it is not certain that Josephus has in mind that the mad Galileans engaged in same-sex intercourse (the passions or experiences of women could be a misogynistic reference to giving in to "lasciviousness"), the picture of transvestite assassins carousing in the city is remarkable. Galileans even before the time of Jesus had the reputation for rebelliousness (Luke 13:1–2) and one of Jesus the Galilean's followers was said to be a zealot, also named Simon (Luke 6:15). Here at least it is clear that transvestism is associated with excessive behavior of other kinds, including violence, carousing, and sexual extremes.

In the *Jewish Antiquities* Josephus tries his hand at making the destruction of Sodom intelligible to his Greco-Roman allies. Josephus' treatment of the story begins from what we earlier saw to be the standard treatment of the text in Hellenistic Judaism, a tradition that had also been the foundation for Philo's reading: "The Sodomites, overweeningly proud of their numbers and the extent of their wealth" (95). Pride and avarice is then connected to the violation of the ethos of hospitality to the stranger: they "showed themselves insolent to men and the divinity [*theion*], insomuch that they no more remembered the benefits that they had received from Him, hated foreigners and declined all intercourse with others" (194). This then is made to be the motive for the divine wrath: "Indignant at this conduct, God accordingly resolved to chastise them for their arrogance [*huperathanias*]" (195). Moreover, Josephus correctly notes the contrast with the hospitality of Abraham who earlier had greeted the travelers: "taking them to be strangers [*xenous*] arose and saluted them and invited them to lodge with him and partake of his hospitality" (196). It is precisely Abraham's example of hospitality that is then imitated by Lot: "Lot invited them to be his guests, for he was very kindly to strangers [*tous xenous philanthropos*] and had learnt the lesson of Abraham's liberality" (200). Thus, it is precisely in the context of the question of strangers that we get the atrocity of the sodomites that confirms their arrogant and hostile character: "But the sodomites, on seeing these young men [*neaniskous*] of remarkably fair appearance [*euprepeia*] whom Lot had taken under his roof, were bent only on violence and outrage [*hubrin*] to their youthful beauty" (200–201).

Thus far Josephus' reading of the text has steered away from an explicitly homophobic discourse save for what will become a surprisingly significant detail: the imagined youthful beauty of the strangers that is somehow associated with the attempted violation of them on the part of the whole population of Sodom. Is Josephus suggesting that the beauty of young men is the cause of their rape (blaming the victim)? Or is he suggesting that those who find these young men beautiful (homoerotic desire) inevitably cross over into gang rape? In terms of his treatment of the text it may be more likely that he is simply underscoring the violence of the assault as one that aims to attack what is lovely. On this reading of Josephus, he is taking it for granted that his readers will be moved by the imagined sight of these lovely lads in peril. That is, he may be taking certain elements of homoerotic passion for granted as a way of embellishing his story.

That, however, is not the way his reading of the text plays out in subsequent history. To give an indication of this we may take the reading of the story of Sodom by one of the most respected Old Testament theologians of the twentieth century, Gerhard von Rad. Von Rad's reading of the text is heavily shaped by the subsequent history of homophobic exegesis. Here, even though the issue of hospitality has not entirely disappeared, we see placed at the forefront what appears to be homophobic exegesis: "The older form of the saga reported only one judgment on Sodom which came upon the city because of the unchastity which did not stop even with divine messengers."[10] Here von Rad ignores the fact that the story is understood in biblical witnesses as referring not to unchastity but to arrogance and hostility. But then he continues: "One must think of the heavenly messengers as young men in their prime, whose beauty especially incited evil desire" (217). Here we have beauty as that which is the motive of the attack, thus associating homosexuality as the motive for rape. For evidence to support this extraordinary claim, he cites Hermann Gunkel, who in turn had cited Josephus. Von Rad attempts to make this even more credible by suggesting that in Canaan "sexual aberrations were quite in vogue" and associates this with fertility cults.

How we are to get from unchastity and orgiastic sexuality (something no longer attributed to fertility cults) to homosexual rape is unclear. Or rather it works only on the supposition that the erotic is implicitly rape, especially the homoerotic. What stands between Josephus and von Rad is the notion of sodomy, which Mark Jordan has shown is largely a medieval invention.[11]

It will take several centuries before this application of the story of Sodom to male same-sex desire and practice will be accepted into Christian discourse. Indeed the first assertion that the sin of Sodom is to be understood in these terms appears to come with Augustine, who in the *City of God* affirms that the sin was *stupra in masculos* (16.20). But even this may not entail a blanket association of all same-sex practice with Sodom, as we shall see in a later chapter. It is with John Chrysostom, also in the fourth century, that the sin of Sodom will be unambiguously associated with male same-sex practices.

When Josephus turns to write a philosophical defense of Judaism to its cultured despisers (*To Apion*), he clearly supposes that the Law of Israel corresponds to the perspectives of philosophically informed pagans: "The Law recognizes no sexual connexions, except the natural [*kata phusein*] union of man and wife, and that only for procreation. Sodomy [*pros arenas arrenon*] it abhors and punishes any guilty of such assault with death" (24). The translator has supplied the connection to Sodom or sodomy (instead of "male with male" under the influence of much later medieval interpretation. Note that Josephus has supplied the notion that sex is "only for procreation" of children, since no such provision is present in the Law. He has also added, "according to nature." Now where do these two conditions come from? We discovered them in the *Laws* of Plato. They are in Musonius Rufus, the prominent first-century Stoic who was an almost exact contemporary of Josephus. But neither "only for procreation," nor "according to nature" are conditions found in Leviticus nor are they found elsewhere in the Bible that Josephus is reading. We may also wonder at this stage whether Josephus's characterization of same-sex practice in this text is to be understood as assault ("any guilty of such assault") or if he intends this characterization to apply to any and all same-sex sexual practices. As it stands the text allows for a certain ambiguity.

## Pseudo-Phocylides

Another text from first-century Judaism that may shed light on the emergence of homophobic discourse within that context is the short collection of sayings that the writer attributes to the sixth-century

B.C.E. Greek philosopher-poet Phocylides. The text shows the influence not only of certain biblical texts (Leviticus, Exodus, and Proverbs) but also of Sirach. In this text we can see a writer at work who seeks to demonstrate the harmony of certain Jewish ideas with pagan philosophical ideas to the point of putting in the mouth (or pen) of a pagan writer the views of Hellenistic Judaism (just as conversely Moses can be seen with as anticipating the same philosophical ideas in the work of Philo and Josephus.) The text may be dated sometime between 50 B.C.E. and 100 C.E., a period overlapping the work of Philo and Josephus. There is some evidence that it may come from Alexandria as well.[12]

The text is composed as a series of hortatory maxims that are to be a guide for life. They include exhortations to justice and mercy, warnings about the love of money, affirmations of the usefulness of labor and self-restraint, and so on. The text begins with what seems to be a sort of summary, in pagan language, of the Decalogue. In this summary we find inserted in parallel with the counsel to avoid adultery and before counsels to avoid treachery and murder the admonition not to incite passion for the male (*arsena Kuprin opinein*), which the translator offers as "rouse homosexual passion." We will see that such insertions into accounts of the Decalogue become a regular trope of second-century Hellenistic Christianity. Here, however, there is no attempt to invoke the authority of Moses (it is an ancient Greek poet who is supposed to be speaking, after all). The point is that this might well have been written by a Greek moral philosopher, and our investigation thus far demonstrates that this suggestion has some foundation. Thus the reference to the (male) lust for the male here serves to "paganize" the rephrasing, if it is that, of the Decalogue (rather than to "judaize" Greek philosophy as is often maintained).[13] Indeed this may be of a piece with the author's odd views on the immortality of the soul and on the divine being of the departed (97–115).

Much later in the text (175–206) we have a series of maxims and exhortations devoted to family life and sexual practices. The governing idea is expressed as follows: "Do not remain unmarried, lest you die nameless. Give nature her due, you also beget as you were begotten"

(175–76). The view that marriage is an obligation is of course consonant with Musonius, perhaps even with Plato in the *Laws*. The view
that this is the means of ensuring procreation, which in turn ensures
a continuation of one's own life, is also familiar to us from Plato and
later Hellenistic sources.

There follow some admonitions that may seem rather strange, for
example, the admonition not to prostitute one's wife, since this will
produce progeny "not in your likeness." There are also admonitions
not to have sexual relations with one's stepmother or one's father's
concubines or with sisters or stepsisters, which offer elaborations on
incest taboos. The reader will also be exhorted concerning when and
how to have sexual relations with a wife (the readers are presumed
to be male): not when she is pregnant, not with unbridled lust, not
with shameful means of intercourse, and so on. As Plato suggested in
Socrates' first speech in the *Phaedrus* (and Diotima's in the *Symposium*), "Eros is not a god" (194). Oddly the reader is, on the one hand,
encouraged to love his wife (for what could be sweeter and better) and
encouraged not to multiply marriages because that adds "calamity to
calamity."

It is within this context that we read about same-sex relations. "Do
not transgress with unlawful sex the limits set by nature, for even
animals are not pleased by intercourse of male with male" (190–91).
We have met with the argument that male same-sex sexual relations
are unnatural because not found among animals in Plato's *Laws*. It is
an argument not found in biblical literature. There is also an admonition against women adopting the sexual practices of males. Since
this immediately follows the admonition concerning male same-sex
practices, we might understand it as warning against women having
sexual relations with women. In this case it would parallel what we
found in book 1 of the *Laws* of Plato. But we may also understand
it as suggesting that women not be the active or aggressive partners
in sex with males, something of concern in the *Dialogue on Love* by
Plutarch. Such a concern would echo Pseudo-Phocylides' provisions
about men not being too sexually aggressive with their own wives.

We find a number of admonitions regarding sons that seem to have
a similar frame of reference. One is not to castrate one's male children

(187), which seems somehow to be connected to the admonition not to have sex with animals. The latter we have seen in Philo (and of course it exists in Leviticus as well as ancient Hittite laws), but the admonition concerning castration is not biblical. Castration was practiced in the Greco-Roman world for a number of reasons, including the prolongation of youthful beauty, but it also was a way to secure advancement in administrative and military ranks where the inability to procreate would ensure that the official would not become a rival to hereditary rank.[14]

This admonition may be connected to a series of subsequent admonitions about protecting male offspring from certain dangers. We have admonitions concerning cutting boys' hair because "long hair is not fit for boys, but for voluptuous women" (212). We are then warned to "guard the youthful prime of life of a comely boy, because many rage for intercourse with a man [pros arsena mexin erotos]" (213–14), an admonition paralleled by one about keeping virgin daughters safely indoors. Now all of this seems intelligible in a Greco-Roman rather than a specifically Jewish context. Short hair for males was a Roman rather than a biblical custom. The admonition to guard comely youths from the untoward advances of unwelcome suitors was the basis of the custom, already a commonplace in ancient Athens, of providing youths with older guardians, often slaves, who accompanied the lads for just this purpose. If the readers are presumed to be Jewish males then they are being exhorted to adopt gentile customs.

This odd text reinforces the impression that Hellenistic Judaism's perspectives on male same-sex sexual practices are in harmony with, and most likely derived from, Greek and Hellenistic philosophical sources. The supposition that we have here a specifically Jewish homophobia distorting (or correcting) a Greek homophilic perspective is without foundation.

What then has Hellenistic Jewish reflection added to the development of homophobic discourse? On the one hand we may say that it has adapted themes and perspectives from Greek and Hellenistic sources, for example: that male same-sex practices are against nature, or that natural sex is for procreation, or that same-sex practices threaten masculine gender identity. On the other hand, Hellenistic

Judaism has added the possibility of harmonizing biblical hermeneutics with this Greek and Hellenistic homophobic tradition — thus the adaptation of the story of Sodom to fit this mold (against the tradition of previous Jewish interpretation) or the explanation of Levitical prohibition in conformity with Greek and Hellenistic homophobic projects. In this way Plato's suggestion about devising stories (Sodom) and sentences (Leviticus) that would contribute to making male same-sex love an object of reproach and shame has been undertaken in ways that will make certain elements of biblical material available for this purpose, just as in Greek sources discussions about how to understand the stories of Zeus and Ganymede, or Achilles and Patroclus, or even the legislation of Solon have also been marshaled to this effect, not by Jews, but by pagan writers who have prepared the way for this (homophobic) hermeneutical project.

In the next chapter we consider whether the homophobia attributed by some to Paul has any connection with the homophobic project we have been tracing, or whether it will have any influence on the emergence of a specifically Christian homophobia. It will become clear that Paul's perspective is quite different from the Greek or Hellenistic homophobic project and that the emergence of Christian homophobia is a development not from Paul but from the very same Greek and Hellenistic sources that we have been examining.

# Part Three

# The Case of Paul

IN THE PREVIOUS CHAPTER I identified a variety of perspectives that bear witness to the development of homophobic discourse in traditions influenced by Plato's homophobic project outlined in the *Laws*. That project dates from more than four centuries before Paul. The Hellenistic discourses that we have examined come from the same century as Paul. In this chapter we turn to examine Paul as a possible source of the homophobia that will eventually come to be carried by the Christian movement that owes so much to his mission to the gentiles.

In a previous book I sought to demonstrate that the traditions concerning Jesus contained in the Gospels do not contribute to homophobic discourse.[1] In fact they contain a number of elements that are antithetical to homophobic attitudes and perspectives. I have, for example, drawn attention to the story in Matthew of the centurion whose love for his *pais*, or "boyfriend," leads him to take such risks in approaching Jesus as to make him exemplary of faith according to the narrative itself. I have also shown that the deliberate flouting of gender conventions in the Gospel of John separates the Jesus of that narrative from the gender discourses that are a regular subtext of Greek and Hellenistic homophobia. And it is obvious that Jesus, in all the traditions associated with him, is utterly opposed to the "marriage and family values" that provided such a staple of Roman and Jewish traditions and that is invoked in some types of homophobic discourse.

In what has proven to be the most controversial aspect of that earlier discussion of the narratives about Jesus I have shown that the Gospel of John may be fairly read as depicting Jesus as having a homoerotic relationship with the man known only as "the disciple Jesus loved." I have even shown that there are traces of this tradition in the Gospel of Mark.

I think that I have shown that these are plausible readings of the narrative texts of the New Testament. They are, moreover, readings that carry forward the rather nonchalant use of homoerotic themes in the narrative literature of the Hebrew Bible that I have discussed in *Jacob's Wound.*[2] Within that vast corpus, I have maintained, the only texts that may be plausibly construed as giving some expression to homophobic perspectives are two otherwise isolated verses in Leviticus, verses that are embedded in the Holiness Code, which probably does not predate the time of Plato's *Laws.*

But if the narrative traditions of ancient Israel or those of emergent Christianity seem rather accepting of homoerotic themes, we seem to be left with only the writings of Paul (and those who wrote in his name) as a possible biblical origin of Christian and Western homophobia. Yet here again we are left with only a few fragments: three verses from all of Paul's letters, one word from all those letters that subsequently claim Paul as their (pseudonymous) author. In fact, when Robin Scroggs wrote his landmark study *The New Testament and Homosexuality,* these were the only texts that could be brought forward as having a bearing on the question.

This is itself rather remarkable since the whole edifice of Western homophobia seems to depend upon the isolation and privileging of these few fragments. That these fragments stand in stark contrast to anything that can otherwise be discovered about the New Testament writings that are the chief source of testimony to the mission and ministry of that same Jesus regarded by Paul as the messiah of Israel should give some pause to those who wish to make Christian identity dependent upon a homophobic project and program.

In order for a homophobic reading of Paul to make sense we must either suppose that Paul is the apostle to the gentiles of an Israelite faith that is reducible to the Holiness Code of Leviticus (Paul as the transmitter of Levitical legislation to the gentiles), or that Paul is an exponent of the Greek and Hellenistic homophobia that we have examined in previous chapters. Each of these views, or any combination thereof, seems to me to be highly implausible.

In chapter 9 I will be looking at these fragments of Pauline texts to ask how they might be understood on their own terms and within their own literary context. I will try to show that the homophobic reading of these texts is not self-evident and that other readings may be far more plausible.

This will render only the more acute the question of how these texts do come to be read in homophobic ways. In later chapters I will show how the homophobic discourses of the Hellenistic world come to be assimilated into emergent Christianity. This ideological "framing" will subsequently enable later readers of Paul to appropriate these texts by means of a homophobic hermeneutical strategy. The point of this is not to suggest that Christianity did not become the bearer of homophobia. It is rather to suggest that it did so not on account of Paul (or Leviticus), but on account of its appropriation of Platonic and Hellenistic homophobic discourses.

In the chapters that follow I look first at the two words that appear in 1 Corinthians 6:9–10, one of which reappears in a text attributed to Paul but written decades after his death (1 Timothy 1:9–10). I suggest that malakoi has nothing whatever to do with homosexuality but refers to "self-indulgence." I also suggest that arsenokoitai is very unlikely to be a translation of Leviticus and, instead, should be understood to refer to male predatory sexual behavior including, but not restricted to, the rape of other males.

Turning to the text of Romans 1:26–27, which is most often cited as representing Paul's views on same-sex love, I maintain that it is best understood as a reference to the notorious lifestyles of the emperors (and "their women") who were known to Paul and under whose authority Jesus had been executed and the Jesus movement persecuted. It is the egregious behavior of those at the top of the Roman order that makes their passing judgment on Jesus illegitimate and thus sets the stage for Paul's argument concerning true justice.

I propose that Paul does not pass judgment on the generally accepted or tolerated same-sex behavior of the Hellenistic world. Although it is possible for Paul to come into contradiction with major elements of the Jesus tradition, and it is virtually certain that he did not know of the traditions I have considered in my earlier study of the Gospels, still there is no reason to conclude that Paul himself comes into (inadvertent) contradiction to the Jesus tradition at this point. Moreover Paul's view of "sexuality" is at considerable variance, and indeed irreconcilable, with Hellenistic homophobic discourse.

# – 9 –

# In a Word:
# *Malakoi* and *Arsenokoitai*

In the modern period homophobic biblical interpretation has seized upon two words found in a series of terms in 1 Corinthians (one of which recurs in 1 Timothy) to justify fear and loathing of persons who engage in same-sex erotic relationships. The terms appear in what are called vice lists. There are a number of lists of prohibited patterns of behavior in the New Testament. In the Gospels these lists often follow the outline of the Ten Commandments, although they focus not on relationship to God but on relationships among persons (for example, Mark 10:19 and parallels). Paul also has similar material (for example, Romans 13:9). In addition there are a number of lists that seem to be constructed on the spur of the moment or for purposes of argument (1 Corinthians 5:9–11; 1 Corinthians 6:9–10; Galatians 5:19–21; Ephesians 5:3–5; Colossians 3:5; 1 Timothy 1:9–10; 2 Timothy 3:3; 1 Peter 4:3; and so on).

Of these lists, none has any word that in Hellenistic Greek was associated with same-sex behavior. This is not because there were no such terms. There were, and they were widely used. But they do not appear in New Testament vice lists. The general term that would have been employed was "pederasty." We have also discovered other less common ways of referring to male same-sex practices and relationships in Plato and in Hellenistic literature. In addition we will discuss another term used in early Christian literature to refer to some kinds of same-sex relationships, namely, those that identify the seduction or corruption of minors: *paidophthoros*.[1] However, these terms do not occur anywhere in the New Testament. This is a fact seldom noted in discussions of "homosexuality" in biblical texts and, I believe, is never given the weight it deserves.

113

Modern translators have compensated for the absence of such terms from these lists by identifying homosexuality with two terms that do occur in two of these lists. The two terms that have been made to carry the weight of homophobic interpretation appear in a list from 1 Corinthians. The list, in the NRSV translation, is as follows:

> Do you not know that wrongdoers will not inherit the kingdom of God? Do not be deceived! Fornicators, idolaters, adulterers, male prostitutes [malakoi], sodomites [arsenokoitai], thieves, the greedy, drunkards, revilers, robbers — none of these will inherit the kingdom of God. (1 Corinthians 6:9–10)

One of these terms reappears in the later list found in 1 Timothy:

> This means that the law is laid down not for the innocent but for the lawless and disobedient, for the godless and sinful, for the unholy and the profane, for those who kill their mother or father, for murderers, fornicators, sodomites [arsenokoitai], slave traders, liars, perjurers, and whatever else is contrary to the sound teaching. (1 Timothy 1:9–10)

What are we to make of these terms and of their increasingly common association with same-sex practices or relationships? We will attend first to malakoi.

## *Malakoi*

Only in the first list, from 1 Corinthians, does the term *malakoi* appear, and only in the twentieth century has it become customary to translate this term with reference to any same-sex practice. This interpretation is first offered in 1826 by Alexander Campbell, who translates this as "catamites" (using "sodomite" as the translation for *arsenokoitai*). After James Moffat's translation of the 1930s the association of this term with same-sex activity becomes standard practice.[2]

Prior to this innovation in translation the principal sexual meaning given to this term was that of "masturbation," a view that surfaced in the Middle Ages and still predominates in Catholic moral handbooks.[3] This was also the basis for Protestant panic concerning masturbation in the nineteenth century.

Alongside the view that *malakoi* may be understood as reference to the "solitary vice," and preceding it in the tradition, is the view that the term means "effeminate." This view takes gender roles as fundamental and regards the relaxation of male gender roles with special horror.

But what does the term mean? In this case we are able to see how the term is otherwise employed in Hellenistic Greek. Its use is by no means confined to same-sex practices. Indeed, when some variation of the term is used in a specifically sexual context, it may be applied equally to practitioners of cross-sex and same-sex eroticism. Thus in Plutarch's *Dialogue on Love* (*Erotikos*), it is used to refer to youths who seek the passive position in same-sex intercourse (751e) and of men who are seduced by the charms of women (753f). In both cases it is paired with another term for effeminate, making clear that *malakia* refers to softness or self-indulgence rather than effeminacy as such.

Something similar occurs in the case of Philo, who, like Plutarch, was a near contemporary of Paul. Philo calls a man who takes back an adulterous wife *malakias* (translated in Loeb as "degeneracy") and *anandrias* ("lack of manhood") in *The Special Laws* (3.31). Although Philo spends considerable energy discussing effeminacy of various kinds in the next several paragraphs, including the effeminate partner in same-sex relations, he does not use the term *malakoi* in that connection.

This is further confirmed by recalling the text of Musonius Rufus, again a near contemporary of Paul. In the very first of his teachings recorded we find Musonius Rufus explaining why it is easier or harder to learn the virtue that philosophy exists to inculcate and thus the difference between the need for many proofs and the need for few and direct proofs. The example he gives is of two youths who have had quite a different upbringing. The one who has been raised in a somewhat Spartan style will quickly grasp that work is not an evil and that pleasure is not (always) a good. But another who "has been reared in luxury, his body effeminate [*tethalumenon*], his spirit weakened by soft living [*malakian*]," will require much convincing and so many proofs (p. 34).[4] It is in this connection that Rufus uses the term *malakian*. What is instructive here is that the term has no sexual connotation at all. It refers precisely to indolence, luxury, and self-indulgence.

In a subsequent conversation that claims that exile is not an evil, Musonius suggests that in some cases it may even be a benefit: "To others who were in poor health as the result of overindulgence and high living [*malakias*], exile has been a source of strength because they were forced to live a more manly [*andrikoteron*] life" (9.10–15; p. 71). Similarly, in discussing the value of hard work with one's own hands (on the land), he says: "You may be sure that no one who was not demoralized by soft living [*malakos*] would say that the labor of the farmer was degrading or unfit for a good man" (11.201; p. 81). In the same teaching Musonius refers to the false philosophers who do not labor but live indolently in the city to whom he refers (according to the translation) as spoiled and effeminate [*malakoi*] (11.5; p. 84). Again there is no hint here of sexuality.

As in the case of Philo, when Musonius does touch on the question of same-sex love, he does not use the term *malakoi*. We should also beware of the suggestion about "effeminacy" in the translation. Musonius Rufus in any case is not one to suppose that women are fundamentally different from men. In subsequent teachings he insists that training in philosophy (which for him means virtue) should be the same for males and females, who equally have a disposition to virtue, including self-control, justice, temperance, courage, and so on. He is not therefore a representative of the gender system that appears so rigid in many authors, including Philo (and, to a certain extent, Paul). Thus the term *malakoi* or *malakia* should also not be confused with the issue of gendering. As we have seen, where this is the issue even Philo does not use the term.

The meaning of the term in 1 Corinthians can be confirmed by its meaning elsewhere in the New Testament. It occurs in sayings by Jesus about John the Baptist. Matthew and Luke each have slightly different versions of this saying. Since this is the only New Testament usage it is instructive to look at these texts first from Matthew:

> What then did you go out [into the wilderness] to see? Someone dressed in soft [*malakois*] robes? Look, those who wear soft [*malaka*] robes are in royal palaces. (Matthew 11:8)

Then from Luke:

> What then did you go out [into the wilderness] to see? Someone dressed in soft [*malakois*] robes? Look, those who put on fine clothing and live in luxury are in royal palaces. (Luke 7:25)

The word itself means "soft." The context makes clear that it is soft in the sense of luxurious. The term then refers to those who indulge themselves in luxuries. Or put more simply: the self-indulgent.

This is the way the term was used and employed in early Christian literature. Later, when Christian literature came under the sway of gynephobic prejudice, the attraction to luxury was self-evidently attributed to women, and so men who were attracted to luxury could be deemed "effeminate." Nevertheless it was still possible for women to aspire to be manly in the sense of self-disciplined or self-controlled. But men who were not self-disciplined or self-controlled were not manly but "soft, effeminate."

Only in the late Middle Ages, with the growing intrusion of the church in the sphere of lay sexuality, did it seem possible to give to the concept a decidedly sexual meaning. The initial candidate for this, as we have seen, was masturbation, the vice of sexual self-indulgence.

Only in the modern period with the emergence of stereotypes about males who engaged in same-sex sexual behavior, namely, that they were a "third sex" and so congenitally "effeminate," would it make sense to transfer a term previously restricted to self-oriented sex behavior or gender slippage to practitioners of same-sex behavior. This seems to occur just as the modern notion of "the homosexual" was being constructed and consolidated at the end of the nineteenth and beginning of the twentieth century. The application of the term to homosexual identity or to same-sex practice is thus an invention of modernity.

Now some have attempted to qualify what was perceived as Paul's exclusion of "homosexuals" by restricting the term to male prostitutes, perhaps especially effeminate call boys.[5] But this seems to be without merit. If Paul had wanted to say male prostitute it would have been good to use the term that his readers would have understood: *kinaidos*. Paul surely wanted to be understood. Nor could delicacy have restrained him, for the language that Paul uses is typically blunt. He knows the term for female prostitute (*pornae*) and uses it (1 Corinthians 6:15–16).

It is thus clear that the translation of *malakoi* as homosexual or as catamite or as effeminate boy prostitute is unwarranted.[6] It means precisely those who are self-indulgent.

## *Arsenokoitai*

In the case of *malakoi* the meaning of the term is clear from its use. We know it is used to mean soft, luxurious, and self-indulgent. Things are less clear when we come to the other term that has been interpreted to license homophobia. The difficulty is that the word does not appear in Greek literature prior to or contemporaneous with Paul. Nobody else uses the term.

The rarity of the term has meant that scholars often have had to fall back on the analysis of the components of the term to get at its meaning. This is an exceedingly difficult and chancy enterprise. Take, for example, the components of the term "fireman." There is "fire" and there is "man." But what does that tell us of the meaning? Are we to think of men who set fires? of men who are "fired up"? of men who are "on fire"? of men who play with fire? Is the "man" generic or gender-specific? If we didn't already know, how would we guess that it refers to men who put out fires?

In this case we have some reference to males (*arseno* = *arreno*) and some reference to coitus (*koitai* = bed). How shall we decide if this refers to men who bed, men who are bedded, men who bed women or men who bed men? The term itself will not tell us; only its use will. But the usage is of little help. We do know that the term is not used in reference to same-sex acts otherwise. That is, the term is not employed in contexts where pederasty or prostitution is under discussion.

Recently two modern scholars have proposed that the term is coined, perhaps by Paul, to correspond to the phrasing of Leviticus. Robin Scroggs (p. 108) suggests that the term is a Greek equivalent used by Paul to translate *mishav zakur,* a term derived from the Levitical passages by the rabbis. David F. Wright suggests that the term is invented by Paul based on the Septuagint version of Leviticus 18:22 and 20:13.[7]

However, only in Leviticus 20:13 are the component terms adjacent to one another, and even there they do not belong to the same grammatical clause. The emphasis in Leviticus falls not on "male-type sex" but on "female-type sex."[8] Thus the attempt to construct *arsenokoitai* on the basis of Leviticus is implausible on the face of it. Certainly if Paul had hoped to be understood by reference to Leviticus he could have been clearer. However, we cannot rule out the Septuagint proposal on purely formal grammatical grounds. It is implausible but perhaps not impossible.

What will render the association with Leviticus still more unlikely is a consideration of Paul's relationship to Leviticus in other passages. Thus it may be helpful to look at how Paul does argue when we know that he could well appeal to Leviticus to make his point. We have such a case in 1 Corinthians itself, indeed in the same context within which this vice list occurs.

In 1 Corinthians 5, Paul is confronted with the case of a man who is having a sexual relationship with his father's wife. The passage is as follows:

> It is actually reported that there is sexual immorality [*porneia*] and of a kind that is not found even among the pagans; for a man is living with his father's wife. And you are arrogant! Should you not rather have mourned, so that he who has done this would have been removed from among you? (1 Corinthians 5:1–2)

We are not told that the woman is his mother. Nor do we know whether the man's father is alive (the offense is not termed adultery). The woman then seems to be the man's stepmother. The man is knowingly breaking a taboo. He apparently believes that the breaking of this taboo shows that he is set free from the law and able to live in Christian liberty. It appears that members of the Corinthian Christian community agree that the relationship demonstrates Christian liberty. It is likely therefore that the relationship is one of "mutual consent," one that is not a violation of the other person. But this is still conjecture.

Paul's attitude is quite different. He views the relationship as an intolerable one. He claims that it is a transgression not otherwise known among the gentiles. In this Paul is mistaken. The tale of Phaedrus is precisely the story of the ill-fated love of a young man for his stepmother, which, of course, ends in tragedy (as had the relationship that Oedipus unknowingly had with his mother). Nor is this kind of relationship unknown in the Hebrew Bible. Rueben, one of the sons of Jacob, is reported to have had sex with one of Jacob's wives/concubines (Genesis 35:22; Bilhah, the mother of Dan and Naphtali). The Genesis story shows no evidence of knowledge of the kind of prohibition that we find in Leviticus since there is no suggestion of the imposition of any penalty, still less the death penalty. In fact Rueben will subsequently be something of a hero in his attempt to prevent his brothers' murder of Joseph. Of course Genesis does regard the relationship as an infringement upon the dignity of Israel/Jacob, but no penalty is exacted beyond Jacob's curse upon his eldest son that he "shall no longer excel" (Genesis 49:4).

But now notice what Paul does not do. He does not refer to Leviticus. The relevant passages in Leviticus are located in the very same passages from which Paul has allegedly constructed the term *arsenokoitai* to refer to same-sex behavior. The passages are as follows:

> You shall not uncover the nakedness of your father's wife; it is your father's nakedness. (Leviticus 18:8; the presumed reference to same-sex behavior is 18:22)
>
> The man who lies with his father's wife has uncovered his father's nakedness, both of them shall be put to death (Leviticus 20:11; the alleged reference to same-sex behavior — with the same penalty — is 20:13).

The Levitical passages are clear and severe. But instead of referring to them, Paul relies upon his own authority in the community:

> For though absent in the body, I am present in spirit; and as if present I have already pronounced judgment in the name of the Lord Jesus Christ on the man who has done such a thing. When you are assembled, and my spirit is present with the power of

our Lord Jesus, you are to hand this man over to Satan for the destruction of the flesh, so that his spirit may be saved in the day of the Lord. (5:3–5)

The very passages from which it is alleged that Paul has derived his strange reference to same-sex acts is one to which he does not appeal (or even mention) when we clearly have a case that falls under its purview.

Now surely it is curious that the Paul we are to imagine is so under the sway of Leviticus that he must coin a new Greek term to apply Leviticus to same-sex behavior in Corinth is the same Paul who in dealing with a case self-evidently falling under the authority of Leviticus passes over Leviticus in silence.

Of course we know that Paul has no intention of applying the law from Leviticus 20:11. He does not call for them both to be put to death. In fact he calls for no punishment for the woman at all and only asks that the man be (temporarily) expelled from the community. Even this punishment may seem too severe to Paul, who in 2 Corinthians seems to say that the man should be brought back into the community; he had only been testing the community in any case:

This punishment by the majority is enough for such a person; so now instead you should forgive [welcome] and console him, so that he may not be overwhelmed by sorrow. So I urge you to reaffirm your love for him. I wrote for this reason: to test you and to know whether you are obedient in everything.

(2 Corinthians 2:6–9)

Paul doesn't appeal to Leviticus because he has no intention of enforcing Leviticus on a gentile congregation.[9]

Nor is this simply a matter of a particular case. Paul's entire project is understandable only from the point of view that Leviticus does not and cannot apply to gentile converts. The entire mission to the gentiles, as Paul understood it, depended on the suspension of the rules of Jewish particularity for gentile converts. Even circumcision is abolished (Galatians), let alone the application of ritual and dietary laws.

A further illustration may be helpful. According to Acts, the council in Jerusalem agreed to Paul's mission to the gentiles on the following conditions:

> For it has seemed good to the Holy Spirit and to us to impose on you no further burden than these essentials: that you abstain from what has been sacrificed to idols and from blood and from what has been strangled and from fornication. (Acts 15:28–29; see also verses 19–20)

Of these conditions only the one concerning fornication is enforced by Paul. The issue of meat sacrificed to idols does concern him but only insofar as it may divide the community. Thus he only tells those who eat this food that they should not flaunt their freedom in the face of those who have scruples about it (1 Corinthians 8:1–13; 10:23ff.; Romans 14).

With respect to any other dietary restrictions, including those concerning blood, which are so important to the council and to Leviticus (Leviticus 17:1–16), Paul is clear that he sees no ground whatever for observing them (Romans 14). And in this view Paul is followed by the author of 1 Timothy (4:1–5). Thus not only Paul but also his more conservative followers are quite clear that the dietary restrictions based on Leviticus (and presumably reinforced by James the brother of Jesus and the Jerusalem council) should be disregarded.

A final concrete illustration of Paul's attitude toward Leviticus may be instructive. In the course of his argument in Romans, Paul has occasion to refer many times to the books of the Torah, the books "of Moses." However he only twice seems to refer to texts from Leviticus. Whenever he does so it is to contrast his own views and the perspective of the gospel as a whole from the perspective represented by Moses in Leviticus. Thus in Romans 7:10 he refers to the promise of life from obeying the commandments (Leviticus 18:5) and claims that instead it produces death. Similarly he contrasts the saying of "Moses" (Leviticus 18:5) that "the one who practices the justice based on the law shall live by it" and contrasts this with "the justice based on faith" (Romans 10:5–6). Not only is the perspective of faith contrasted with the view articulated in Leviticus, but the contrast is with the Holiness Code

and indeed with the very chapter within which we encounter the proscription of (some) same-sex acts that has allegedly served as the basis
for Paul's invention of the term *arsenokoitai*! Nor is this contrast one
that concerns only incidental matters. It has to do with the very heart
and center of Paul's gospel.

These illustrations are not isolated instances. Rather they are indicative of a fundamental policy. Paul is the apostle to the gentiles. His whole
project depends on not making the gentiles into imitation Jews. This
is why in Galatians he is so upset about the idea that gentiles might
wish to be circumcised. He is committed to developing a gentile form
of faith that will in no way be an imitation or ersatz Judaism. This
is not because of any antipathy to Judaism. Paul remains a convinced
and practicing Jew. But he is persuaded that a gentile does not have
to be a Jew to become a follower of Jesus or to be a recipient of grace
through faith. This means that the last thing that could occur to Paul
would be to impose Levitical legislation on gentile Christians. This is
precisely what the Pharisees did in their mission to the gentiles. And
this is precisely what distinguishes Paul's mission to the gentiles from
his former life as a Pharisee.

The suggestion that Paul is so enamored of Leviticus and of its
universal applicability to gentiles as to invent a new term based on
Leviticus is one that depends upon forgetting what Paul is doing in this
and in all his letters. The proposal that *arsenokoitai* refers to same-sex
practices as such depends on the Leviticus connection. No other justification for it exists since the word is otherwise unattested in the first
century and the structure of the term is itself ambiguous. But making
the Leviticus connection would seem to make nonsense of Paul's life
project as an apostle to the gentiles.

If the term is not based on the LXX of Leviticus what can it possibly mean? We are left where we were at the beginning. It seems to
connect males with male-type sex. What is this? One possible explanation is that it means men who are seducers, or perhaps rapists, of
women. This has the advantage that it connects to the wider context
of Paul's argument. For in this part of the epistle he is referring to sins
of heterosexuality (*pornai*). If the term is to fit in its context it might
more naturally refer to heterosexual vice.

This interpretation also has the advantage that it fits Roman law and thus pagan custom. Since Paul is dealing with a gentile audience he should argue in terms that are understandable from this point of view. This is precisely what he does in the case of the man who is sleeping with his (step)mother. Since Roman law forbids seduction or corruption, especially when this involves violence and violation, it would be appropriate to refer to this in this context as *arsenokoitai*.[10] Given the context any reference to same-sex behavior would only be implicit insofar as this would be a subset of the seductive or violating activity generally (which has a primarily heterosexual form).

Alternatively, but less likely, Paul does depart in a one-word gesture from what is otherwise his theme (heterosexuality), in order to take a swipe at a particular form of same-sex activity. But what form? Not prostitution, as this is either already covered (*pornoi*) or else he has terms available that would be clearer. Not the general love of youths (pederasty) by which same-sex liaisons were universally known. For he does not use the term. What then? Once again we may have to do with relationships of assault. *Arsenokoitai* then would be men who prey upon other males. This is possible so long as we are aware that it means that Paul must have abandoned his own theme briefly to include these in his consideration of heterosexuality.

If this is the meaning then it certainly does have resonance with Roman legislation concerning *stuprum*, which criminalized predatory behavior in which men turned other males, usually younger free males, into sexual prey either through rape or through overbearing seduction.[11]

How does this guess compare with the use of the term in later Christian literature?[12] Most of the occurrences of this term in the two centuries following Paul are simply quotations of Paul, and early commentaries on these passages do not seem to identify the term with homosexual practices. Moreover these authors, when they do discuss same-sex practices, do not use the term *arsenokoitai*.

There are, however, two cases in patristic literature where the term is actually used in ways that give it a context. They are the *Apology* of Aristides (ca. 130–38) and the *Refutatio* of Hippolytus (ca. 222–35). In a fine discussion of these passages William Petersen notes that "both of these sources — the two earliest to place the word in a context — offer Zeus as the archetype of the *arsenokoitas*. In the taking of Ganymede, Zeus is the model of someone who commits *arsenokoitai*."[13] In the story of Zeus there is, of course, no question of a consenting relationship. Zeus simply swoops down on the young Ganymede and carries him off to the abode of the gods, where Ganymede becomes Zeus's boy toy and decorative slave (cup bearer). The term rape indeed comes from this story, where Zeus is disguised as a "raptor" (eagle) who kidnaps the beautiful boy.

The *Apology* of Aristides is further evidence that what is involved in *arsenokoitai* cannot possibly include every kind of male same-sex behavior. To be sure, Aristides is mostly concerned with the misdeeds of the gods, misdeeds that then serve as models for mere mortals. Aristides offers only a very glancing treatment of Zeus and Ganymede, being primarily interested in adultery. But when he comes to his conclusion in chapter 13, he maintains that we must either say that the gods broke the laws, or that the laws have no divine sanction. It is in this connection that he refers to the law of the Greeks against adultery and *arsenokoitai*. Now we know that the Greeks at least had no law against same-sex behavior as such. On the contrary. But we can suppose that predation and rape were proscribed, the very activities of which Aristides is accusing Zeus. Once again it is evident that *arsenokoitai* cannot be understood as anything other than rape.

Although Roman society clearly tolerated same-sex behavior, including relationships between older and younger men, the predatory seduction of youths seems to have been regarded as criminal behavior under the law of *stuprum*. The predatory sexual violence given expression in the legend of Zeus and Ganymede was condemned even (often especially) by those who celebrated the nobly courted and freely given love between older and younger men. One of the clearest indications of this is the life of the very emperor to whom Aristides writes his *Apology* for the Christian faith and in which Aristides believes he may reckon with a favorable reception to his criticism of the behavior of Zeus. The emperor Hadrian did seek to curb abuses relating to the castration of males, whether free or slave, for purposes of supplying brothels. But he was also quite famous for his exclusive love of young men. Indeed one of these affairs was the most famous of the century: his love for Antinous, whose untimely death provoked the emergence of a cult in the name of the young lover now proclaimed a divinity.[14] The point here is that one of the most famous practitioners of same-sex eroticism could be expected to join with Aristides in condemning the behavior exemplified by Zeus, which Aristides (following Paul) called *arsenokoitai*.

*Arsenokoitai* then refers to that class of sexual predators who overwhelm their victim with superior force in order to make them sexual property. Even if the term is restricted to that group of predators whose prey includes other males (though of course Zeus engages in similar behavior with female victims), we are still very far from a stigmatization of same-sex eroticism as such, even of the cross-generational (pederastic) form that this often took in antiquity.

Now how does this identification of *arsenokoitai* with sexual predators fit with the context within which we first encounter the term in the New Testament? In 1 Corinthians 6:9 Paul introduces the list by saying: "Don't you know that the unjust (*adikia*) will not inherit the reign of heaven?" The list then goes: "*pornai* [fornicators], idolaters, adulterers, the self-indulgent [*malakoi*], sexual predators [*arsenokoitai*], thieves, the greedy, drunkards, revilers, robbers." Here the sexual predator is linked with thieves and the greedy. That is, the predator is one who is concerned only to please himself (linking with the *malakoi* and including fornicators, the greedy, and drunkards) and whose behavior toward others is rapacious (adulterers, thieves, revilers, robbers).

The appearance of *arsenokoitai* in 1 Timothy tends to confirm this interpretation. For here the term is preceded by a series of violent crimes: murders of fathers and mothers and murders in general. Its immediate context is as follows: "the promiscuous [*pornai*], *arsenokoitai*, and kidnappers." This last term refers to those who capture people for the slave trade. The capturing of people for sexual purposes and the capturing of people for the slave trade then are linked in a way that makes good sense of the generally violent character of the crimes suggested by the list.

Thus the use of the term *arsenokoitai* in the first, second, and third centuries clearly points us toward the sexual violation of another person. We have a term for that in English: rape. The condemnation of rape is no invention of the twentieth century. Both Athenian and Roman law adamantly legislated against such behavior whether its object were male or female. This legislation has nothing to do with the question of same-sex eroticism as such any more than it has to do with cross-sex eroticism as such.

Now we should notice here a certain irony. The term *arsenokoitai* is translated in the NRSV as sodomites. Were it not for nearly two thousand years of the exegetical violence that has identified this term with same-sex eroticism one would have to say that this might be a useful translation. For the crime of Sodom was the violation of the vulnerable, culminating in attempted gang rape. In the interpretation of this tale that prevailed until the time of Philo, the gravity of this crime has to do with the outrageous commitment of an entire city to the violation of the vulnerable. In a later chapter we will see how this text comes to be read as a pretext for the condemnation of same-sex behavior in general.

Our study of terms in the New Testament that have been regarded as offering a clue to understanding the attitude toward same-sex erotic practices has had the result of showing that terms that were intelligible in antiquity as designating persons who engaged in same-sex erotic practices are in fact never used in the New Testament. Although some have attempted to make up for this lack by identifying two other terms with same-sex practices, we have found that there seems to be no good reason for doing so. The first term (*malakoi*) seems to refer to the sort of self indulgence characteristic of the prosperous who pamper themselves with small or large luxuries. The second term (*arsenokoitai*) seems to be concerned with the forcible seduction or rape of a vulnerable object of (male) lust.

It is unlikely that Paul knew of the dangerous memory of Jesus that is later transmitted by the Gospels and that suggests Jesus' openness to and possible practice of same-sex erotic attachment. The letters of Paul show little acquaintance with any of the traditions concerning Jesus' actions, teachings, or relationships with other people. However, there is, at this point at least, no necessity to drive a wedge between Jesus and Paul. If our interpretation of *malakoi* and *arsenokoitai* is correct, then even if Jesus approved of same-sex relationships (as Matthew and Luke suggest) or, indeed, was involved in such a relationship himself (as hinted at in Mark and openly suggested by John), Jesus would still have utterly rejected both the luxurious self-indulgence of the prosperous and the violation of other persons for purposes of rendering them sex objects.

Indeed, Jesus does condemn predatory sexuality generally by his extension of the commandment against adultery to include "everyone looking at a woman with a view to desire her" (Matthew 5:28). What is in view here is not a "look of love" but a predatory lust that seeks to possess the other whether in reality or in fantasy. Obviously the domain of predatory lust in this saying is heterosexual. And as we have seen, this may also be true of Paul's use (and that of later early Christianity) of the term *arsenokoitai*. Even if this term were designed to apply primarily to predatory males whose prey was other males, this would not be inconsistent with the Jesus tradition's warning about male predatory sexual behavior, though it would certainly be an extension.

The analysis of these terms shows that their appearance in Pauline literature does not itself suggest a commitment to a homophobic project. The terms are far better understood as indictments of the wealthy and arrogant. In this way they would fit well with wider currents of Jewish and Christian ethical reflection.

However, the terms eventually will be assimilated into a homophobic perspective — although in the case of *malakoi* this will await the modern period. This assimilation requires the preexistent authority of a tradition of homophobic interpretation. While such a tradition does not derive from these texts, that tradition once fully developed will seize upon these texts to buttress its authority with the name of Paul.

# – 10 –

# When in Rome:
# The Interpretation
# of Romans 1:26–27

In order for Pauline texts to be appropriated into homophobic discourse something more than the bare mention of *arsenokoitai* in vice lists will be needed to establish Paul as an authority for such discourse. That "something more" will come in the interpretation of Romans 1:26–27. In a later chapter we will see that this interpretation does not gain currency before the late fourth century, nearly 350 years after Paul. Yet the weight of subsequent homophobic tradition will have the effect of making the homophobic interpretation of this passage seem self-evident.

In this chapter the task is to show how the passage can be read otherwise. In part this will have to do with seeing the ways Paul's position differs from that of the homophobic discourses we have already encountered. Later interpretations of Paul will have to overcome these differences in order to gain Paul as authorization for later Christian homophobia. Two other related moves will also enable a homophobic reading. One is to isolate these verses from their context in Paul's letter and the other is to separate them from the social-political context within which Paul is writing. Accordingly, in this study it is important to restore, so far as possible, these contexts so that it will be possible to see how the passage may have had a nonhomophobic significance before being appropriated by a homophobic hermeneutic.

The passage, usually quoted in isolation from its context in Paul's argument, is as follows:

For this reason God gave them up to degrading passions. Their women exchanged natural intercourse for unnatural, and in the same way also the men, giving up natural intercourse with women, were consumed with passion for one another. Men committed shameless acts with men and received in their own persons the due penalty for their error. (Romans 1:26–27 NRSV)

On the face of it this passage seems to indict all persons, male or female, who engage in same-sex practices. To a certain extent Paul appears here to repeat the attitude of Leviticus 18:22 and even 20:13. For the whole indictment of pagan civilization concludes with the assertion: "They know God's decree, that those who practice such things deserve to die" (Romans 1:32). If this concluding phrase were to be transferred from the context Paul gives it (the third indictment of 28–31) and attached to our verses (as sometimes happens in homophobic exegesis), the position of Paul would appear to agree with that of Leviticus 20:13. The main difference between the attitude suggested by this passage and that of the Leviticus legislation would be that Paul sees fit to include lesbian practice in the proscription. Giving that sort of priority to female same-sex practice would be an innovation not only for Judaism but for pagan homophobia as well.[1] Paul thus would become the first "equal opportunity" homophobe in history. This is certainly the way he is seen by many homophobic, and even some anti-homophobic, interpreters.[2]

In addition to the innovation of including female same-sex erotic practices in his alleged condemnation of same-sex practices, Paul is here credited with grounding this prohibition in a view of natural law, which comes to prevail in later theological ethics. In this view the sexual activity that Paul has in mind is "against nature" in the sense that it is nonprocreative in character. Thus, all nonprocreative sexuality is against nature in this sense (including nonprocreative sexuality between persons of "opposite genders").

Before engaging in a critique of the appropriation of this passage for homophobic purposes let us first ask what such an interpretation would mean for our understanding of the attitude toward same-sex erotic practices based on our study thus far. It is of course possible that Paul did feel a strong repugnance toward same-sex behavior. Some have supposed that this would be virtually inevitable given Paul's own

Jewish background and especially his adherence to Pharisaic Judaism. Even though my earlier study of Old Testament materials demonstrates that a variety of perspectives on homoeroticism were possible within the literature of ancient Israel, the normative Judaism of the emergent pharisaic type may well have included a strong opposition to same-sex eroticism on a basis similar to that reflected in Leviticus. Moreover it is quite possible, indeed likely, that Paul was aware of those strands of Hellenistic philosophy, including some forms of Stoicism, that rejected nonprocreative sexual activity as unnatural.

Let us then suppose that this mixture of Pharisiac and philosophical ideas combine in Paul to produce a blanket rejection of same-sex eroticism as unnatural. Let us further suppose that in some otherwise unknown way Paul has extended this perspective not only to include lesbianism but to actually make it the lead example of his views. Just how plausible is this combination of views?

## Against Nature: Looking Closer

It may be helpful first to provide a more literal translation of the passage to get a clearer sense of the words that Paul is using:

> Therefore God handed them over to dishonorable passions; for even their females changed the natural [*phusikein*] use [*chreisin*] to that against nature [*para physin*], likewise also the males leaving the natural [*phusikein*] use [*chreisin*] of the females burned in their desire for one another, males among males, working unseemliness (unfittingness) and receiving back the punishment which fit their error.

In reflecting on this oddly constructed passage we should first note that the term usually translated "against nature" refers to the activity of females. But here he does not explicitly refer to same-sex behavior. He does not say that "their females" have left off the "natural use of the male and instead burn in lust for one another," etc.[3] Paul leaves completely unspecified what it is that the females do that is against natural "use."

We should also note that the term that the NRSV has translated as intercourse (*chreisin*) is normally used in Greek to mean the use or serviceableness of an object or a person. It almost never has the meaning of sexual use. To translate it as intercourse and to introduce the idea of sexual intercourse as the type of intercourse intended is to impose an interpretation on the text without adequate justification.

Only by way of analogy with what is supposed to be referred to concerning the males is there ground for supposing that Paul has referred in verse 26 to female same-sex practices. But what Paul says is that the women have "changed natural use" to that which is "against nature." The males, however, do not *change* natural use but are said to "*abandon* the natural use of the female" in order to do whatever it is they do with other males. If what he says of the males (that they burn in lust for one another, males with males) is to be regarded as "against nature" it is only by analogy with what he says about the females. The phrase "against nature" applies directly to the females and only by implication to the males.

Because of this grammatical asymmetry and because of the unmotivated innovation that would be required for Paul to actually deal with lesbianism as equal to male same-sex behavior, some contemporary commentators have concluded that it is unlikely that Paul has in mind lesbian sexual practices in verse 26.[4] It is likely that Paul is not thinking here of sexual practices at all but rather of behavior that is contrary to female nature generally. If Paul does have in mind some sexual practices, then it is not lesbianism but some other sexual behavior that he regards as contrary to "natural use."

Now what is it that is "against nature"? As we have seen, the text does not tell us what the women are doing that is exchanging natural use for unnatural. Tradition has supplied the view that what is unnatural here is nonprocreative sexuality generally. However, this is a view that is unattested in biblical literature. The supposition that sex is natural when used for purposes of reproduction is one that was developed in Hellenistic thought, both Jewish and gentile. In a later chapter I will trace the adoption of this view into Christian thought by Clement of Alexandria.

Now is this the view that lies behind what Paul is referring to here? This seems most unlikely. When Paul engages in an extended discussion of sexuality in 1 Corinthians 7, he does not refer to procreation as the purpose of sexual activity between male and female. Instead Paul seems to be of the view that sex has the purpose of giving pleasure and comfort to the partner, of assuaging desire and expressing delight.

In order to see how this is so it may be helpful to refer to Paul's words here. His basic point of view is that it is best not to marry since marriage makes one anxious about the affairs of the household (7:32–35). However, he does agree that those who find their sexual desire to be overwhelming (and thus productive of its own form of anxiety or distraction) should marry. In this way he seems to think that the man and the woman will be delivered from the obsession with desire that would distract them from their commitment to the life of the community.[5]

That the aim of marriage is to control but not eliminate desire is evident from his advice to those who are married: "The husband should give to his wife her conjugal rights [debt], and likewise the wife to her husband" (1 Corinthians 7:3). Paul even warns against depriving one another of this right except for short times for prayer! At no point does Paul suppose that the rationale for marriage has to do with procreation. He does not provide comfort for those who later will maintain that husband and wife should refrain from sexual practice except for the purpose of producing progeny. He explicitly warns against what will later become (in the second and third centuries) the practice of cohabiting without sex. For Paul this would amount, as he says, to offering an opening to satanic temptation. Paul's views here seem rather more in accord with a Jewish and biblical realism about the significance of sexuality in the life of persons, a realism enshrined in the creation account of the delight that male and female find in each other (Genesis 2:23–24). As Puritan readers would later discover, the point of sex is to give appropriate expression to desire and delight in and through one another's bodies. Moreover in this Paul retains a manifest equality (1 Corinthians 7:4).

Only by way of inattention to Paul's own expressed views about sexuality is it possible to imagine that he has adopted the Stoic view of sexuality. But this means that *para physin* cannot mean that the activity of females (and perhaps by extension of the males) is against nature because it is nonprocreative sexual activity.[6]

But Paul does use the phrase *para physin*. If it does not refer to nonprocreative sexuality then to what does it refer? If this were the only context in which Paul used the phrase we might be left to speculation. But Paul uses this phrase in another context in Romans. It comes in his discussion of the divine plan by which the gentiles come to be included in the covenant of divine grace. Here Paul uses the analogy of the growing of olives and speaks of the branches of Israel being (temporarily) cut off so that the branches of the gentiles may be grafted in.

What is noteworthy is that it is the activity of God that is here described as "against nature" (Romans 11:24). For it is the divine plan that has made provision for the extraordinary engrafting of wild branches onto domesticated root stock. If going against nature were such an obviously terrible thing then one would hardly use this as an expression of what God is doing, especially since this activity is the very activity that Paul has devoted his life to furthering. He is of course the exemplary apostle to the gentiles. It is God who has called him to this work. It is his entire reason for being. And it is, as he says, "against nature."[7]

To this point, then, it is clear (a) that "against nature" refers directly to the behavior of women and only indirectly, if at all, to the male behavior of verse 27. Moreover (b) the term cannot refer to nonprocreative sexuality generally since Paul does not hold the view that sex is for procreation. We have also learned (c) that being against nature does not mean being contrary to some immutable law established by God in creation since God is also represented as acting "against nature" and Paul has made that activity the center of his work and life.

The results so far are negative as far as "against nature" is concerned. But there is more that we can learn from his use of the same term in Romans 11:24. In the latter passage Paul is making use of a metaphor based on agriculture. The practice of grafting branches onto root stock is common in horticulture, especially with grapes and olives. But what is uncommon is that Paul suggests that *domesticated trunks* have *wild branches* engrafted into them. This is what he calls *para physin.* It is "against nature" because it is exactly the reverse of common horticultural practice, which grafts *domesticated branches* into *wild trunks* or uncultivated root stock. What is against nature is not the activity of grafting but rather the reversal of horticultural practice. Against nature is not "against biology" but contrary to (universal) custom.

Thus also in Romans 1:26, the women may be said to be acting in such a way as to alter or reverse "general or universal custom," what is expected as a matter of course. Just as God has acted in such a way as to fly in the face of universal custom (by grafting wild branches into domesticated root stock) so also the females in Romans 1:26 are said to fly in the face of universal custom or expectation. Now a moment's reflection will suggest that any behavior that is, from a general cultural standpoint, "unwomanly" could be regarded as in this sense "against nature." If what is in view here is general gender expectations, then any behavior that flies in the face of gender role expectations could be so regarded. If what is in view is sexual behavior, then any sexual activity that transgresses gender expectations in this sphere would be against nature.

That Paul is concerned with gender role expectations and that he relates these to "nature" is something we also encounter in 1 Corinthians 11:2–16. The specific context for reference to nature in this argument is as follows:

> Does not nature itself teach you that if a man wears long hair, it is degrading to him, but if a woman has long hair it is her glory? For her hair is given to her as a covering. (1 Corinthians 11:14–15)

To what is Paul referring when he speaks here of "nature"? Certainly not biology since both female and male hair grows until it is cut (or falls out). He is referring to what he took to be the generally approved practice or custom of the Hellenistic world. This practice was to cut the hair of males and to allow the hair of females to grow without interference. Moreover this custom was specific to the Roman Hellenistic world. It had nothing to do with the customs of those outside that world or civilization, who would have been regarded as "barbaric" or uncivilized.

We have learned two more things about "nature" here. The first is that it refers to civilized custom. The second is that Paul uses it to refer to gender role expectations within that framework of civilized custom. This suggests that Paul is concerned that "their women" are outraging civilized custom through behavior that violates the gender role expectations of women.

The connection between Romans 1:26–7 and 1 Corinthians 11:15–16 is even stronger. For in Romans 1:26 Paul introduces his theme by speaking of what the NRSV translates as "degrading [*atimias*] passions." In 1 Corinthians 11:15 he says that for a man to have long hair is degrading [*atimia*] to him. What is at stake in both cases is activity that brings one into disrepute or makes one the object of ridicule.

Taken by itself, verse 26 will not get us much further in identifying specifically what it is that Paul has in mind here. We know that it is the females who have somehow changed natural use into something against nature. We know that against nature most likely refers to that which seems to go against the grain of universal custom or expectation (remembering that this is also capable of having a positive sense). We know it is very unlikely that Paul is referring to nonprocreative sexual activity generally. Indeed, the only reason for supposing any sexual practice to be involved here is the connection to verse 27. By itself the changing of something "natural" into something unnatural could refer to any general or presumably universal attribute of females into what appears to be a perversion of that expectation or role. This may involve sexual practice; for example, women may be regarded as "naturally" passive so that a more extreme sexual activism such as sexual predation could be regarded as a distortion of feminine sexuality. But other features of universal expectations of women might be involved: being cruel rather than nurturing, for example. Or the motherly role of women could be involved, as in violence against their children or incest abuse. Taken in isolation the verse does not tell us.

We should also note one of the most curious phrases used by Paul. The women are described as "their" females. Whose females are we talking about here? Since answering this question requires attention to the overall context of the passage we only note it here. But those to whom these females "belong" are presumably some group of males. And it is to their behavior that Paul next turns.

Paul does not say that male behavior is against nature but that the behavior of "their" females is. But the males, while acting badly in Paul's view, are not directly acting "against nature." What the males are doing, however, is "leaving off the natural use of females." Now, we should not presuppose that Paul approves of "the natural use of females." The customary use of the female to gratify male lust is more or less universal practice (and in *that* sense natural) but also inexcusable.[8]

Is Paul referring to sexual practices among the males? Some have doubted this. After all he does not use any term for sexual relations in this passage. He says "male with male" but uses no verb at all, still less one that would suggest lying with (as in Leviticus) or bedding. Paul knows these terms, but he does not use them here.[9] Paul does say that these males "burned in their desire for one another." This may be regarded as a desire that is specifically sexual in character even though Paul does not himself say so.

We are also told that this consuming desire for one another is one that produces, as it were spontaneously, a fitting retribution. Those who fall into this obsessive desire already get their just deserts. That is, this passion produces its own fitting comeuppance. Notably Paul does not say that God punishes this behavior (whatever it is), still less that Christians ought to do so. Rather, the activity produces its own punishment. It sets up some kind of vicious circle. Indeed, the whole catastrophe of Roman civilization of which this is a symptom is really due to the way that people have been left by God (temporarily) to their own devices. Whatever is going on here, Paul views it as a kind of madness that follows from abandoning the way of justice known by all people as the will of God.

Neither in the case of the females who change natural (customary) practice for that which is against nature nor in the case of males who abandon the natural (customary) use of the female and burn in their desire toward one another do we have to do with isolated criminal activity. Rather what we encounter here is a symptom of the sort of madness that follows from rejecting the Creator for the creature and choosing injustice instead of justice.

In order to understand this more clearly it is important to attend to the context within which Paul makes the presumed reference to same-sex practices among males.

## The Unjust Social Order:
## Looking at the Context

We may begin with the way in which Paul's overall argument is traditionally understood. In the traditional view, Paul is in the process of demonstrating that *all people,* whether Jews or gentiles, have come into such serious opposition to the justice or righteousness of God as to merit divine wrath and destruction. He goes on to maintain that this death sentence is, however, suspended through the act of God in Jesus, which then offers to humanity a way to salvation that depends not on the fulfillment of the law but upon the grace that awakens faith in and gratitude to God.

The argument that begins in 1:18, then, is the opening intended to demonstrate the sinfulness of the gentile world, whose capital is the city of Rome and whose Christian adherents are the audience for Paul's letter. In any version of this traditional understanding of the argument of Paul in Romans it would be obtuse to extract any one element from Paul's indictment of the gentiles in order to attempt to distinguish between sinners and nonsinners. For it is Paul's point that all are sinners, all need grace, all receive the offer of salvation in Jesus.

Closer attention to the immediate context of our verses casts further light on the kind of distortion of human being with which Paul is concerned. Paul's indictment of gentile civilization begins by asserting that the gentiles know God and God's will on the basis of their own understanding (not on the basis of Judaism or Christianity), "so they are without excuse" (1:20b). Paul then goes to the presumed root of the problem, namely, that the gentiles have turned away from God as they knew God and instead of honoring or being grateful to God, have substituted images of mortal beings for God. That is, the gentiles turn to idolatry.

There follow three articulations of an indictment of which our verses are the second. The first is:

> Therefore God gave them up in the lusts of their hearts to impurity, to degrading of their bodies among themselves, because they exchanged the truth about God for a lie and worshiped and served the creature rather than the Creator, who is blessed forever. (24–25)

The indictment then reaches its climax (and greatest degree of specificity) following our verses:

> And since they did not see fit to acknowledge God, God gave them up to a debased mind and to things that should not be done. They were filled with every kind of wickedness, evil, covetousness, malice. Full of envy, murder, strife, deceit, craftiness, they are gossips, slanderers, God haters, insolent, haughty, boastful, inventors of evil, rebellious toward parents, foolish, faithless, heartless, ruthless. (28–31)

And it is in reference to *this* indictment (rather than the verses that most concern us) that Paul concludes:

> They know God's decree, that those who practice such things deserve to die — yet they not only do them but even applaud others who practice them (32)

One of the first things to note concerning these three parallel indictments is that they are meant to demonstrate the same thing: the exchange of the immortal for the mortal and thus the descent into a kind of social madness. We should also be aware that where Paul is most specific in his indictment we do not encounter sexual misconduct at all. The extended indictment that concludes and climaxes the series is devoted to an astonishing array of symptoms of generalized human strife and meanness. It is with this, rather than the presumed sexual misconduct of verses 26–27, that Paul is most concerned. It is this that demonstrates the moral bankruptcy of those he is describing. And it is this that they themselves are said to know brings on utter destruction because it flies in the face of what they know to be the "decree of God."

If we are to make headway in interpreting the references in verses 26–27 then we must anchor the passage in the specific context of verses 28ff. If Paul has anything sexual in mind in our verses it is a sexuality that comes to expression in the context of an extreme rapacity of people in relationship to one another. It is this rapacity that Paul believes his readers will recognize as both inhuman and as contrary to even gentile "piety."

Now we may pause at this point to note that whatever Paul is referring to in verses 26–27, it is most unlikely to be same-sex eroticism in general. He is not likely to be referring to female same-sex behavior in verse 26, which becomes a topic of significant Roman comment only in the following century (in the satires of Martial, Juvenal, and Lucian). The reference to male behavior should not be construed as applying to those sorts of same-sex behavior widely regarded as acceptable or within the range of customary male behavior. The more likely way same-sex behavior can be a part of this indictment is if it shows the signs of behavior that Romans knew or believed to be beyond the pale of civilized conduct. Thus pederasty as modified by Roman custom (adult males and young adult or older adolescent males) and even prostitution (generally protected by the State even later under Christian emperors) is unlikely to be in view here.[10]

Already the rapaciousness that Paul refers to in verses 28ff. offers pointers toward the kind of behavior to be referred to in verses 26–27. The inclusion of items like "insolent, haughty, boastful" point us toward a certain class of people: those of the ruling elites.

That we do have to do with a certain class of people here and not with each and every Roman is made clear by a number of ways in which Paul discriminates between those who are unjust and those who are just. In spite of the difficulty that this causes for the traditional interpretation of Romans, it is crucial for Paul's argument. Thus he maintains:

For he will repay according to each one's deeds: to those who by patiently doing good seek for glory and honor and immortality, he will give eternal life. (2:6–7)

Later he returns to the same theme:

When gentiles who do not possess the law, do naturally [*physi-kon*][11] what the law requires, these, though not having the law, are a law to themselves. (2:14)

Paul clearly supposes that there are some gentiles who act decently and justly and that these are not the enemies of God to whom he has been referring in the indictment. The ground of their action is not compliance with the laws of Judaism, nor is it the "faith in Jesus Christ," which he intends later to commend. It is the traditional pagan goal of "glory and honor and immortality" (2:7).

There appear then to be two groups here: those who act rapaciously and those who act honorably. Both are gentiles. How then can Paul suppose that the rapaciousness of some warrants the conclusion "that all, both Jews and Greeks, are under the power of sin" (3:9)? This works only if those who are decent are under the power of those who act dishonorably and if those who act dishonorably are somehow the legitimate representatives of the people as a whole. Then it would follow that the rapaciousness of the powerful and socially dominant elites characterizes the society or civilization as a whole.[12]

This means that if we are to understand the sort of behavior Paul has in mind in verses 26 and 27 we must identify the behavior of the imperial court in whose name justice is both applied and perverted in the civilization as a whole. The same of course would be true of Paul's use of prophetic materials to indict "the Jews." For what is going on there is not an indictment of all Jews as Jews but of the leadership elites whose behavior tarnishes the nation as a whole.

We may note in passing that what Paul is up to here is showing that the authorities in whose name the law is applied to condemn and execute Jesus are themselves corrupt. It is for this reason that law itself (whether Jewish or Roman) comes into suspicion as incapable of producing justice and that therefore a way that is outside the law must be found if justice is to be actualized and divine wrath averted.[13] Thus again it is the behavior of those at the top of the social pyramid — in whose name the death sentence against Jesus was carried out and the persecution of Christians perpetuated — that invalidates the presumed justice of that sentence and of the whole system of law that it represented.

## In Caesar's Court

Now we know exactly where to look for the behavior that Paul has in mind in verses 26–27 and indeed throughout his indictment of Roman civilization.[14] It is the activity of the imperial court from the time of Tiberius (under whose authority Jesus was executed) to the time of Nero (during which time Paul may be writing to a group of people in the capital). Those to whom Paul is writing, as "citizens" or at least inhabitants of Rome, may be expected to know something of the widely circulated rumors concerning the goings on of the imperial household. As it happens we have good information too, at least about the sort of rumors then current. It is this material (from Suetonius, Tacitus, and Dio) that provides the correct context for interpreting Romans 1:18–32 and especially verses 26–27.[15]

Two of the historians to which we turn (Tacitus and Suetonius) wrote in the following century and regarded their labors as having been impossible in the preceding century due to the arbitrary violence to which all who spoke out were subject. Tacitus, for example, writing around 120 C.E. recalled that "the histories of Tiberius, Caius [Caligula], Claudius and Nero, while they were in power, were falsified through terror" (*Annals* book 1.1). His description of the reign of Tiberius is true of the succeeding accounts as well: "I have to present in succession the merciless biddings of a tyrant, incessant prosecutions, faithless friendships, the ruin of innocence, the same causes issuing in the same results, and I am everywhere confronted by a wearisome monotony in my subject matter" (book 4.33). Virtually the entire period from the time of the death of Augustus until the assassination of Domitian was characterized as a reign of terror in which literally no one was safe from false accusation, from the arbitrary loss of position, property, and even life. Even a cursory reading of Suetonius, Dio, or Tacitus confirms the characterization of Paul in Romans 1:28–32 of rapacious cruelty, arbitrary violence, and ruthlessness.

Dio, for example, reports that "Tiberius employed all the citizens without exception against one another, nor, for that matter, could anyone rely upon the loyalty of any friend" (58.16.5), and Tacitus likewise reports that "the force of terror had utterly extinguished the sense of human fellowship, and with the growth of cruelty, pity was cast aside" (6.19).

It is this climate of fear that the historians blame for the silence of contemporaries about the events in question. And it is the passing of this climate of fear and the cultivation of the letters associated with the ascendancy of the "good" emperors — Trajan, Hadrian, Anoninus Pius, and Marcus Aurelius — that provides the context for the emergence of a historical accounting of the years of turbulence that were beginning to recede in favor of a period of veritable renaissance. This background helps us to understand both the audacity of Paul in adverting to the behavior of the imperial court and the understandable caution with which he veils his references to these activities.

## Unnatural Women

In order to better understand Paul's reference in Romans 1:26 to "their women" who have transformed "natural use" into that which is against nature (or against civilized custom), it is important to know what the people of Rome themselves thought of the behavior of the women associated with the emperors that contravened their sense of rightness or fittingness. As it happens the histories of the time provide ample evidence of the view that the women of the emperors played a major role in the tale of terror that characterizes the history of this period. While the sources do not provide us with a broad social history, concentrating as they do on the imperial household, they do give us strong evidence of the breakdown, from a Roman perspective, of the natural or customary role of women at the top of society. Here we will briefly attend to the career of three women who dominated this period: Livia Druscilla, Messalina, and Agrippina the younger.

Livia Druscilla was the last wife of Augustus. She had been married to another man but was ordered by Augustus to divorce her husband and marry the emperor himself. Her first son by the previous marriage, Tiberius, was ordered to divorce his wife and marry Augustus's daughter Julia, a woman famous, like her mother of the same name, for her flagrant adulteries. Eventually both Julias were exiled and Livia became the undisputed power behind the throne.

The death of Augustus was regarded by some as having been hastened by Livia when she feared that Augustus would reconcile himself with a grandson (Agrippa) rather than leave the empire to Tiberius, whom he had adopted (Dio, LVI.30.1). In any case she was widely credited with the death by poisoning of that grandson as Augustus himself was dying in order to clear the path to the throne for Tiberius. In the aftermath the deification of Augustus was secured by Livia and Tiberius acting in concert, and she acted more and more openly not as the power behind the throne but as the co-emperor. It was supposed that she had secured the throne for Tiberius, even against Augustus's wishes, and she fostered this impression to the extent that "she always declared that it was she who had made Tiberius emperor; consequently she was not satisfied to rule on equal terms with him but wished to take precedence over him" (Dio, LVII.12.3). In an act that was especially galling to Tiberius, the senate called him not only "son of Augustus" but also "son of Livia" (Suetonius, *Tiberius*, chapter 50). Her constant up-staging of Tiberius (who was no child after all but a man in his mid-fifties when he became emperor) is given as a primary reason for Tiberius's abandoning of Rome and removal to Capreae in 26 C.E. (Tacitus, 4.59). Even Livia's death three years later did not effect reconciliation. Tiberius's protegé Caligula referred to her as "a Ulysses in petticoats" (Suetonius, *Gaius*, 23). Claudius, however, later decreed divinity for her.

The same Claudius himself appears to have been ruled by a small circle of former slaves and by successive wives. Messalina, his second wife, appears to have run the empire as a private fiefdom. She collaborated in the sale not only of citizenship but also of "military commands, procuratorships and governorships" (Dio, 60.17.6). In addition she worked on Claudius's naturally timid nature to induce fear of rivals, which enabled her to secure the deaths of multitudes of men, women, and children, using slaves to inform on their masters and children on their parents. Dio calls her "the most lustful and abandoned of women" (60.14.3) and claims that she induced other Roman women to engage in adultery at the palace in front of their husbands (the latter receiving her favorable treatment). She is even said by Dio to have sat as a prostitute in the palace and coerced other women of high station to do the same. This behavior was apparently well known to all but Claudius himself. Dio reports that "the people . . . were grieved to think that he alone failed to realize what was going on in the palace — behavior so notorious, in fact, that news of it had already traveled to the enemy" (60.28.4).

Her flagrant behavior eventually caught up with her, however. She apparently had betrayed one of her own paramours, securing his execution even while she was still having an affair with him. This understandably persuaded her confederates that she could not be trusted. She had in the meantime arranged to publicly marry her lovers, especially one Silius, who was particularly ambitious (Tacitus, 11.26–28). Her henchmen in the palace used this as a pretext for claiming to Claudius that she was on the point of having Claudius assassinated so that she and her new husband could inherit the empire. He fled at the news (being always timid) but gave the go-ahead for an attempt to nip the plot in the bud. Messalina was thus herself slain by those who had been her confederates in terror (Tacitus, 11.38).

Claudius plunged immediately from the frying pan into the fire by marrying Agrippina the younger. Agrippina's mother (Agrippina the elder) had herself been rather formidable in protecting her own brood of imperial fledglings. She had, it was claimed, actually commanded armies when her husband, Germanicus, was unable to do so and had quelled riots among the troops (Tacitus, 1.69). After Germanicus's death she had fiercely protected her children from Tiberius's jealous attempts at removing all plausible rivals to his throne. This met with some success as her youngest son, Gaius (nicknamed Caligula), lived to eventually become the successor of Tiberius. Agrippina the younger was Gaius's sister. Caligula had illicit sexual relations with his sisters. Agrippina then married Lepidus, who was also Caligula's lover (the one case where a person is claimed to have been both "top" and "bottom" in the same relationship in this history).

When Messalina was killed, Agrippina, who was still relatively young, was referred to by the middle-aged Claudius as his daughter, though she was in fact his niece. Claudius managed to get the senate to pass a new law that permitted the marriage of uncle and niece (previously regarded as incestuous and strictly prohibited in Rome) so that he could marry Agrippina. Agrippina required as the price of this matrimony that Claudius would adopt her son Nero as his own son thereby making Nero a candidate to succeed Claudius, whose own son (Britannicus) was still quite young. The same source maintains that Agrippina pushed Claudius to even greater extremes of cruelty, continuing the work of Messalina in playing upon the timid emperor's fears (Tacitus, 12.59).

According to Tacitus, it was well known that Agrippina subsequently secured the death of Claudius in order to prevent his passing over Nero and granting inheritance to Britannicus (12.64–67). Following the assassination of her husband, Agrippina became virtually the undisputed ruler of the empire, as Nero was still only seventeen. She insisted on prerogatives never before granted a woman, including signing decrees, receiving ambassadors, and entering upon senate business. She continued the tradition of Livia and especially Messalina in securing the death of all who stood in her way.

When Nero as a young man began to exercise more imperial power and to resent the intrusion of his mother in affairs of state, she sought to regain control over him by flaunting a sexual relationship with her emperor son. Although it is unclear whether she was actually engaged in an incestuous relationship with her son or was simply feigning such a relationship in order to give the impression of having him under her control, the relationship was widely known and talked about (Tacitus, 14.2).

As Nero himself chafed under the arrogance of his mother, it became clear that the only way to escape her clutches was to have her assassinated. A variety of attempts failed. But finally Nero managed to have his own mother murdered on the pretext that she was attempting to have him assassinated in order to take over the empire. This ruse was apparently successful; Agrippina was sufficiently unpopular as to cause Nero to be hailed as a conqueror merely for having successfully assassinated his own mother.

This brief survey of the exploits of some of the women who earned notoriety in the period between the death of Augustus and the reign of Nero is sufficient to indicate how Paul could suppose that people with common sense in Rome would have agreed that "their women" had transformed natural service or use into that which was decidedly against nature. Even one who was less ambivalent than Paul about the role of women in the world might have supposed that the dominant role of women in the corruption of the state and in the reign of terror of this period went against civilized custom.[16] The role of wife and mother exchanged for that of assassin of husband and would be assassin of son; the role of matron for adulteress and prostitute, the role of sister for that of paramour. The "dishonoring of their bodies among themselves" (verse 24) and the "dishonorable passions" (verse 26) of which he speaks are well represented here. There is no need to imagine some reference to female same-sex relationships. Something far more obvious, far more public, far more notorious, is quite adequate to explain how it is that Paul can foreground the unnatural behavior of prominent women well known to his readers in Rome. This behavior, moreover, is not simply a parenthesis but is deeply reflective of the violence and violation pervasive in the society as a whole.

## Burning with Desire

"Likewise the males...." The behavior of imperial women is reflected in the behavior of imperial males. A similar connection is made in a speech reported by Dio Cassius and attributed to Boadicea, the female war chief who united the Britons in an uprising against imperial Rome in the time of Nero. Because it makes a very similar connection it is worth investigating for insight into the way in which the imperial court may have been viewed both by outsiders (like Boadicea) and by insiders like Dio. The partial congruence of these views with those of Paul helps to show how Paul might have supposed that his readers would find his categorizations rhetorically effective.

Boadicea initially refers to the way in which the Romans have been ruled first by Messalina "and afterwards Agrippina and now Nero (who though in name a man, is in fact a woman, as is proved by his singing, lyre-playing and beautification of his person)"; she prays for "preservation of life, and liberty against men insolent, unjust, insatiable, impious, if indeed, we ought to term these people men who bathe in

warm water, eat artificial dainties, drink unmixed wine, anoint themselves with myrrh, sleep on soft couches with boys for bedfellows —
boys past their prime at that — and are slaves to a lyre-player and
a poor one too. Wherefore may this Mistress Domitia-Nero reign no
longer over me or over you men; let the wench sing and lord it over
Romans, for they surely deserve to be slaves to such a woman after
having submitted to her so long" (Dio, 62.6.3–5).

In this speech the domination of women, the rule of vicious cruelty,
and the sexual habits of the emperors are linked together in a way that
is not unlike the rhetorical connections made by Paul. These elements
are differently organized to be sure and it is difficult to know how
much of this connection was a part of the historical tradition.[17] But
the parallels are instructive.

Paul's concern is primarily with the social disorder and with the
connection between that unjust social order and the worshiping of
mortal creatures (like the emperors themselves). But he also sees a
connection between the unjust social order and the total subversion
of gender role expectations among imperial women and suggests that
this has a certain impact on the sexual behavior of the males as well,
behavior he is confident that the Romans themselves will understand
to be "dishonorable."

Now we have already seen that this cannot mean a wholesale indictment of all same-sex practices. Whether or not Paul felt that all such
practices were repugnant would be extraneous to the case he is trying
to make. He is trying to link a general subversion of justice to the sexual practices of the emperors of this time. Do the sources indicate that
these emperors and their households engaged in sexual practices that
would have been regarded by their fellow Romans as beyond the pale
of civilized conduct, whether or not these same Romans practiced or
approved of the legally condoned forms of same-sex behavior?

Again, we know perfectly well that the behavior of these males was
beyond the pale of what other Romans would have regarded as civilized
custom, even if these same Romans approved of some forms of same-
sex relationships. The same sources that shed light on the unnatural
behavior of some imperial women also shed light on the behavior of
the emperors themselves.[18] Again we will not attempt an exhaustive

recounting of this behavior amply documented in the sources. Only a few illustrations will suffice to show the situation within which Paul's argument could have been expected to be rhetorically persuasive to his readers.

It was widely believed that Tiberius retired to Capeae (Capri) in order to escape his mother, Livia. Suetonius also suggests that "having found seclusion at last, and no longer feeling himself under public scrutiny, he rapidly succumbed to all the vicious passions which for a long time he had tried, not very successfully, to disguise" (*Tiberius* 42). Suetonius continues:

> On retiring to Capeae he made himself a private sporting house, where sexual extravagances were practiced for his secret pleasure. Bevies of girls and young men, whom he had collected from all over the empire as adepts in unnatural practices, known as *spintriae*, would copulate before him in groups of three, to excite his waning passions. . . . He furthermore devised little nooks of lechery in the woods and glades of the island, and had boys and girls dressed up as Pans and nymphs prostituting themselves in front of caverns or grottoes. . . . Imagine him training little boys, whom he called his "minnows," to chase him while he went swimming and get between his legs to lick and nibble him. (43–44) (See also Tacitus, 6.1)

Suetonius's account brings together the general Roman aversion to oral sex (widely regarded as unnatural) together with extreme cases of pedophilia. The Romans, like the Greeks, abhorred pedophilia, although their definitions varied. In classical Greece boys under twelve were regarded as decidedly off-limits. In Rome fourteen appears to have been the minimum age for sexual relations.[19] The pederastic or cross-generational structure of relationships often referred to in antiquity was carefully distinguished from the unacceptable corruption of minors. Greeks seem to have favored youths in the sixteen to seventeen range while Romans seem to have favored young men who were noticeably older, usually eighteen or older. In either case the activity of Tiberius would have been regarded as reprehensible.

A later emperor, Vitellius, who ruled for much of 69 C.E., had "spent his boyhood and adolescence on Capreae, among Tiberius's male prostitutes. There he won the nickname "Spintria," which clung to him throughout his life; by surrendering his chastity, the story goes, he secured his father's first advancement to public office" (Suetonius, *Vitellius* 3). I quote this later reference in order to make clear how it was that the emperor acquired his children (by offering advancement to their fathers who had absolute power over them) and thus how it happened that his habits would have become public knowledge.

Vitellius's father, it is said, had first instituted the practice of worshiping Gaius Caligula as a god (Suetonius, *Vitellius* 2). Gaius, nicknamed Caligula ("little boots") from his infancy spent in the army camp where his father, Germanicus, was general, managed to survive Tiberius's paranoid hatred of his family by becoming Tiberius's youthful protégé on the infamous island of Capreae, where he learned an early passion for watching torture and executions. It was later reported that he had himself turned on his adoptive father and, to hasten the work of poison, actually strangled Tiberius to death. Caligula in any case became emperor at the age of twenty five. He was initially regarded as a hero. But Caligula soon became not a name of endearment but one of terror. He insisted on the deification of Tiberius but then went beyond what had only recently become customary (the deification of a dead emperor) to insist on being deified himself while in the bloom of youth and health. He was known to commit incest with all of his sisters but especially loved Druscilla, whom he treated as his lawful wife. When she died he insisted on her divinity.

He was known for his delight in cruelty and torture and for threatening all who were close to him with his power to take their heads. He especially wanted those whom he killed to be killed slowly or with many cuts so they would know they were dying. His upbringing on Capreae led him to astonishing levels of debauchery. He was the first to be publicly known as the lover and beloved of the same man — something shocking to Roman sensitivities. His sexual exploits, both active and passive, with a variety of people were widely rumored. But he was most given to rape, especially the rape of other men's brides. Indeed, apart from his incestuous relationship with his sister, he seems to have had sex with women primarily in situations of rape. He met his end in a rather fitting way, being assassinated by a group of young knights, some of whom had been raped by him, others of whom had had their wives raped by him. He was stabbed thirty times, "including sword thrusts through the genitals" (Suetonius, *Gaius* 58). It was the sort of death that Paul might well have described as "receiving in their own bodies the fitting recompense."

Claudius, who was regarded as the weakest and most timid of men and who was ruled by women and slaves, does not enter into our account of sexual nonconformity. He was supposed only to delight in ordinary cross-sex adultery.[20]

Nero, however, was another story. He was only seventeen when he became emperor and ruled until he was thirty one. He seems to have been a young gangster. In his early years as emperor he liked to go out disguised as a commoner to engage in highway robbery and rape of passersby. In this way he instigated a kind of crime wave in the city with other young nobles either accompanying him on his nightly raids or imitating him. As he grew into adulthood he became both more vicious and at the same time more complex. He loved the theater and himself became a musician, poet, and actor, even playing the roles of women and slaves, to the dismay of the more traditional of the aristocracy. He self-consciously modeled himself after his hero Gaius-Caligula, seeking to outdo him in cruelty and debauchery.

After the death of his wife (whom he had kicked in the womb), his affections were transferred to a slave boy, Sporus, who bore a strong resemblance to his late wife. He had Sporus castrated and married him with great ceremony. This relationship was the only lasting one of his life. Sporus was one of the handful still with him when he was hunted down and killed at the age of thirty-one.

The relationship with Sporus was one that directly replaced marriage for Nero. But it was not his only marriage to a man. Suetonius reports:

Nero practiced every kind of obscenity, and after defiling almost every part of his body finally invented a novel game: he was released from a cage dressed in the skins of wild animals, and

attacked the private parts of men and women who stood bound
to stakes. After working up sufficient excitement by this means
he was dispatched — shall we say — by his freedman Doryphorus.
Doryphorus now married him — just as he himself had married
Sporus — and on the wedding night he imitated the screams and
moans of a girl being deflowered. (*Nero* 29)

Several points are combined here. Nero has outraged Roman sensibilities by finding a way to combine oral sex (repugnant to Romans) with
rape and torture (and execution). This is the novelty by which Nero
completes the work of "defiling every part of his body." The other point
is that Nero has now managed to substitute marriage with a man in
both senses for the conventional "use of the female."

Again this brief survey of the reign of terror suggests the climate and
culture that Paul was characterizing in writing to people who lived in
Rome. His audience would have been familiar with these and probably
more outrageous rumors about those who exercised supreme authority
in the city and the empire. Our sources no doubt pale in comparison
with what was widely circulated about imperial goings on both in the
city and in the empire at large. But the sources that we do have are
sufficient to show us, as in a mirror dimly, the kind of behavior that
Paul could assume his readers knew about and deplored and that he
could assume was deplored by Romans of common sense and decency
wherever they lived.[21]

## Conclusion

In order to clarify Paul's supposed references to same-sex sexuality in
Romans 1:26–27, it is first helpful to see what Paul is up to in his
argument as a whole. I believe that when we take his argument as
undermining the legitimacy of Roman condemnations of Jesus and the
Christian movement (just as he will also seek to undermine similar
condemnations on the part of normative Judaism), we are able to get
much clearer about how his eventual argument about the law and
about a form of justice that supersedes structures of legality could be
taken as both pertinent for the readers in Rome and as effective in

establishing the need for an extralegal way of establishing justice and so wholeness in the human community.

Within this wider context, then, Paul's argument in Romans 1:18–32 demonstrates that the administrators of Roman law (and thus justice) have become the enemies of justice as they themselves understand justice. Thus he argues on Roman-Hellenistic (gentile) grounds that the system has become corrupt. He regards this corruption as due to the specific forms that idolatry has taken (most egregiously in the deification of emperors and members of the imperial household). The ultimate disorder, however, is the total breakdown of society disclosed in verses 28–32. It is this breakdown that marks the society as bound to destruction, as any thinking citizen could (in Paul's view) recognize.

A middle term in this argument is the breakdown in gender and sexual roles. Once we know that Paul is talking about the governing elite we know where to look for the symptoms he is describing. And this leads us to the way in which Roman historians themselves diagnosed the society that they described. And here we find significant confirmation of Paul's own diagnosis as well as clarification of what that diagnosis meant. For the historians agree with the diagnosis of the near total breakdown of law and order, the perception of the complete subversion of justice, resulting in the loss of all humane social interaction.

It is within this context, I believe, that we can best understand the references to "their women" in 1:26. Here there is no need to propose an unlikely preoccupation with female same-sex behavior to account for the text. Instead, it seems more plausible to suppose that it refers to the total subversion of the gender role expectations on the part of imperial women. Their behavior subverts nature or transforms the natural into that which is against nature in that the women become the models not of virtue but of cruelty and murder. Moreover, they are so far from being the models of matronly virtue that they actually transform the role of wife into that of assassin, of mother into that of seductress, and so on. Paul's own nervousness about gender role conformity in a matter so small (to us) as hair length fully accounts for his willingness to foreground female subversion of gender role expectations in this forceful way. And we know that the sort of behavior he was likely to be referring to was regarded in a very similar way by the Romans themselves.[22] Thus the text is much clearer without supplying a condemnation of lesbian relationships. (I do suppose that as some concern about these relationships emerges in second-century Rome and Alexandria, it would become easier for Christian readers of this text to supply a sexual meaning. Even so, as we shall see, many patristic interpreters do not read the text in this way.)

Even though Romans 1:26 does not seem to refer to female same-sex relationships, I have agreed that 1:27 does include reference to some male same-sex behavior. I agree with those who suppose that this is not specifically directed against the pederastic model of same-sex behavior. But I also do not believe that it is plausible to read here a blanket condemnation of all same-sex behavior. What Paul is referring to, I believe, is the distortion of sexuality, including the outrageous forms taken by same-sex activity, on the part of the ruling class and especially the emperors and their households. The same texts that help us understand how Romans might have been appalled by the behavior of imperial women help us to see how the same Romans might have been appalled by imperial sexual activity, perhaps especially the activity of "males with males." But it is critical for the forcefulness of Paul's argument here that we do not import into the discussion some imagined views about same-sex behavior as such. If this is what Paul wanted to talk about, he would have to develop an argument at much greater length. For many, perhaps most, Romans of the time regarded some forms of same-sex behavior as quite legitimate. But virtually all, irrespective of their views on same-sex behavior as such, would have held that the emperors were behaving very badly indeed. And the behavior of the emperors that we are in some position to document was quite likely to be but the tip of the iceberg among the ruling classes as a whole. Thus I do not suppose that Paul is referring only to the behavior of Tiberius, Caligula, or Nero but that he is referring to the sort of behavior that we happen to know about in their cases but that may very well have been multiplied within the class from which they were drawn.

Now of course it is possible that Paul himself regarded any and all same-sex behavior with repugnance, or that he supposed that it contravened the will of God. It is possible. But I do not think that Paul tells us what he thought about this. He does tell us what he thought of the behavior of those in whose name Roman justice was administered. And he tells us that his view of the matter was one that other Roman citizens like himself and those who lived in Rome (like his audience) would recognize and agree with without requiring a lot of complicated explanation.

In short, though Paul may have been personally homophobic, we can't tell this from what he says in Romans 1:26–27. We do know that Paul does not apply Leviticus to gentiles, as a matter of principle. We do know that he does not buy the Stoic argument (accepted by Jews like Philo and Pseudo-Phocylides) that sex is for procreation. We know that he does not accuse the Romans of violating Jewish law and custom but of violating Roman law and sensibility (law that permitted and even protected many forms of same-sex behavior). What Paul's private views of the matter of same-sex behavior were we have no way of knowing — only the guesses of scholars, homophobic or not, Paul-phobic or not.

This leaves unsettled the question of how it comes to pass that Paul is nevertheless read in ways that contribute his authority to homophobic discourse. In the next part of this study I will seek to examine how Hellenistic homophobic perspectives come to be assimilated into Christian perspectives and how that framework begins to make plausible a homophobic appropriation of Paul's texts.

## Part Four

# Christian
# Homophobia

I N CHAPTER 11 we take up the question of the appropriation of homophobic themes in the second century of Christian beginnings. We will want to inquire regarding to what extent these emergent themes are traceable to the biblical traditions that Philo had recruited for a Hellenistic homophobic project or to the Pauline materials that are often alleged to inaugurate a specifically Christian homophobia. On the other hand, we will want to inquire to what extent the themes that we will investigate are drawn from a preexisting or developing Hellenistic or Greco-Roman philosophical discourse. And we will want to discover any new themes that are introduced into the discussion.

We will begin by looking at the earliest documents that seem to bear traces of homophobic discourse and that may seem to introduce a new topic, the expansion of the Decalogue to include a prohibition related to same-sex sexual practices: the treatise attributed to Barnabas and the *Didache*, transmitted as the teaching of the twelve apostles. These documents, closely related in method and in content, add the idea of the corruption of youths to their renditions of the Decalogue, an addition that will also be found in Clement.

We will then turn to another new context for the presentation of homophobic discourse, Christian criticism of the emperor Hadrian's love affair with Antinous. As we shall see, this theme will have a longer hold upon the discourse of Christian intellectuals than the apparent tampering with the Decalogue. Indeed, tracing this theme will take us into the beginning of the fourth century of Christian origins.

We will then turn to the ways in which Clement (and to a certain extent Tertullian) adopts the Hellenistic and Stoic discourses concerning sexuality and incorporates them into perspectives that will have a significant impact upon emergent Christianities. It will finally be Clement who establishes the general ideological context within which elements of Christian homophobia can begin to gain a certain currency.

# – 11 –

# The Corruption of Youths

We noticed in the work of Pseudo-Phocylides the insertion — in what appears to be a "Hellenizing" of the Decalogue — of a prohibition against rousing passion for males that seemed to parallel the prohibition of adultery. In second-century Christian literature we see a similar move, which is both more explicit in its citation of the Decalogue and which introduces what appears to be a new technical term for the prohibited offense: *paidophthoreo*. This term is often translated in English as homosexuality, pederasty, and so on, but seems to have a somewhat more narrow meaning: the corruption or seduction of boys (or youths, or children). This more narrow meaning may indeed comport well with the actual concerns of Pseudo-Phocylides, since that document evinced an interest in the protection of young males from the attentions of unwanted male suitors or predators.

*Paidophthoreo* makes its first appearance in Christian literature in the closely related texts of Barnabas and the *Didache*, both of which are commonly dated as written between 70 and 135 C.E.[1]

The little book of Barnabas, which Clement of Alexandria regarded still in the late second century as an authoritative scriptural document written by the companion of Paul, is a witness to this practice. The text may well derive from Alexandria and employs a method of allegorical biblical interpretation that is reminiscent of Philo of Alexandria's treatment of the "Special Laws." Barnabas deals with the restrictions regarding food that are found in the Septuagint, including Leviticus 11:7–15 and Deuteronomy 14:8–11 (although some of the food taboos have an unknown origin). Unlike Philo he does not seem to regard the literal meaning of the texts as of any further use and concentrates instead on rather fanciful allegorical applications. One of these that gives a flavor of the whole and that also concerns our subject is as follows:

"You shall not eat the hare." Why? Do not become, he means, one who corrupts boys [*paidophthoros*], or even resemble such people, because the hare grows another opening every year, and thus has as many orifices as it is years old (10.6). Again neither shall you eat the hyena. Do not become, he means, an adulterer or a seducer [*phthoreus*] or even resemble such people Why? "Because this animal changes its nature from year to year and becomes male one time and female another." (10.7)

It is possible that the writer has in mind that one who pursues both women (an adulterer) and youths (a seducer) is changing the object of attraction (from male to female) and is in this way similar to that which changes (its own) gender; but the term "seducer" here does not specify the gender of the seduced, so any interpretation seems to require something of a stretch.

Thus eating is assimilated to "becoming," which is then connected to behavior, in these cases, probably to sexual practice.[2] Although, as we shall see, the idea of seducing or corrupting youths may have a possibly nonsexual meaning, the connection between seduction and adultery in the following interpretation does argue in favor of such a connection, as does the rather odd idea of a new orifice or anus among rabbits.

When Barnabas turns to exhortation concerning the "two ways," we have what appears as an enlargement upon the Decalogue: "This is the way of light . . . you shall love him who made you . . . you shall not be sexually promiscuous; you shall not commit adultery; you shall not corrupt boys. The Word of the Lord shall not go forth from you among any who are unclean. You shall not show partiality" (19.4). Here we see that the corruption or seduction of youths is clearly situated within the field of sexual transgression, though it may still be unclear precisely which transgression is thereby indicated.

The *Didache*, or teaching of the twelve apostles, which was also often cited as authoritative for Christians in the second century, does not engage in allegorical interpretation of Old Testament texts, unlike Barnabas, but does show a similar inclination to insert a prohibition of the seduction of youths into a context reminiscent of the Ten Commandments.

The second commandment of the teaching is: "You shall not murder; you shall not commit adultery; you shall not corrupt boys [*ou paidophthaseis*]; you shall not be sexually promiscuous [*ou porneuseis*]; you shall not steal; you shall not practice magic, you shall not engage in sorcery" (2.2). This list seems to alternate between texts from the Ten Commandments (which the translator/editor puts in quote marks that of course are not in the Greek text), and additions that may well suggest a Jewish-Christian provenance (magic, sorcery).

The overall tone of the text is serious and shows connections to the Sermon on the Mount and to the New Testament letter of James. For example: "Do not become angry, for anger leads to murder" (3.2), or: "Do not be foul-mouthed or let your eyes roam, for all these things breed adultery" (3.3). There is an admonition reminiscent of 2 Peter 2:18–21: "Slaves be submissive to your masters in respect and fear as to a symbol of God" (4.11). There are also admonitions that go further than specific texts of the New Testament but are consonant with later patristic teachings: "you shall not turn away from someone in need, but shall share everything with your brother, and not claim that anything is your own" (4.5).

Since these texts have a different style and tone yet come from the end of the first or beginning of the second century, they may be regarded as independent witness both to the use of the somewhat technical term "corruption of boys" and to the insertion of this term into lists of commandments that derive their form and some of their content from the Decalogue.

This will reach a certain culmination at the end of the second century, in the work of Clement of Alexandria, who will generally cite the Decalogue as if it contained this specific term and prohibition. Clement adopts from Barnabas and the *Didache* the theme of the corruption of youths and the tendency to locate this in his citations of or references to the Ten Commandments. Thus in the *Exhortation to the Heathen* we have the list: "Thou shalt not kill, thou shalt not commit adultery, thou shalt not [corrupt] boys, thou shalt not steal, thou shalt not bear false witness" (chap. 10). This rather blatant smuggling of *paidophthoria* into the Decalogue is not an isolated practice for Clement. In *The Instructor* we read, "Thou shalt not commit adultery, thou shalt not worship idols. Thou shalt not corrupt boys, thou shalt not steal...," etc. (book 3, chap. 12) and a similar sort of list of commandments of the Law is also found in the *Stromateis* or *Miscellanies:* "The law given to us enjoins us to shun what are in reality bad things, adultery, uncleanness, corruption of youths [the translator substitutes pederasty], ignorance, wickedness, soul disease" (book 2, chap. 8). The reference to the "law" here is odd since this text does not actually seem to be a version of the Decalogue but instead an ad hoc collection of items in which only adultery seems to be from that source while others are of unknown provenance (ignorance, soul disease). In the same text he cites the Decalogue, uncharacteristically, in its more familiar, canonical form (book 4, chap. 16), although he subsequently adds the command "thou shalt not corrupt boys" (book 4, chap. 36). Of course in no known version of the Bible does such a commandment anywhere appear. It seems to be a way of making the biblical witness conform to an already existing and prestigious condemnation of the "corruption of youths."

The placement of such a commandment in the context of Mosaic legislation appears to have arisen as a way of updating that law so as to conform to the philosophical wisdom of certain strands of Hellenistic discourse. Since in these contexts there is no independent treatment of the prohibition it seems not to be a defense of Mosaic legislation so much as an attempt to square that legislation with what non-Jewish and non-Christian readers would take to be something that it would have been good or wise for the commandments to have included.

However, this will by no means be its only context. Indeed, while the habit of citing this as if it had been promulgated at Sinai will seem to disappear after Clement, the category itself seems to have been available for use in a variety of contexts. Before attempting to more closely identify its meaning or range of meanings, it may be helpful to survey some of the other places where it appears in second-century Christian texts.

One text that is undecidably Christian or Jewish but that does appear to come from this period is the "Testament of Levi," a part of the *Testaments of the Twelve Patriarchs* that we examined in connection with the invention (by Philo) of a homophobic reading of the story of Sodom.[3] In this text there is a discussion of the priesthood that is to follow in the steps of Levi. A list of vices of the priestly class, the Levitical priesthood that will in turn prepare for the coming of the true priest (Christ?), includes the following: "And in the seventh week the priests will come, [who are] idolaters, contentious, lovers of money, arrogant, lawless, lascivious, abusers of children and beasts" (17:11). The commentator notes the list "contains a number of Hellenistic terms which occur only here in the Testaments," but makes reference to several of the texts where the corrupters of youth (which has here been translated as "abusers of children"!) appears in the literature we are considering. The connection between some same-sex practice and the sexual use of animals is reminiscent of Philo.

There are other texts whose Christian provenance is more certain where this term also appears. The celebrated Christian apologist Justin Martyr, who had been trained as a philosopher and who continued to wear the distinctive garb of the philosopher even after his conversion to Christianity, makes use of this term in his dialogue with Trypho, a representative of Hellenistic Judaism: "how much more shall all the nations appear to be under a curse who practice idolatry, who seduce youths, and who commit other crimes?" (95.1). For now we will simply notice the connection between the worship of false gods and the seduction of youths. We will discover that such a connection long predates Paul and, indeed, has a Platonic/Socratic provenance.

Tatian (110–70 C.E.), who may have been a student of Justin Martyr and who later became a spokesperson for the Encratite or self-controlling school of Christianity — a group that forbade all sexual intercourse of any kind, including heterosexual marriage — carries forward this term into new contexts. In addition to being one of those we will discuss in the next section who makes reference to the strange case of Antinous, Tatian also disparages the gods of the Hellenistic world, arguing that they are obviously mere mortals who have been divinized. Here he makes apparent reference to Zeus when he writes of a god as "he who marries and is a pederast and an adulterer" (8). That Zeus is recalled as one who was married to Hera, who seduced or raped Ganymede, and who had numerous liaisons with women makes this identification of the god all but certain. (In this case the translator in the *Ante-Nicene Fathers* has substituted "pederast" for "corrupter of youths.") Tatian appears to be referring to the abduction of Ganymede. In that case the corrupter of youth has a meaning that will overlap with the way Paul's reference to *arsenokoitai* is also understood, as referring to a classic case of rape. Of course for Tatian, for whom any sexual practice at all was abhorrent, it was not a problem to class marriage along with adultery and the corruption (or rape) of youths, since it was all the same for him in any case. In another context Tatian writes, "Pederasty is condemned by the barbarians, but by the Romans, who endeavor to collect herds of boys like grazing horses, it is honored with certain privileges" (28). Once again the translator has substituted pederasty for corrupter of youths. The "barbarians" may refer to Israel (as non-Greeks), but the idea of boy herds seems odd. On the one hand it may refer to certain ancient practices in Crete and or Sparta where youths were segregated from the general population until they were taken on by male mentor/lovers. Or it may refer to something like the celebrated case of Tiberius, whose "Life" by Suetonius (written 121 C.E.) may have been published by this time and who, as we noticed in discussion of Paul, kept something like a herd of boys for his pleasure at his retreat on Capri.

Another of the Christian apologists of this period, Theophilus of Antioch (115–168/181 C.E.) in his letter to Autolycus also adds "do not corrupt boys" (1.2) to his version of the "commandments." In an indictment of Hellenistic culture he also asks: "Why, then, do Epicurus and the Stoics teach incest and sodomy ... [literally corruption of youths] so that from boyhood this lawless intercourse is learned?" (3.6). Now this is rather odd. It demonstrates the continued association of the Stoics with pederasty and/or the corruption of youths, at least in the minds of those who wished to portray Christianity as a superior philosophy.[4]

Now what are we to make of the use of this rather odd term, "corruption of youths"? What range of meanings might we reasonably suppose this to have had either for the writers or the readers of these texts? Since these texts do not expound upon its meaning, any attempt to

specify that or those meanings will necessarily be inferential in character. Nevertheless we do have some ways to get our bearings. The
most obvious place to begin is by noticing that it has almost the opposite meaning of the term "pederasty" (corruption vs. love), which, as
we have seen, translators sometimes substitute for it. Certainly the
term "pederasty" continues in use both by its defenders and by its
detractors. Is *paidophthoria* simply a more effective way of pejoratively
naming the same set of practices and customs, or is its range more
narrow, pointing instead to certain abuses that occur within pederastic
settings?

We might note first that no less a personage than Socrates himself
seems to have been indicted precisely for the corruption of youths. In
the *Euthyphro* (2d–3b) Socrates tells a friend who accosts him as he
is leaving the "law courts" that he is to be accused of corrupting the
youth of Athens (*neous diaphtheironta*). The corruption in question,
according to Socrates' account here, has to do with "making new gods
and not believing in the old ones" (3b). This is expanded upon in the
*Apology* or Defense of Socrates (written of course by Plato) in which
the charge brought by a certain Meletus is several times characterized
as "corrupting the young." The first statement of this largely repeats
what we have heard in the *Euthyphro:* it says that "Socrates is guilty
of corrupting the minds of the young and of believing in gods of his
own invention, instead of the gods recognized by the state" (24b). The
term appears again many times in this text (24c, 25a, d, 26b, 30b, 33d,
34b, and so on.) Obviously it is a charge that has some sting to it. It is
interpreted here as having to do not with a literal seduction that aims
at a sexual relationship (though Socrates in other situations that we
have earlier examined is not averse to associating himself with that
practice). Rather the sting of the term is directed toward the denial of
the old gods and the veneration of new ones.

Is it not precisely some such charge as this that may have been
brought against the early Christians? For what, after all, do they do
but deny the existence of the traditional gods, offer in their place some
new god, and eagerly reach out to all who will hear with the "good
news" of this new god? Thus if the term has been used in this Socratic
or, rather, Platonic sense against Christians it might be understandable

that they would turn it back against their accusers, perhaps with a somewhat more literal or sexual meaning.

We get an idea of this in the text from Tatian, who, we recall, characterized Zeus as one who marries, is a corrupter of youth, and an adulterer (8). In this case, if the reference is to Zeus's abduction of Ganymede, then we have a specification of the term as involving forcible coercion for sexual purposes. We have already seen that this was a characterization of the story that commended itself independently to pagan writers (who did not share Tatian's horror of all, including marital, sex).

In any case we are in a position now to see that the association of the worship of false gods with a way of designating at least some same-sex practices predates the association presumably made by Paul in Romans as well as any presumed connection to Hellenistic Judaism. It is deeply etched in the Platonic tradition, even if the specific terminology undergoes some change.

But has the term gained a different meaning in the Greco-Roman world? Eva Cantarella indicates a number of sources that suggest to her that it was a crime in Rome to attempt to seduce a freeborn Roman male.[5] Sexual relations with slaves or freedmen or foreigners, however, were not subject to legal penalty. Cantarella maintains that this prohibition applied also to consensual relations: "*Stuprum* did not consist in imposing sex by force: it simply consisted in having an illicit relationship even with a consenting person" (104–5). However, the evidence she cites seems typically to involve attempted coercion. Thus she cites the case of a certain Titus Venturius, who was the object of the (unwelcome) attentions of Publius Plotius in 330 B.C.E. The latter even had the former whipped in order to induce him to submit to sexual advances. The use of the whip does not seem to persuade Cantarella that this was a case of attempted rape! The next case cited for which any detail is offered is that of Caius Lusius, who in 102 B.C.E. attempted to force a young soldier under his command to have sex. The latter killed his senior officer. When witnesses were produced to show that the officer had repeatedly attempted to seduce the young man and had been consistently rebuffed, the young soldier was honored rather than punished for the murder of his superior officer. This seems to be a fairly straightforward case of sexual predation ending in attempted rape, rather than courtship. Cantarella offers another example concerning the origin of the law in question: "Plutarch relates that Caius Scatinius Capitolinus tried to seduce the son of Marcus Claudius Marcellus" in 227 B.C.E. (108). Scatinius was "found guilty of attempted seduction." The law was applied to a case of someone "arrested for committing a sexual outrage against a lower magistrate" (109). Again we have a case of the attempt of a superior to force his will upon a subordinate.

If the ancient and obscure *lex scantinia* had been directed against coercive same-sex relationships, this would help to explain how consenting amorous relations could be celebrated by no less a court poet than Virgil and by the later poetry of Catullus without fear of contravening any known law.

In any case it would appear that Roman law had long had a provision that criminalized some kinds of attempted "corruption of youths," most likely of the sort that did not elicit consent on the part of the youth or subordinate. Of course the prohibition did not extend to slaves, foreigners, or freedmen, as we have seen.

How does this help us to illumine the use of the term *paidophthoria* in the literature that we have been examining? These authors may well have believed that they were simply adopting a Roman rule and showing that they were in fact more in line with ancient Roman custom and law than were many of their tormentors. It does not seem likely, however, that Christian writers would have applied the sorts of exceptions (slaves, foreigners, and so on) that had been a part of the Roman perspective since most Christians at this time may have belonged to these classes of persons. Thus they might have supposed, whether on Stoic or specifically Christian grounds, that slaves had the same rights to bodily integrity that the law granted to Roman citizens.

But this leaves open the question of whether the term as they used it entailed a certain degree of coercion. In the case of Tatian that we have noted, the reference to Zeus suggests a strong degree of coercion; there is no evidence that Ganymede was even courted by Zeus before being taken away to the abode of the gods. However, it may be that the term is one that permits a certain degree of slippage from courtship, to seduction, to harassment, to predation, to rape. If, as many scholars have suggested, the basic structure of Roman sexual relations was that of rape, that is, the imposition of indomitable will and strength, then "seduction" may have often been rather heavy handed, at the least.

Slippage may also occur in other ways. The term *paidophthoria* refers to boys or youths. But what does this mean exactly? The Roman age of consent appears to have been about fourteen. But young men of eighteen to twenty-two or so were supposed to be the most desirable objects of erotic desire (somewhat older than for the Greeks, perhaps). Are the "boys" to be understood as under the age of consent (younger than fourteen therefore), or does this include those who are the more appropriate age of consent (over fourteen but younger than, say, twenty-five)? Put another way, are we dealing with what the Greeks would have called pederasty or with the sexual abuse of prepubescent children (pedophilia) or something in between?

Certainly modern homophobic discourse has capitalized on this slippage. The celebrated case of Anita Bryant's "Save our Children" crusade in Florida in the 1970s made considerable use of the stereotype that "homosexuals" were an imminent threat to the well-being of young children. Even counter-homophobic authors like Bernadette Brooten could characterize the traditions of pederasty as "the sexual abuse of children," thereby falling into the all too familiar homophobic trope.[6]

In general the texts do not tell us if they have in view a blanket condemnation of all pederastic relations, renamed as *paidophthoria*, or if they specifically have in mind situations of actual or implied coercion. In any case there is no reason to suppose that the introduction of a prohibition of corruption of youth is an innovation of a specifically Christian form of homophobia. As it stands it seems to be in line with a Roman insistence on the bodily integrity (especially as regards sex) of its citizens. Even if the extension of the same protections to noncitizens was beyond the scope of the original law there is no reason to suppose that this would not have been something also agreeable to certain pagan philosophical perspectives (like Stoicism) to which early Christianity looked for approval. If this has the added force of turning the charge of corruption of youths in the sense given it in the

Platonic dialogues (innovation in religion) away from Christians and upon those who attacked them, so much the better.

Although the habit of introducing a prohibition of corruption of youths into the Decalogue does not seem to have survived the second century of our era, this prohibition itself survives into the first attempt in a council of the church to legislate sexual morality. The Synod of Elvira in Spain around 306 (or 324) C.E. contains a number of provisions related to sexual practices of the laity and the clergy. One of its provisions declares that those who corrupt youths (*stupratoribus puerorum*) shall not be given communion, even at the end (that is, as they are dying).[7] Again, we are not in a position to know whether what is in view here is coercive behavior or consensual romance. (The former seems to me to be far more probable, since there is more likely to be a plaintiff in the case of coercive or predatory behavior). But the very imprecision of the declaration may have given it added force in the direction of making even those involved in consensual relations eager to avoid the spotlight of public (ecclesiastical) notice.

We should also note that the condemnation of *paidophthoria* continues into the early work of Athanasius in *Contra Gentes* (written between 325 and 337), in which he details the exploits of the gods and the divinized emperors. In the conclusion to his catalog of the folly of these "gods" he refers to adultery (as a species of assault), incest, and *paidophthoria* (translated as pederasty).[8] He refers to these as acts "which the laws do not permit men to indulge" (12.40). The linkage to adultery regarded as a form of assault upon other men's wives and to incest (with sisters) may recall the exploits of Caligula. It appears that what is at stake in *paidophthoria* is assault (as in adultery) and the contravention of universal law and custom. This again suggests that what is at stake here is a form of assault that outraged pagan sensibility as well as law and thus has in view sexual predation rather than less violent (and perhaps more customary) forms of pederasty.

# – 12 –

# The Case of Antinous

The second-century Christian discourse on same-sex love differs from previous Greco-Roman and Hellenistic homophobia on account of attention that is given to the strange case of Antinous (the beloved of the emperor Hadrian), whose deification in 131 brought with it the rise of the last pagan cult to rival the emergent Christianities of the period. Christianity in this period and for some time to come is decidedly plural. In addition to Gnosticism there were also the Marcionites (an ascetic Paulinism that only at the end of the century might be said to be no longer the dominant form of Christianity), a neo-spiritualist and apocalyptic Montanism, as well as multiple amalgams of Judaism and Christ-followers, and of course inevitable mergers with some forms of already existing pagan cults. The texts that survive are generally from the recognized antecedents to that form, or those forms, of Christianity that were ultimately victorious in securing imperial patronage: "Catholic," Orthodox, but also Arian, Monophysite, and so on.

This helps us understand what is at stake in many of the texts that we read: the identity of something to be called Christianity was by no means a settled matter. And even in its sheer multiplicity, Christianity in any form was a very small minority even at the end of the second century. It was striving for respectability and this will explain its desire to appropriate respectable discourses concerning same-sex love.

There are intriguing hints that a different way was possible. I will point to a couple of these hints before looking at the story and cult of Antinous, which closed off the chance for a homophilic form of Christian faith, at least as far as surviving witnesses can tell us about.

We find the first of these hints in the Gospel of Matthew. As I have suggested elsewhere,[1] Matthew is remarkably open to various forms of eroticism, including same-sex eroticism in the case of the centurion and his beloved youth. Jesus is said to address the crowds in the words of the prophet Isaiah (Isaiah 42:1–2): "Behold my servant whom I chose, my beloved in whom my soul was well pleased. I will put my spirit upon him and he will announce judgment to the nations" (Matthew 12:18). What the translation obscures is that Matthew's text has actually changed "servant" to "lad" (*pais*). Thus we have: "Behold my youth whom I chose, my beloved in whom my soul was well pleased."[2] When we recall that "soul" is the word for the seat of yearning or desire we have a pretty good approximation to pederastic rhetoric concerning the beloved youth in whom the lover's desire finds pleasure. The haste with which the translator "corrects" the text is an indication that the text as it stands might lead readers astray.

The second hint of the same type comes in the form of an anonymous defense of Christianity perhaps written in the time of the emperor Hadrian, who had been responsible for the attempt to recover the now ancient traditions of noble (as he thought) Greek pederasty. In the early years of his reign, he presided over a cultural and economic revival of the empire that made the bad old days of imperial tyrants seem a thing of the past. The defense is addressed to one Diognetes, which may even be a pseudonym for the emperor himself.[3] The goal is to persuade the reader that Christianity, far from being a threat to the public weal of the empire, is the very salt and savor of that empire. Thus we read: "what the soul is to the body, Christians are to the world" (6.1). Moreover the discussion of the manner of God's acting and the character of the divine nature is quite significant. God acts "as one who saves by persuasion, not compulsion, for compulsion is no attribute of God" (7.4). In this and many other ways it is theologically one of the most interesting and rewarding of second-century texts.

In this text there is an attempt to defend the association of Jesus with God. The text makes use of language that will become familiar to describe this relationship as that of Father and Son. But it also makes use of a different language to identify the object of Christian adoration: that of beloved youth! Thus we read, after again hearing that God is kind, good, without anger (8.8), that "God communicated the plan of saving action to his lad (*pais*) alone" (8.9). When the plan is disclosed through his beloved youth (*agapatou paidos*) this knowledge is communicated to the world. The writer will also say that God and his "youth" planned the whole thing together (9.1). The daring use of this language is obscured by translation which, even in the best of cases, uses "child" to translate *pais* in contrast to son to translate *huios*. For the writer does use the more traditional language as well, especially when alluding to the more conventional formulas of Christianity. Thus we get the allusion to Pauline language: "He gave up his own Son as a ransom for us" (9.2) or again: "In whom was it possible for us, the lawless and ungodly, to be justified, except in the Son of God alone [*mono tou huio tou theou*]?" (9.4). Later we read "he sent his one and only [begotten] Son [*ton huion autou monogena*]" (10.2). There seems to be a fairly clear use of "Son" in the context of citations of traditional language, and the substitution of "beloved youth/boy" in more "free-form" expositions to the pagan reader of the relationship between God and Christ.

If pederastic language had been undergoing a revival during the time of Hadrian, and if it was understood as embodying the noblest of classical virtues, then it is understandable that an apologist might make use of it to speak of Christ and God. Certainly it had some advantages over the Father–Son language that will give Christianity much trouble in the years ahead. For Father–Son language will suggest that, as the chant of the Arians would have it: "there was a time when the son was not." Moreover, it led to a hierarchical perspective that would spawn subordinationist heresies. But lover/beloved could be an attractive alternative in that it was also associated with friendship, thus pointing toward equality and mutuality — something Christologies and trinitarian theologies have long sought to make intelligible within the counterintuitive framework of Father–Son.

If, as these hints might suggest, there had been the possibility of assimilating Christianity to the best traditions of same-sex love, then it may be that the case of Antinous puts an end to these experiments.

A brief review of the case will be useful for our consideration. Antinous was a Bithynian youth who, when he was about seventeen, became the beloved of the emperor Hadrian about 127 C.E., when Hadrian had been emperor for ten years and was about fifty years old. They became close companions, hunting together and traveling together (Hadrian was never a stay-at-home emperor and in fact seldom visited Rome.) Hadrian had gone with his beloved companion to Egypt, in part in a campaign to stamp out male circumcision, which he apparently regarded as male genital mutilation. (Hadrian had also made illegal the practice opposed by Philo of castrating young male slaves in order to make them marketable as boy prostitutes.) All of this coheres with Hadrian's admiration of the male form as represented in classical Greek sculpture. This campaign against circumcision would meet with only some resistance in Egypt, which was the home of the custom, but with fierce resistance on the part of the Judeans, who saw it as a return to the policies of the hellenizing emperor Antiochus Epiphanies nearly three hundred years before.

In the course of this campaign and when things may have been going badly for the emperor both with respect to the empire and with respect to his health, Antinous drowned in the river Nile (about 130 C.E.). Some said this was his voluntary self-sacrifice for the welfare of his lover and for that of the empire. Others said he had been sacrificed for this purpose by the emperor himself. In the event astrologers reassured the grief-stricken emperor that they had seen a shooting star that signaled the resurrection of Antinous to the realm of the immortals.

The grief of the emperor shook the very foundations of the empire. And the word of the astrologers set him upon the course of deifying the beautiful and beloved youth. This was the first time a "commoner" had been deified by an emperor. Moreover, he commissioned statues to bear the image of Antinous, thereby provoking the last renaissance of classical sculpture in antiquity. The graceful and beloved body of Antinous was everywhere, and his lovely features were stamped upon imperial coins, again the first time a mere commoner had been so honored.

Beyond this the emperor founded in Egypt a city, Antinouopolis, built to rival Alexandria. This city, built to astonishing proportions, was lined with images of the godling and boasted a temple to which those in need of the divinity's aid could repair. Not only here, but throughout the Greek-speaking portion of the empire, there sprang up shrines of Antinous. The athletic games held in his honor would last well into the third century. These games were not only athletic contests but occasions to rehearse the marvelous story of his self-sacrifice and ascension into the heavens and of the many benefits of healing conferred upon those who worshiped at his shrine or wore the medallions bearing his youthful visage.

This, in brief, is the story of the emergence of a god even newer than the Jesus talked about by the Christians. And already we can see the grounds for rivalry. For Antinous was a new and young god who had given his life for the benefit of the whole world and who had ascended into heaven to take his place in the heavenly realm from whence he conferred benefits of health and prosperity upon his adherents.

At least as soon as Hadrian had died (eight years after Antinous, 138 C.E.), Christian apologists went after Antinous as a false god. And it was his life as boy toy of Hadrian that gave them the most grist for their mill. Of course they were not acting entirely on their own in this regard. A great many imperial subjects had reason to feel glad that Hadrian had died. His attraction to Greek ways made him enemies among those who felt the old Roman ways and privileges had been abandoned. His constant time away from Rome gave his rivals free rein and gave him few allies there. His devastation of Jerusalem earned him the enmity of Jews everywhere and of Jewish Christians as well. His remarkable accomplishments (Hadrian's wall in England still stands) earned him considerable jealousy. His deification of Antinous and patronage of his cult seemed excessive by patrician Roman standards, and a threat to the old forms of worship. (In this way he was, even in the Socratic sense, a corrupter of youth.) The establishment of Antinouopolis as a rival to Alexandria would earn him the hostility of all, Christians, Jews, and pagans, who honored that city's tradition as the cultural and intellectual capital of the empire. Even though Hadrian appointed his next two successors through a complex process of adoption, they could not be counted on to defend his hellenized ways. Indeed, the second of these, the philosophically inclined Marcus Aurelius, had no use at all for the revival of pederasty (or, for that matter, for Christians). Thus Christians were on increasingly safe ground in echoing the distaste of many of their pagan contemporaries in execrating the cult of Antinous — especially, as we shall see, when these same pagans developed the tendency to lump the cult of

Antinous together with that of Jesus as new cults that divinized mere commoners and near contemporaries at that.

The first of these Christian references to Antinous seems to come from the philosopher and converted Christian Justin Martyr, who writes in an account of the superstitions of the pagans, "We think it is not improper to mention among these things also Antinous, our contemporary, whom everyone was coerced to worship as a god on account of fear, although they knew who he was and where he came from" (*First Apology*, chap. 29). The picture of the possible consequences of defying the grief stricken emperor (coercion/fear) and the indication that this is now in the past, helps us situate this text. Now that the emperor is dead it is possible for Justin to mention a subject that would also have been embarrassing to the pagan intellectuals to whom he was addressing himself.

In this reference he is echoed by his pupil, Tatian, "And how was the dead Antinous fixed as a beautiful youth in the moon? Who carried him thither: unless perchance, as men, perjuring themselves for hire, are credited when they say in ridicule of the gods that kings have ascended into heaven, so someone, in like manner, has put this man also among the gods, and been recompensed with honor and reward?" (*To the Greeks*, chap. 10). At least Tatian does not use this as an occasion to wax eloquent about the sexual practices that presumably elevated the young man to the pantheon. Instead he focuses on the political corruption involved, as he supposed, in that deification.

Theophilus, who in his letter to Autolycus had alleged that even the Stoics were corrupters of youth (the *ANF* translator has "sodomy"), initiates what looks like a reference to Antinous when he writes: "And, indeed, the names of those whom you say you worship, are the names of dead men. And these, too, who and what kind of men were they?" (1.9). Later the reference is far more specific: "I am silent about the temples of Antinous, and of the others whom you call gods. For when related to sensible persons, they excite laughter" (3.8). Of course Theophilus has not been entirely silent, although compared to some later writers on this subject he is rather laconic in his reference. However, he does tell us that "sensible persons," which he undoubtedly expects to include his readers, find the cult of Antinous laughable, although he does not tell us whether this has to do with the recent elevation of a commoner to heroic status, or the emperor having exhibited too much grief over the death of a mere boy toy, or because sensible persons would regard the whole idea of a renaissance of Greek pederasty with derision.

However, there were other Christian writers of the second century who were rather more circumspect in their references to Antinous. Thus Athenagoras attributes the elevation of Antinous to the pantheon to the love for humanity (philanthropy, benevolence) of Hadrian: "Those, therefore, to whom either the subjects gave honor or the rulers themselves [assumed it], obtained the name, some from fear, others from revenge. Thus Antinous, through the benevolence of your ancestors towards their subjects, came to be regarded as a god. But those who came after adopted the worship without examination" (*Supplication* 30.2). Of course, he does this in writing to Marcus Aurelius, who owed his imperial career to Hadrian.

Not surprisingly, as an Alexandrian, Clement uses the trope of Antinous to considerable effect, although this is written three-quarters of a century after the deification of Antinous. But there remains some ambivalence here. He too can come under the spell of the beauty of Antinous and then turn this into outrage at what Hadrian did to him (that is, made him the object of erotic attention).

"In Egypt there is another new God, and almost in Greece, too, since the Roman king (Hadrian) reverently elevated to Godhood his lover [*eromenon* = beloved] Antinous, an exceedingly beautiful boy, whom he worshiped, as Zeus did Ganymede, for lust is not easily prevented if it has no fear; and now men celebrate the 'Sacred Nights of Antinous,' in which those who love shameful things lawlessly stay awake together. And why do you choose for me a god who is to be honored by fornication? And why have you appointed him to be mourned as a son? And why do you go on and on about his beauty? That shameful beauty is withered by wantonness. Do not become a tyrant, my friend, nor act wantonly with the beauty of young boys just grown of age; keep it pure, in order that it may be beautiful.... But now there is a grave for Hadrian's lover (*eromenou*), as well as a temple and a city of Antinous, for graves are held in awe by the Egyptians like shrines" (*Protrepticus* 4.49).[4]

The charge that Antinous was worshiped through shameless fornication might seem to have a certain plausibility to the outsider. Yet it has no support in anything otherwise known about the cult of Antinous, which appears to have more to do either with athleticism or with healing than with the image of orgies evoked by Clement. Of course, this is simply putting the shoe on the other foot since this charge was also made against Christians, whose nocturnal meetings, and perhaps the custom of nude baptism, excited prurient speculation on the part of their enemies. In the case of Antinous, this may have had to do with rumors about the mysteries of Eleusis into which both the emperor and his companion may have been initiated (in 128) and/or with the assimilation of Antinous into the cult of Osiris.

Clement does seem to recognize the allure of youthful male beauty. Statues of Antinous were by now rather common. His perspective indeed seems to evoke compassion for the youth in the warning to the (long dead) emperor to protect rather than exploit that loveliness. That is, unlike some other Christian writers who assail the character of Antinous, Clement seems to want to defend his beauty from the despotic predation of the emperor ("keep it pure so that it may be beautiful"). It is thus of a piece with his use of the theme of the "corruption of youths."

The reference to the city that had been erected in honor of Antinous to rival the glory of Clement's hometown of Alexandria could at least be expected to earn him a glad hearing among the partisans of Alexandria.

Tertullian, Clement's contemporary, though distant in North Africa and even more distant as a writer of Latin rather than Greek, had also heard of Antinous and his cult. In his treatise "To the Nations," in which he takes up the task of defending Christianity to Latin-speaking intellectuals, he writes, "After so many examples and eminent names among you, who might not have been declared divine? Who, in fact ever raised a question as to his divinity against Antinous? Was even Ganymede more grateful and dear than he to (the supreme god) who loved him? According to you heaven is open to the dead. You prepare a way from hades to the stars. Prostitutes mount it in all directions, so that you must not suppose that you are conferring a great distinction upon your kings" (*Ad nationes*, 10).

In this text we see the joining together of the myth of Zeus and Ganymede with the love of Hadrian and Antinous. In spite of the obvious difference that Ganymede was abducted and Antinous appears to have loved his lover to the point of willingly sacrificing his life for him, the parallels that Tertullian is exploiting are also all too plausible. For the habit of divinizing emperors together with the near absolute power they wielded in life makes the comparison between the "kings" and the high god at least superficially plausible. And of course, both stories may have been used as recommendations for pederasty. Tertullian is also either misinformed or engaging in a rhetorical flourish when he asks "who raised a question as to his divinity as to Antinous" since several Christian and pagan authors had already done so.

What is especially odd here is the suggestion that "prostitutes" are going into the heavens. It may be that Tertullian has allowed his rhetoric to betray him. It may be that Tertullian intends to suggest that Antinous was a prostitute (thereby taking the opposite tack of Clement, who had blamed the despot rather than the beautiful youth). And others have insinuated something similar (recall Theophilus's question about divinized men: "What sort of men were they?"). The charge that Antinous was a prostitute was, of course, an easy enough charge against one who becomes the favorite of any wealthy benefactor, not to mention the most wealthy and powerful of the day. But whence the idea that (apparently quite many) prostitutes are ascending to the stars? This necessarily must remind Christian readers of the words of Jesus in Matthew to the religious and respectable folk (and Tertullian is nothing if not religious and respectable) that "prostitutes and tax collectors are entering the kingdom of heaven ahead of you!" (Matthew 21:31). Does this mean that since according to Jesus even prostitutes enter into heaven, it is therefore no big deal that the kings are divinized, or does it mean that it is correct to say that Antinous has ascended to the stars since that is, according to Jesus, the privilege of prostitutes; or, that pagans go so far as to divinize prostitutes — or what exactly?

The whole thing seems like a time bomb set to demolish Tertullian's own presumed point.

Perhaps the most instructive of all Christian commentators on the story and cult of Antinous comes from the pen of Origen, Clement's successor as Christian teacher in Alexandria and the greatest biblical scholar that early Christianity produced. Some of his rather daring speculations in his youthful *Principles* would, many centuries later, earn him denunciation in councils of bishops. His early speculations about the soul's transmigration, an attempt to reconcile God's justice with the divine aim of saving all of humanity, owe something to the speculations that we encountered in Plato's *Phaedrus*. But nothing dimmed his reputation as among the greatest of the early theologians.

Origen undertook to answer charges brought against Christianity by the pagan philosopher Celsus. It is in this book that we find the discussion of Antinous. While some earlier (and later) apologists had simply referred to the story to show how silly (or perhaps corrupt) pagan religion could be, Origen must respond to a gifted pagan philosopher who had pointed out the similarity of the Antinous legend and cult with the Jesus story and cult, to the discredit of Christianity. That is, Celsus represented those pagan intellectuals who found the Antinous story and its aftermath to be a rather tawdry affair (and supposed that his readers would agree with that assessment) but goes so far as to claim that Christianity is no better and indeed may be regarded as in some ways even worse.

Although Origen can suppose that Antinous was all too familiar with "unnatural lusts" (3.36), he seems to share the view of Clement that he is to be pitied as having been corrupted by the emperor as one of those who "constantly passed their life, from their earliest youth, either as the favorites of licentious men or of tyrants, or in some other wretched condition which forbade the soul to look upwards" (3.38). What is, however, most instructive is the evidence of the comparison between Christianity and the cult of Antinous. "What is there in common," Origen asks, between Hadrian's boy toy and one of whom nothing had ever been alleged concerning a "tendency toward what is licentious" (3.36)? And Origen later returns to the question of this comparison between Antinous and "our Jesus" (3.63), something that clearly rankles him.

The comparison seems to be based upon the divinization of ordinary (and unfortunate) mortals. In each case this divinization seems to result in a certain reputation for healing (at least after the fact), so that Origen will claim that the healings at the shrines to Antinous are the work of "demons claiming prophetic or healing power" (3.36). The healings are even more suspect because no one ever alleged that Antinous performed any healings (or anything else miraculous) during his lifetime.

One of the claims of Celsus appears to have been that Christians were far less circumspect in the honors paid to Jesus than the Egyptians were in the deification of Antinous. The Christians make Jesus to be the equal of the One God, creator, while those who honor Antinous simply deal with him as a lesser god, not the equal of "Apollo or Zeus." That Antinous is not compared to Zeus, Origen denies (although it would seem that in this case Celsus is more likely to have the facts on his side) (3.37). Thus, if Antinous is simply worshiped as one among many gods or even as a deified hero then Celsus may be right to see the honors paid to Jesus as far exceeding anything a pagan of any sense would claim about Antinous.

Origen's trump in this case is that it was just a bunch of lying astrologers seeking to curry favor with the emperor who proclaimed Antinous's divinity while in the case of Jesus "the Architect of the universe himself, in keeping with the marvelously persuasive power of his words, commended him as worthy of honor" (3.36).

It is not clear that Origen's arguments would have persuaded pagan sympathizers with Celsus, but this work of Origen's proved an invaluable resource for Christians responding to the kinds of charges brought by pagan philosophical critics of the new religion of Jesus.

For our purposes what may be most instructive is the strongly felt necessity of distinguishing, as far as possible, the Christian worship of Jesus from the cult of Antinous. This, together with the pederastic relation between Hadrian and Antinous, however it might be characterized, would seem to make Christian rhetoric more disposed to separate itself from any association with pederastic practices.

Origen, writing in the middle of the third century (and thus more than a century after the apotheosis of Antinous), gives testimony to the enduring allure of this competitor to emergent Christianity. Into the fourth century we still find Christian authors finding it necessary to make reference to this story and cult. Thus Athanasius, like Clement and Origen from Alexandria, writes in his youthful but extremely influential "Against the Nations" (*Contra gentes*, a text we have already encountered in the discussion of the corruption of youths), "Still others, as if rivals of the worse, had the effrontery to deify their rulers...and now the Roman emperor Hadrian's favorite [*paidikos*], Antinous. Although they know he was a man, and not an honorable man but one filled with wantonness yet they worship him through fear of the ruler. For when Hadrian was staying in Egypt, Antinous the servant of his lust died, and he decreed that he should be given a cult, for he loved the youth [*eron tou paidos*] even after his death" (9.40–45). It is not clear how to reconcile the reference to the wantonness of Antinous and the lust of the emperor with the fidelity of a love that "loved the youth even after his death" (certainly not the sort of fidelity one might normally associate with wantonness or lust).

Later in the fourth century the famous church historian and imperial toady Eusebius, whose adoration of Constantine knew no bounds, retells the story in his *Ecclesiastical History* (4.8.2), citing the venerable Hegesippus, from the second century.

In a catalog of odd customs of diverse peoples Jerome notes that the Egyptians have even welcomed Antinous as a god and named one of their cities "after Hadrian's favorite" (*Against Jovinianus*, book 2.7). Insightfully, however, he concludes that "each race follows its own practice and peculiar usages, and takes that for the law of nature which is most familiar to it" (ibid). (We will return to Jerome's views about the relation of nature and custom later.)

Thus late into the fourth century Christian intellectuals are clearly stung by the comparison of their faith with the cult of the rival Antinous. Their invective is not different in kind from that of the philosophically inclined pagans, who meant the comparison with the Christ cult to be invidious. But it may for all that be different in degree as Christians sought to distance themselves as much as possible from this rival cult. In this they were largely successful. The cult of Antinous slowly faded and his city crumbled into ruins. Only the astonishing statues bear mute testimony to the beauty and attraction of the young boy-god. Only after the Renaissance would Christian artists begin to depict Jesus as himself beautiful — and young.

# – 13 –

# Clement on Nature

Although our investigation of the opposition to corrupters of youth and, still more, of the execration of the boy-god Antinous have taken us beyond Clement of Alexandria, we must return to him. It is in Clement that these themes, together with those of the Hellenistic notion of sex according to nature aiming at procreation, come together in ways that will influence subsequent Christian discourse about sexuality generally and about same-sex love in particular.

In *The Instructor*, Clement indicates his indebtedness to the Platonic and Hellenistic traditions, which we have discussed in previous chapters. This comes in his discussion of sexual relations focused on the question of marriage. He juxtaposes quotes from Plato (*Laws*) and "Moses" (Leviticus!) in admonishing the (male) reader about proper sexual relations with his wife. He borrows the image of sowing seed for sexual relations from Plato, as had Philo, and uses the sort of interpretive strategies pioneered by Philo for appropriating Mosaic Law in this respect. That is, the Mosaic restrictions are understood as having to do with restricting sexual activity to that which will procreate progeny. He by no means slavishly follows Philo, however. For example, in explaining why one should not have sex with a menstruating woman he doesn't use the sowing seeds in water analogy but develops the prohibition in an even more transparently sex-phobic way: "It is wrong to contaminate fertile seed destined to become a human being with corrupt matter from the body, or allow it to be diverted from the furrow of the womb and swept away in a fetid flow of matter and excrement" (chap. 92).[1] The emphasis on procreation leads him to go beyond Philo in arguing that Moses forbade sex with wives who were pregnant. Indeed, he calls this sexual practice "contrary to nature" (see also *Stromateis* 3.11.71). It is the idea of having sex with a pregnant wife that

183

leads him into a riff about "wantonness" and the dissolute in which he still seems to have in mind what we might term "heterosexuality."

But the problem seems to be sexuality as such since we then get a digression into the way sex is exhausting, and Clement quotes "the sophist of Abdera" to the effect that it is like epilepsy (chap. 94). Here he seems to go further than he had intended for he must then add: "marriage in itself merits esteem and the highest approval." This qualification is necessary because he is also at pains to distance himself from the opinion of Tatian and other "Encratites," who in the name of self-control opposed sex even for procreative purposes. Yet "to indulge in intercourse without intending children is to outrage nature" and Clement even terms it "contrary to law" (chap. 95).

Clement cautions against what he terms "the mystic rites of nature" during the day. Sex should be practiced only under cover of darkness, even for procreation. In a warning that echoes Pseudo-Phocylides Clement warns that even with one's wife one should "avoid every indecency in intimate embraces" (chap. 97). In general Clement is quite suspicious of sexual practices that might give pleasure since this suggests wantonness. In this he reminds us of Musonius.

Despite the fact that those Clement seems to be citing in this connection (Plato, Leviticus, Philo, Musonius, even Phocylides) mention same-sex sexual practices in this connection, Clement's only reference in this discussion to those practices comes in the form of a citation from the Sibylline Oracles, which he calls the "poetry circulating among you." The quoted lines declaim, "Wicked city, all unclean, adulteries and lawless lying with men and illicit effeminacy dwells in you" (Orac. syb. 5.166–68); this is juxtaposed with another passage regarding the chaste "who have neither base lust for other men's wives, nor passion for the loathsome and abominable sin committed with men" (Orac. syb. 4.33). Although Clement is at pains to cite Moses or Paul whenever possible, his only reference to same-sex sexual practices in this discussion of sex according to nature is a citation, upon which he does not comment, from what he takes to be pagan poetry. A bit later he will juxtapose Paul and Plato in his condemnation of giving in to sexual passion, which then leads him back to the theme of having sex with one's wife only when "the season is favorable for sowing"

(*Instructor* chap. 102) — something totally at odds with Paul's actual advice concerning marital relations.[2]

In the third book of the *Strometeis* — or "Miscellanies of Notes of Revealed Knowledge in Accordance with the True Philosophy," as he styles this collection — Clement is concerned with defending marriage. His chief opponents are those Christian writers, like Tatian, Marcion, and Julius Cassian, who maintained that sex in marriage was no different than fornication and should be renounced by true Christians. It is perhaps difficult for most modern readers to have a sense for how attractive these arguments seemed for a great many people in the second (and later) centuries. The rule of total celibacy for all Christians seemed actually to draw people to Marcion and others who took that position.[3] For some centuries lay celibacy would be of such attraction that every congregation could boast significant groups of lay men and women who pledged never to marry (the virgins), and these seem to have been greatly revered. Thus for writers like Clement and Tertullian to actually defend marriage and to insist on the legitimacy of sexual practices so long as they aimed at procreation (and did not indulge a desire for pleasure) was to take the more "liberal" approach. Christians who defended marriage could be attacked by large numbers of other Christians as making concessions to the flesh, to the world, to lust.

Whatever we may imagine about actual sexual practices it seems clear that in Antiquity there were a great many people who found marriage an unattractive option. For women, marriage put them at risk for all the dangers of pregnancy as well as placing them under the dominion of a man who in Roman fashion may have imagined himself as having the right to total domination of the bodies placed at his disposal. Men may have preferred to avoid entanglements in household responsibilities that they found distasteful or may have even found sex itself repugnant. One may indeed speculate that, given the absolute domination of the bodies of both slaves and children in Roman households, the incidence of the sexual abuse of children was such as to produce a horror of sex on the part of many people in the empire. For others the desire to escape the body as the site of suffering and death had such a hold as to make the pleasures of sex seem a snare that affixed one inexorably to the body that must decay. In any case, this flight from the body (and sexual practices) was not invented by Christians. Eva Cantarella is correct to recall: "The Christians, it has been said, did not make the world ascetic. Rather it was the world in which Christianity found itself at work which made Christianity ascetic."[4] The tide of sexual asceticism in the Greco-Roman world made a renunciation of sex attractive also to Christians.

Clement's task is to defend marriage while making considerable room for those new Christians who, for whatever reason, would find the life of celibacy honored among Christians the most alluring option. In the *Instructor* Clement had been seeking to show that Christians agreed with philosophic standards that emphasized sex for procreation only. In the *Miscellanies* he argues against those who forbid sex even for procreation. This will help to account for the somewhat more positive tone of the latter when writing about sexual pleasure. In combination Clement articulates the position that will be celebrated as the Clementine compromise, which allowed Christianity to honor both the celibate and the married. Thus he writes: "One man may make himself celibate; another may join in marriage in order to have children. Both ought to have the end in view of remaining firmly opposed to any lower standard" (79.3). He then adds: "Celibacy and marriage have their distinctive services to the Lord, their different ministries" (79.5). In this he thinks he can posit two equally fallacious perspectives to be avoided: "Those who out of hatred refrain from marriage or misuse their physical being indiscriminately, out of desire, are not in the number of the saved with whom the Lord is found" (70.4). In any case: "God through his Son is with those who responsibly marry and produce children, and it is the same God who in the same way is with the man who shows self-control in the light of the Logos" (68.4).

In both books his principal authorities are Plato and either Moses or Paul, but as we would expect, both of the biblical writers are read through the eyes of Plato. This will be a bit tricky since his opponents appear to use the same sources. In order to make Paul conform to his view he is required to offer a "supplement" to Paul's teaching about marriage. He will maintain that the aim of marriage is not a mere containment of desire but "actually of mastering desire by self-control" (57.1).[5] Clement then supplements this by adding the view (perhaps derived from Musonius Rufus as well as Plato) that this includes procreation. He makes these goals compatible with one another by maintaining that "If a man marries in order to have children he ought to practice self-control. He ought not to have a sexual desire even for his wife, to whom he has a duty to show Christian love." He concludes by saying, "He ought to produce children by a reverent, disciplined act of will." It will be the impossibility of doing just that which will be the basis for Augustine's view that the act of procreation transmits the disordered desire through which it is accomplished thereby ensuring the transmission of "original sin."

Clement will thus need to supplement Paul's view that married people ought not to refrain from sexual relations with one another by saying "he does not want them to deprive one another of the help offered towards childbirth through divine dispensation" (97.2). He later insists that when Paul says "do not deprive one another" (1 Corinthians 7:5), he says the meaning is to show "the due obligation of marrying, the production of children" (107.5).

One of the curious effects of his valiant attempt to make Paul agree with Musonius Rufus and others regarding the procreative function of sexual practice is his insistence that Paul was married. He has had to concede that Jesus was not (because as the only son he had no need of physical progeny, and because he was married to the church; see 49.3). But he supposes that Paul was married and takes the phrase yokefellow, which Paul uses in Philippians 4:3, to refer to Paul's "wife" (53.1). The irony of course is that Paul is here referring to another male (Epaphroditus), which would then make Paul an early example of male same-sex marriage!

In the course of his advocacy of reproduction, Clement does not take the opportunity, as had Plato, Musonius, or Philo, to comment upon same-sex sexual practices as a violation of that natural aim or goal. Indeed, even the most ardent defender of same-sex love could agree that sex with women is or ought to be only for the production of progeny! This is the position that Plutarch has Protogenes take in the *Dialogue on Love* (750c) and that (Pseudo-)Lucian puts in the mouth of Callicratidas (33 and 35), who even goes so far as to say, "Let women be ciphers and be retained merely for child bearing" (38). Clement, who maintained that women could be philosophical Christians in the same way as men, would not have endorsed the misogyny of Callicratidas but does not seem to see how close to such a position his view of sex with women being only for procreation might come.

Even so, Clement's views regarding sex according to nature will not govern Christian attitudes toward sexual practices for many centuries. Indeed it is only in the Middle Ages that such a view will be taught as something like Christian doctrine, and it will be the subject of canon law only in the modern period. As the view comes to be enshrined as doctrine through the work of Thomas Aquinas, or later as church law, it will also be available to use in specifically homophobic ways. But this is by no means the situation yet at this early stage of Christian doctrinal development.

Clement's view that marital sex must be oriented toward reproduction is not the only one that might find a welcome among partisans of same-sex love. Given the slippage that we have seen that is possible with the notion of the corruption of youths, those who felt that same-sex love ought to aim at friendship and virtue would no doubt have felt it important to condemn sexual predation, harassment, and, of course, rape. As we have seen, Plato can put even more stringent restrictions in the mouth of no less a defender of same-sex love than Pausanius. The deification of Antinous may have also seemed to be going too far for many of the defenders of same-sex love.

In short we cannot but be struck at how mild the homophobia of Clement is, compared to those whom he frequently cites with approval: Plato, Musonius, or Philo. Even at the end of two centuries of Christianity we have yet to encounter any discourse that takes advantage of the resources for homophobic discourse that are already widely available within the culture of the Greco-Roman world.

As we have seen, Clement does not take the opportunity afforded by a discussion of procreation as the natural goal of sex to comment upon same-sex love. In this entire book of the *Strometeis* devoted to questions of sex he makes mention only once of the command not to seduce or corrupt youths. This comes in his discussion of groups that he takes to be licentious in their approach to sexual practices, especially the mysterious Carpocratians. This may be an aberration since other Christian writers do not follow Clement in ascribing same-sex practices to the Carpocratians.[6]

Even though Clement combines a number of elements that might be deployed for homophobic purposes, we are still a long way from discovering a specifically Christian homophobia. In order for this to arise still more work will be necessary to Christianize the Hellenistic homophobia that remains better attested in pagan than in Christian circles at the end of the second century. This will occur through the gradual adoption of a homophobic hermeneutics in the centuries that follow.

# – 14 –

# The Emergence of Homophobic Hermeneutics: Origen to Chrysostom

As we turn to a discussion of the emergence of homophobic discourse in the third and fourth centuries, we recall that we have already seen that the figure of Antinous continues to perplex or rankle Christians, even as the precipitating events recede into the past. There will continue to be occasional reference to *paidophthoria* as well, although without the temptation to smuggle it into a recital of the Decalogue. Most significant is a new development: the emergence of a homophobic hermeneutics that reads biblical texts in ways that stigmatize same-sex relations. We have seen that there are antecedents to this in Hellenistic reinterpretations of traditional stories of the gods or of heroes and that Philo of Alexandria pioneers ways of appropriating biblical texts like the story of Sodom for homophobic purposes. In the material to which we turn our attention now we will see the very gradual appropriation of the Sodom story into homophobic discourse as well as a slow process of interpreting Paul's references in Romans 1:26–27 in a similar way. This process will take several centuries to be consolidated to the point that these interpretations will come to be seen as self-evident. It is only with Chrysostom at the end of the fourth century that we will find several of these threads coming together in order to produce a denunciation of same-sex eroticism.

## Sodom

In the discussion of Hellenistic homophobia we noted, in the reading of Philo and Josephus, the innovation of a homophobic interpretation

of the story of Sodom that contrasted with the tendencies of biblical
and Hellenistic Judaism to understand the story as exhibiting the consequences of avarice, arrogance, and violence against the vulnerable.
The innovation of Philo does not have an immediate impact upon the
Christian interpretation of this text. For example, despite his reliance
in other matters upon Philo (and Plato), Clement does not appropriate
this reading of the account of Sodom.

Clement's near contemporary, Tertullian, does make reference on
several occasions to the story of Sodom. At no point does he connect the fate of Sodom to same-sex sexual practices of any kind. In
fact the only sexual practice to which he associates the destruction
of Sodom is that of (heterosexual) marriage! Not all of Tertullian's
allusions to Sodom make reference to sexual practices. The story of
Sodom with the appearance of three angels, then one Lord, then the
two angels/messengers became a text that would come in for discussion concerning the unity or trinity of God. This issue appears for the
first time in Tertullian's *Adversus Praxeas*. Here he disputes the Mar-
cionite supposition that the double mention of God entails two Gods
(chap. 13).

The story also comes into view with respect to the changes in the
face of the earth, including the deluge, the raining of fire, and more
recent examples of earthquake and so on (*De Pallio* 2.4.1). In the
*Apology* this is turned to good effect in countering the charge that
Christians are responsible for natural disasters since the flood and the
fire came before Christianity (40.7). There are also references to these
sorts of examples, especially the flood and the rain of fire, in a reference to God's punishment of the wicked in opposition to Marcionites
who suppose that such punishment is unworthy of God (*Against Marcion* 2.14.4). In this case the reference to the peculiar wickedness of
Sodom is added by the translator but does not appear in the Latin text.[1]
When it comes to identifying the particular sin of Sodom, Tertullian
can revert to the view of Isaiah that this has to do with seeking after
worldly glory (*Against Marcion* 4.27).

But Tertullian's main contribution to the interpretation of the story
of Sodom is to link the spectacular punishment of the city to the rather
carefree undertaking of (heterosexual) marriage. In *Ad Uxorem* (1.5.4)

he interprets the story as an illustration of people dealing in marriage and merchandise (*nuptias et mercimonia*). He seems to link this
story both to Jesus' warning in Luke 20:34–35 against marrying and to
Paul's saying that those who have wives should behave as though they
did not (1 Corinthians 7:29). This basic perspective is then directed
against those who marry, especially against those who marry again
after the death of a spouse: "And marrying, let us be overtaken by the
last day, like Sodom and Gomorrah" (*Exhortation to Chastity* 9.4).

There is then no evidence yet of an attempt to appropriate the
Philonic interpretation of Sodom into a homophobic discourse. Clearly
the main temptation for which the fate of Sodom might serve as a cau-
tionary tale for Christians at the beginning of the third century was
the temptation to marry. This is not to say that Tertullian would have
approved of same-sex love. But it is the case that in his extraordinarily
voluminous writings he does not seem to find it either necessary or
important to marshal a homophobic hermeneutic.

We should note that Tertullian's somewhat younger contemporary Origen, in his *Commentary on Romans*, makes reference to the
Sodomites, who were "endeavoring to commit lewdness even against
angels" (5.6.2). Here the sin of Sodom lies in an attempted rape, not
of (other) males but of angels. This appears to be an echo of certain
forms of Jewish exegesis that we encountered earlier and that comes
to be enshrined in Jude 7's reference to "alien flesh." This reference
will come in for more attention as homophobic hermeneutics grows
in plausibility.

In the third century Hippolytus makes passing reference to Sodom
alongside the great flood and Egypt's treatment of the Israelites to illustrate the reign of sin. However, Hyppolytus connects the sin of Sodom
with threatening violence to strangers, a view that seems entirely consistent with the story in Genesis. He writes of the Sodomites (people of
Sodom) "who, not satisfied with what the land yielded, offered violence
to strangers."[2]

The next reference to the story of Sodom in Latin Christian literature comes in the fourth century in the work of Hilary of Poitiers.
As in some of the references in Tertullian the story of Sodom appears
as a sort of proof text in relation to the doctrine of the Trinity. Thus

in *On the Councils* he makes a point similar to Tertullian's that the double mention of the divine does not mean two gods (par. 38). Similarly in *On the Trinity*, Hilary makes several references to the story but again only in relation to Trinitarian dispute and without any speculation about the particular sin of Sodom (book 4, chap. 29; book 5, chaps. 16, 24; book 9, chap. 63). The story of Sodom, then, with the appearance of angels/messengers who can also be, or seem to be, "the Lord" appears to be far more important as a bone of contention with respect to the doctrine of God than as a signal instance of sin.

With Ambrose, however, we do get discussions of Sodom that underline its sin. Yet the sin here, as in Hippolytus a century earlier, is the crime against hospitality. In *Letter 63* Ambrose suggests that Lot escaped the destruction of Sodom because he (in contrast to the Sodomites) was hospitable to strangers (par. 105). He makes the same point in his treatise *On the Duties of the Clergy* when, after referring to the hospitality shown by Abraham to the messengers, he writes: "Lot also, his nephew, who was near to him not only in relationship but also in virtue, on account of his readiness to show hospitality, turned aside the punishment of Sodom from himself" (book 2, chap. 21, par. 105). In his treatise *Concerning Repentance* Ambrose departs somewhat from this plain reading of the text to offer the suggestion that the sin of Sodom had to do with overabundance of luxury (which he takes to be excessive drinking), which then provokes "lust." However, the exact nature of this lust is not specified. The text seems consonant with earlier biblical and Jewish perspectives that emphasize luxury and violence without any reference to same-sex desire.

Jerome makes many passing references to the story of Sodom but never uses the story to condemn or even mention same-sex sexual practices of any kind. He even repeats the warning of Tertullian against too much marrying (*Letter 123*, par. 13). He also takes up another idea of Tertullian's to suggest that repentance would have spared Sodom (*Against Jovinianus*, book 2, par. 14). We also find the connection between the fate of Sodom and excessive drunkenness (*Letter 69*, par. 9). Most often he uses the story to warn against turning back as did the wife of Lot. Only in *Against the Pelagians* do we get any mention of lust, but this seems to be a reference to Ezekiel 16:55 and the assertion that Sodom's sin derives from excessive wealth that then produces lust. This again seems to be consonant with the traditional Jewish understanding, derived from Ezekiel, that the sin of Sodom is avarice and arrogance leading to violence without any specification of same-sex sexual practices. Certainly if anything like that is in Jerome's mind, it would be cross-sex lust rather than same-sex lust.

With Augustine we complete the review of fourth-century Latin writers on the subject of Sodom. In his enormous body of work there are only a few references to Sodom. Most of these repeat themes that we have already encountered: Sodom as an example of God's judgment (*City of God*, book 20, chap. 5) or as broaching the question of hospitality (*Contra Faustum*, book 22). In this same text Augustine wonders if Lot's daughters had learned the custom of incest from the Sodomites (par. 44)! However, for the first time in Latin Christian literature, Augustine does also identify the crime of Sodom with something like same-sex lust, or perhaps rather rape. Oddly this comes in two texts about lying. The first of these is *To Consentius, Against Lying* in which Augustine takes up the question of Lot's offering of his daughters in place of the angel/messenger/strangers. While those like Jerome and Ambrose who had dealt with the question of Lot's "justice" in showing hospitality to strangers had passed over in silence the difficulty that this took the form of offering his daughters, Augustine tackles this problem head on. It is precisely in this way that the question of some sort of sexual practice comes into view. First we should note that Augustine does not praise Lot for offering his daughters to the violence of the Sodomites. Instead, he offers a sort of comparative scale in which the intended crime against the (male) strangers was a greater crime than the one that Lot offered as a substitute. Thus Augustine maintains that it "is a lesser evil for women to suffer lewdness than for men" (par. 29). The comparison of the two objects of the Sodomites' outrage appears again in the text *On Lying*, in which Augustine again refers to Lot's offer "that the bodies of women rather than of men might be corrupted by them" (par. 10). What is unclear here is whether Augustine reads this story as referring in any way to same-sex sexuality or rather as referring to violation and rape. The most likely reading is that it is rape that is in view here. He does not use the occasion of a close reading of this text to inveigh against the evils of same-sex sexual practices as such (as Philo had seemed to do); rather he keeps to the question of violence, even if the violence is more clearly sexual violence than had before been the case in the Latin patristic literature. It is the case, however, that the sexual violation of males seems to be even more horrendous than the sexual violation of females. It is this perspective that will need to come in for closer scrutiny. Augustine's views of nature and what is "against nature" provide an explanation for this view.

Before leaving Augustine we should return to a consideration of the *City of God*. For it is in this text that we also have an association, even if in passing, with a homophobic reading of the tale of Sodom. The translators make some such association more apparent than it may be in Latin. The key phrase in the Loeb translation is "that place where homosexual practices among males had become as prevalent as any other actions that enjoy the customary sanction of the laws" (book 16, chap. 39). Another translation has: "where custom had made sodomy as prevalent as laws have elsewhere made other kinds of wickedness." What we first note is that whatever "crime" is attributed to Sodom, it is regarded as one among other sorts of practices that have enjoyed the protection of custom and even law and yet which from another stand-point may be regarded as meriting punishment. In any case Augustine does not use the opportunity here to inveigh against any or all forms of same-sex practice. But what is he referring to when translators write anachronistically of "sodomy" or "homosexual practices"? The term used here is *stupra in masculos*. This is the term that we encountered earlier when we asked about the meaning of *paidophthoreo* and noted that the Roman law that was sometimes interpreted as referring to same-sex practices generally seems rather to have in view a range of actions from rape to harassment where the stronger party imposes his will upon another. While it is certainly possible that some may have extended this notion of domination and sexual violation to include what we might term "consensual relations," this does not seem to have been its basic or more obvious meaning. Augustine's fleeting reference here does not give the interpreter much to go on, but it would seem quite plausible to suppose that what he has in view here is the use of rape as a form of domination employed against vulnerable strangers or foreigners, that is, as a privilege of conquest or demonstration of superior will. This would also connect this discussion to the question of rape that we have seen governs his references to Sodom in the letters on lying.

There is one other instance in Augustine's writings where it might appear that there is a direct connection between same-sex sex and the crime of Sodom. This is found in the *Confessions*, in which he explains his distinction among crimes against nature, custom, and law:

> Therefore those offences which be contrary to nature are everywhere and at all times to be held in detestation and punished; such were those of the Sodomites, which should all nations commit, they should all be held guilty of the same crime by the divine law, which has not so made men that they should in that way abuse one another. For even that fellowship which should be between God and us is violated, when that same nature of which He is author is polluted by the perversity of lust.
>
> (book 3, chap. 8, par. 15).

At first it does not seem that Augustine has necessarily in view same-sex acts even though he does appear to refer to the crime of rape ("abuse one another"). But when we consider the fact that he will go on to discuss the idea of "contrary to nature," it seems more likely that Augustine is linking Sodom with male-male sex (as nonprocreative) with or without the attendant violence. If so, then we are moving in the direction of a homophobic appropriation of the story of Sodom. But we again must remind ourselves that it has taken nearly four centuries for the homophobic reading invented by Philo to become a part of Christian discourse.

With Jerome and Augustine we have entered into the fifth century of Christianity. More than 350 years after Philo had offered his homophobic reading of the story of Sodom, it has yet to take hold in that (Latin) form of Christianity that will ultimately produce the story of Sodom as its prime exhibit for grounding homophobia. This is not to say that the writers we have examined would have approved of same-sex sexuality. But there is no sign whatever that this particular form of sexual practice has yet been connected with the fiery judgment of God. (Only in the sixth century will this connection be made.)

But what of the Greek fourth-century writers? This is where we might have expected to find a readier appropriation of some of the homophobic suggestions of Philo concerning Sodom, if only because of a shared language and culture. However, for the most part there is nothing to be found. Athanasius makes reference to the story only in the context of a christological argument with the Arians (*Discourse 2 Against the Arians*). Gregory Nazianzus makes use of the trope of repentance, exhorting his readers to "show ourselves men of Nineveh rather than Sodom" (*Oration* xvi, "On his Father's Silence") and uses the same idea in the Oration on "The Great Athanasius" (21.7). For Nazianzen the sin of Sodom is simply all sin, sin generically (*Oration on Holy Baptism* and *Panegyric on S. Basil*). When Basil does refer to same-sex sexual practice, in Letter 217 ("On the Canons"), he does not refer to any biblical text at all and treats same-sex practice as on a par with adultery: "He who is guilty of uncleanness with males will be under discipline for the same time as adulterers" (fifteen years of various forms of penance).

However, in a text that may date from the fourth century, the *Apostolic Teaching and Constitutions,* we do find a curious blending of the story of Sodom with the crime of *paidophthoria:* " 'Thou shalt not corrupt boys': For this wickedness is contrary to nature, and arose from Sodom, which was therefore entirely consumed with fire sent from God. 'Let such a one be accursed: and all the people shall say, so be it' " (book 7, chap. 2). This text is remarkable in many ways. It appears to have been compiled in the fourth century, although it was unknown in the West until early modern times. The text seems to begin with the second-century formulation of a Decalogue-like prohibition, "Thou shalt not corrupt youths," and then to link this both to the ambiance of pagan homophobic discourse ("against nature") and thence to a homophobic interpretation of the story of Sodom not unlike that of Philo. These interpretive moves anticipate developments that mostly belong to later centuries, although we will see something similar in Chrysostom's sermon on Romans 1:26–27. The connection to fiery punishment here is quite clear in ways that will be applied with lethal effect by the code of Justinian.

## The Appropriation of Romans

In our discussion of Paul, we saw that the homophobic interpretation of Romans 1:26–27 is by no means the only coherent interpretation of that passage, in spite of the place it has come to hold in homophobic rhetoric and even in the interpretation of counter-homophobic commentators. It is our task now to see how an appropriation of this text for homophobic purposes begins to make its way into Christian commentary. To the extent to which same-sex relations come to be associated with what is against nature on the basis of Platonic and certain Stoic views that we encountered in earlier chapters, Paul's references to "against nature" in Romans 1:26 will provide a privileged point of entry for homophobic discourse.[3]

The true beginning of Christian biblical commentary is to be found in the work of Origen. He is not only the first major exegete in Christian antiquity; he is also unmatched both in the quantity and the care of his reading of biblical texts in the first millennium of Christendom. In his extensive commentary on Romans,[4] Origen does spend time reflecting upon this passage. What is remarkable is that while he does several times refer to the words of the text, he shows no interest in developing these words in the direction of a diatribe concerning the evils of same-sex sexual practice. The nearest he comes is a paraphrase: "Moreover in the case of those whose women or men, by abandoning their natural use, who are inflamed with a passion for unnatural use, it is certain that they are of the number of those who serve created things rather than the creator" (I.17.7). There is nothing here to indicate what Origen may think of natural or unnatural "use," nor of what it may be that is used in these ways. Origen's main interest lies in trying to combine the three grounds for God's handing people over to their own evil desire (not honoring God, turning to the creature, not acknowledging God), which he maintains should be taken together as indicating more or less the same thing rather than indicating three different things with three different results. That is, three handing overs, like the three sets of consequences, are to be understood as a sort of parallelism. This is of course quite consonant with the reading I have suggested above. In addition, he has an interest in suggesting that while Paul may have in mind the pagans and their philosophers, the passage can also be taken as presaging certain Christian heresies (6), particularly one that supposes that God has an anthropomorphic form (8).

In *Against Celsus*, however, there appears to be a use of Romans 1:27 that does point in the direction of same-sex sexual practices. The translator has: "those who call themselves wise have despised these virtues, and have wallowed in the filth of sodomy, in lawless lust, 'men with men working that which is unseemly'" (book 7, chap. 49).The Greek text of course does not refer to sodomy but to an extreme and uncustomary (*mei themis*) corruption of youths (*paidos*). Thus, it would appear that for Origen the Pauline text is understood in connection with an egregious form of *paidophthoria*.

In eastern Christianity, there are to be found occasional passing references to the theme of what is against nature that seem to appeal to Paul, but there is no sustained commentary on Romans to match that of Origen until the work of John Chrysostom (d. 407), whose voluminous writings on Romans take the form not of a commentary but of a series of sermons. We will return to him at the end of this discussion.

Among those early theologians who wrote in Latin we find very little until the work of Jerome and Augustine, who are younger contemporaries of Chrysostom. A partial exception to this is found in a brief allusion to Romans 1:25–28 in Tertullian's reflections in "The Chaplet" (or "De Corona"), chap. 6. His main argument is against wearing a laurel or flower "crown" or garland: "It is just as much against nature to long for a flower with your head as to crave food with your ear or sound with your nose. But anything that is against nature deserves to be branded as monstrous among all men; we surely should also consider it as a sin of sacrilege against God the Master and Author of Nature" (chap. 5). Now it is in this connection that he seeks Pauline support for an appeal to nature. Here he cites first the discussion of the veiling of women in 1 Corinthians, followed by the notion of gentiles doing by nature what the law requires, then the passage most relevant to our concerns: "he says that the male and female have changed among themselves the natural function of the creature and descended to unnatural practices" (chap. 6). We may note that it is quite unclear whether this is meant to refer to same-sex practices at all. But in the same chapter he goes on to say: "Perhaps you have some doubt as to whether we should allow nature to be our guide in the enjoyment of God's creatures? To be sure there is a danger that we be led astray in the direction in which God's rival (Satan) has corrupted, along with man himself, the whole of creation."

In interpreting this passage bear in mind that Tertullian is not using an appeal to nature in order to get at the question of sexual practices. Rather he is making use of Pauline references to nature to legitimate his own use of an appeal to nature to argue against men wearing victory garlands on their heads. He thus cites all of those passages where Paul seems to make use of an appeal to nature (including Romans 1:25–28) in order to grant himself access to philosophical, perhaps especially Stoic, uses of arguments from nature. Thus the passage tells us very little about whether Tertullian understood Paul in a specifically homophobic (or lesbi-phobic) sense.[5] It does however indicate that Tertullian is also aware that an appeal to nature may have its limits, something that Jerome will certainly underline.

Jerome seems not to suppose that the appellation "against nature" is itself unambiguously negative. While he can refer to the phraseology of Romans 1:26–27 in *Letter 69,* he does so only in passing to suggest that all sins can be "washed away in the fountain of Christ" (par. 6). But he can also remark that when something is done against nature (here perhaps referring to miracles) "it is a manifestation of God's power and might" (*Letter 108,* par. 24) in a way that recalls Paul's suggestion in Romans 11 that God acts "against nature." It is then no surprise that Jerome can even suppose that it is the duty of the Christian to act contrary to nature in preferring celibacy to marriage (*Letter 130,* par. 10). Thus with Jerome the term "against nature" seems not to have the rather clear-cut moral meaning that it had in the *Laws* of Plato or the reflections of Musonius Rufus.

With Augustine, however, the Platonic and Stoic view of nature comes to have a far more direct influence. In his writings against the Manicheans, Augustine contends that nature is good while evil is that which is against nature. In this way he is maintaining that that which is created (nature) is good. All that is truly evil therefore is to be rejected as against nature.[6] This will then incline Augustine against the rather polymorphic view of what is against nature that we found in Jerome.

The upshot of this is that Augustine will strongly defend heterosexual sexual practices as being in accordance with nature even when he finds them to be in different senses sinful. Thus in an interesting discussion of polygamy in the Bible Augustine writes: "Again, Jacob the son of Isaac is charged with having committed a great crime because he had four wives. But here there is no ground for a criminal accusation: for a plurality of wives was no crime when it was the custom; and it is a crime now, because it is no longer the custom. There are sins against nature, and sins against custom, and sins against the laws. In which, then, of these senses did Jacob sin in having a plurality of wives? As regards nature, he used the women not for sensual gratification, but for the procreation of children. For custom, this was the common practice at that time in those countries. And for the laws, no prohibition existed. The only reason of its being a crime now to do this, is because custom and the laws forbid it" (*Contra Faustum* book 22, par. 47).

This becomes even more acute in his reflections *On Marriage and Concupiscence*, in which reference to Paul becomes unmistakable. This comes in the context of answering an opponent's question as to what is the natural and unnatural use of women:

My answer to this challenge is, that not only the children of wedlock, but also those of adultery, are a good work insofar as they are the work of God, by whom they are created: but as concerns original sin, they are all born under condemnation of the first Adam; not only those who are born in adultery, but likewise such as are born in wedlock, unless they be regenerated in the second Adam, which is Christ. As to what the apostle says of the wicked, that "leaving the natural use of the woman, the men burned in their lust one toward another: men with men working that which is unseemly" (Romans 1:27); he did not speak of the conjugal use, but the "natural use," wishing us to understand how it comes to pass that by means of the members created for the purpose the two sexes can combine for generation. Thus it follows, that even when a man unites with a harlot to use these members, the use is a natural one. It is not, however, commendable, but rather culpable. But as regards any part of the body which is not meant for generative purposes, should a man use even his own wife in it, it is against nature and flagitious. Indeed, the same apostle had previously [Romans 1:26] said concerning women: "Even their women did change the natural use into that which is against nature;" and then concerning men he added, that they worked that which is unseemly by leaving the natural use of the woman. Therefore, by the phrase in question, "the natural use," it is not meant to praise conjugal connection; but thereby are denoted those flagitious deeds which are more unclean and criminal than even men's use of women, which, even if unlawful, is nevertheless natural. (book 2, chap. 35)

Here we have a remarkable insistence that sex with a prostitute or adultery is according to nature (though a sin), whereas nonprocreative sex with one's wife is against nature. Thus presumably oral or anal sex with one's wife is "more unclean and criminal" than adultery or prostitution. He makes this case again in the treatise on the *Good of Marriage* (par. 11–12).

Augustine takes this somewhat further in order to maintain that sex and its associated bodily equipment was a part of the divine creation (*City of God*, book 14, chap. 23). This stands in some contrast to his view that original sin is passed on in the act of procreation itself, but Augustine's point is that it is the way that the sex act is infected with inordinate desire rather than the act itself that is the mechanism for the transmission of original sin. In this way, of course, any sexual act in our fallen state is sinful, precisely because it is always accompanied by excess or disordered desire. But since sex is a part of creation it would be good (as natural) if not so corrupted. In some way, however, Augustine wishes to combine this with the Platonic view that sex for procreation is natural and the Clementine view that any other sort of sex is against nature. Presumably this will then make it possible to characterize nonprocreative sexual practices as in some way even more "sinful" than the natural, but corrupted, acts that may result in progeny. It will fall to Thomas Aquinas to develop this view with systematic rigor in reliance upon more Aristotelian than Platonic views of "natural law."

If the discussion of Romans in Latin Christianity seems to be somewhat hesitant in the appropriation of Romans 1:26–27 for homophobic purposes, Greek Christianity seems rather less hesitant in this regard, perhaps because it is more familiar with a more generalized homophobic discourse among the intellectuals of the Hellenistic world. It is with St. John Chrysostom, writing in Greek at the end of the fourth century, that we find the most fully developed homophobic appropriation of Paul's text in Romans. Chrysostom had been steeped in the traditions of pagan Hellenistic culture, a culture that he appropriated into his homilies to powerful effect. As a priest in Antioch (386–98) and then as a bishop in the imperial see of Constantinople, Chrysostom made his reputation as the greatest preacher of antiquity. His sermons regularly took the form of exposition of books of the Bible. His sermon series on Paul's Letter to the Romans includes thirty-two homilies. Chrysostom's chief preoccupation in his homilies was with the corruption of Christianity occasioned by the temptations of wealth, and his sermons therefore take every opportunity to castigate the wealthy and to turn the attention of his hearers to the plight of the impoverished. His "Homily on Romans 1:26–27" is no exception since it concludes with an excoriation of luxury and wealth, which he takes to be the chief cause of sin, including that which he takes to be the subject of Paul's references in the Romans verses.

Within that context, however, Chrysostom incorporates into his reading of Romans 1:26–27 a great many of the tropes of Hellenistic homophobia that we encountered in our reading of Plato and of Philo. The overriding idea, derived from Paul's language, is that same-sex love is "contrary to nature." This is an idea that Chrysostom deploys no fewer than seven times in the space of a single homily! He does not fail to add the notion that this sort of intercourse is not found among "irrational creatures," not even dogs: "for in no case does such intercourse take place with them, but nature acknowledgeth her own limits." Here Chrysostom is clearly appropriating a trope not from Paul, but from Plato.

Chrysostom also supposes (with Plato) that same-sex passion is the result of an excess of passion (not a deficiency in heterosexual desire): "you see that the whole of desire comes of an exorbitancy which endureth not to abide within its own proper limits." In this case Chrysostom is inclined to maintain that same-sex love is "so much worse than fornication as cannot even be expressed," going so far as to maintain "there surely is not a more grievous evil than this insolent dealing."

Led by Paul's text, but anticipated in Plato's *Laws*, is the linking of male same-sex desire to that of women for one another: "even the women seek after these intercourses who ought to have more of a sense of shame than men."[7]

In order to suggest how this crime is so horrific, Chrysostom will link it to the idea of prostituting oneself, a notion that we encountered in Aeskhines' indictment of Timarkus. But even more, he links it to the feminization of males (he does not make the gender argument against female same-sex relations). He thus addresses the male: "For I should not only say that thou hast become a woman, but also that thou hast lost thy manhood" and in this way "become a traitor" to both sexes at once. Perhaps this is clearer when he maintains that "it is not the same thing to change into the nature of women, as to continue a man and yet to have become a woman; or rather neither this nor that." To this Chrysostom adds the idea that same-sex love exacerbates the war of the sexes against one another, making them resolute enemies of one another.

Toward the end Chrysostom links this discussion to the example of Sodom: "Consider how great is that sin, to have forced hell to appear even before its time" in which the "unnaturalness" of the rain ("fire and brimstone") corresponds to the unnaturalness of the crime. Although Chrysostom's formulation does not appear to be indebted to the perspective we saw in *The Apostolic Constitutions*, it also links fiery punishment with same-sex sexual practice in a way that is in considerable contrast to the use we had seen in Nazianzen, which had made the sin of Sodom a metaphor for any and all sin.

In this sermon, preached perhaps in Antioch around 391 C.E., we have the coming together of Platonic and Hellenistic, and especially Philonic, homophobic discourse in a way that appropriates both Paul in Romans and the Sodom story from Genesis to great rhetorical effect. In this case we are no longer dealing with an issue of violence among males but with the symbolic violence that any same-sex relationship is imagined to entail.

It is noteworthy that homophobic hermeneutics reaches this point in Greek so much earlier than in Latin. We have seen that even the somewhat later work of Jerome and Augustine in Latin is much more tentative in the development of homophobic discourse, including that which appropriates biblical texts for these purposes. And when this does happen in Greek, it appears to betray close affinity to the perspectives already brought forward by Plato in the *Laws* and by the Hellenistic perspectives, especially those of Philo, that derive from Platonic views. The very fact that it takes several centuries for Paul to be read in this way and for that reading to be linked up with the homophobic interpretation of Genesis suggests that this was by no means a natural and necessary consequence of the reading of either biblical text, but that this reading was made plausible within the context of a preexisting Platonic and Hellenistic homophobic project. Once again it is not the Bible that produces Christian homophobia. Instead, over a long and tortuous path the Bible is conscripted for homophobic purposes in order to bring it into conformity with an already existent Platonic homophobic project.

Even here we should not suppose that Chrysostom's views are at all representative of late fourth-century Christianity. Chrysostom himself gives testimony that his views with respect to same-sex sexual practices ran very much against the grain even of Christianity in Antioch. Indeed his own words suggest that the great majority of Christians not only accepted same-sex love but were enthusiastic practitioners.[8]

# – 15 –

# Homophobic Christian Law

Modern Western homophobia has appealed not only to the natural law and to Scripture but also to the legal precedents attributed to the Christian emperors of the early church. When Constantine promulgated the edict of Milan that gave legal protection to Christianity in 313 C.E., a process was launched by which Roman imperial ideologies and Christian perspectives began to mutually transform one another. In this chapter we will look at the ways in which Roman legislation concerning same-sex sexual practices developed from the fourth century until the sixth in order to see how a foundation is laid for subsequent Western homophobia. The material to which we turn is perhaps surprisingly sparse. It is also not easy to determine how it should be interpreted. Although there has been much subsequent reflection on these legal materials, I will take as my starting point the influential interpretations of D. S. Bailey.[1]

In the earlier discussion of the question of the corruption of youths, I argued that Roman legislation concerning male same-sex practices could best be understood as forbidding the imposition of superior will or force upon a free citizen or upon a minor. That is, the law could best be understood as forbidding actual or attempted rape as well as providing legal protection for minors of the class of (prospective) citizens. Christian thinkers seem to have felt that these same protections should be extended to all persons rather than restricted only to free citizens of the empire. One of the effects of the interplay between Christian and imperial institutions would be that all persons were indeed included under the provision of the laws.

The first legal declaration in the context of the Christian empire comes from the brothers who had inherited the empire from their father, Constantine, some decades following the institutionalization of Christianity. Unlike previous Roman statutes, those of the Christian emperors are incorporated in the compilations of laws produced by later emperors such as Theodosius and Justinian. Thus we do have the wording even if this does not always make interpretation easy. The edict of 343 reads as follows in a translation proffered by Bailey:

> When a man marries in the manner of a woman, a woman about to renounce men, what does he wish when sex has lost its significance; when the crime is one it is not profitable to know; when Venus is changed into another form; when love is sought and not found? We order the statutes to arise, the laws to be armed with an avenging sword, that those infamous persons who are now, or hereafter may be, guilty may be subjected to exquisite punishment.

Bailey suggests that the first clause should better be rendered: "When a man marries [and is] about to offer [himself] to men in a womanly fashion." Cantarella suggests: "When a man couples (literally 'marries') as though he were a woman, what can a woman desire who offers herself to men?" The Latin clause is: "Cum vir nubit in feminam, femina viros proiectura quid cupiat?" If something like Bailey's amended translation is accepted then it seems plausible that the edict targets those males who make themselves "female" in order to marry a male.[2]

Although the law is incorporated in the compilations of later emperors there is some doubt that it was meant to be taken seriously. One of the imperial authors to whom it is ascribed was himself believed to have been taken with same-sex sexual practices[3] and the rather "over the top" wording of the statute has suggested to many that it was facetious. Bailey thinks that the reference to marriage here should not be taken literally and Cantarella agrees,[4] but it seems to me that it makes good sense of the terminology to suppose that marriage may be precisely what is in view. Emperors since the time of Nero had outraged (or titillated) public sensibility by marrying castrated slaves who took the place of the female partner more typical of a marriage ceremony. It might well be that some in the aristocratic circles close to the emperors had engaged in such ceremonies and that the edict, whether in jest or in earnest, targeted them or, rather, targeted those males who offered themselves in this way as wives or concubines.

If this edict were to have a basis in prior Roman legislation it would seem to lie in the prohibition of castration of males for sexual purposes apparently promulgated under the emperor Hadrian, whose own opposition to male genital mutilation had led him to try to stamp out circumcision in Egypt and, most famously, Judea. On the other hand Cantarella suggests that the "exquisite penalty" (exquisitis poenis) referred to in the statute may be castration. The logic would apparently be something like the following: if you make yourself symbolically female then the state will more literally "feminize" you. But the statute does not in itself more directly specify the penalty, meaning that it is essentially left to the imagination of the reader.[5]

Although the edict of Constantius and Constans initially may not have had a serious purpose, it was incorporated into the compilation put forward by the Emperor Theodosius, who added a new edict (in company with Valentinian II and Arcadius, his co-emperors) that would extend its provisions while leaving little doubt as to its earnestness. The law was put forward in 390 (roughly contemporary therefore with the sermon of Chrysostom that we have read) and reads as follows, again in Bailey's translation: "All persons who have the shameful custom of condemning a man's body, acting the part of a woman's, to the sufferance of an alien sex (for they appear not to be different from women), shall expiate a crime of this kind in avenging flames in the sight of the people."[6] Bailey is himself uncertain about how the law is to be understood. He suggests that it may have to do with prostitution or that it may refer to an "active sodomist" and so serve as a complement to the previous edict that would then be understood as penalizing the "passive sodomist." Bailey also suggests that it may have to do with "homosexual prostitution" (the reference to "condemning a man's body").

Again it seems to me that the law may be understood as an extension of the legislation of Hadrian except that here it more clearly focuses upon those who force another male to take the part of a woman. This would be entirely consonant with the intent of Hadrian's law. The insistence that the one coerced here "appear[s] not to be different from women" may also be a reference to castration.[7]

However narrowly the law may have been formulated, it was to have far greater effect in subsequent history. The "exquisite punishment" of 342 has become burning in 390. This is the punishment that would come to be inflicted upon those condemned for same-sex sexual practices in the late Middle Ages. While there is no evidence that this law was enforced in the period we are considering, it would become the basis of severe suppression of same-sex behavior in later centuries.

## Gender Troubles

What both these fourth-century edicts have in common is an obvious concern about the feminization of the male. Whether this was understood to have to do with emasculation for transgendering purposes, castration for the preservation of ersatz youthful beauty, or more symbolic forms of feminization, what comes to expression is a horror of the transgendering or feminization of the male. We have seen something similar in the views of Chrysostom, who was contemporary with Theodosius. It is therefore appropriate that we pause to consider the provenance of this fear.

We have already noticed in the case of Leviticus and that of Plato a concern about the male who makes himself female. In the case of Leviticus, this had to do with adopting the sexual role of the female; in the case of Plato, too, there was an attempt to shame practitioners of male same-sex behavior with the suggestion that they feminized themselves either through yielding to passion (in the case of the active partner) or through playing the part of the female with another male. These roughly contemporaneous perspectives may have had similar social causes in that each may arise from a sense of the vulnerability of the male social body to the cultural or political domination of a more virile national entity.

Whatever may have been the case with Plato and the authors of the Holiness Code of Israel, Philo combines these traditions in his own Platonizing reading of the Holiness Code within the context of a quite different social order, that of the Roman Empire. Studies of Roman sexual ideology have regularly remarked upon the rather extreme forms of Roman "machismo." The policing of proper masculine demeanor and

comportment seems to have been something of an obsession throughout the Roman period. The concern about the way a man walked and
spoke, as well as the ways proper to a man to relate to other males,
fills many pages of ancient moral and medical advice.[8]

Many have suggested that this concern for rigid gender dichotomiza-
tion and fastidious gender performance had a good deal to do with the
vocation of the Roman male to rule, that is, to impose his will upon
others, whether women, slaves, barbarians, or even other Romans.
Masculinity was the gender of domination. Thus Eva Cantarella notes:
"To some extent, the Roman male was condemned to a life of maleness — the maleness of a sexual thug who, by imposing his desires
on women and *pueri,* his enemies and those who had wronged him,
proved his sexual potency, indomitable character and social muscle to
himself and to others."[9]

Christianity does a good deal to subvert this gender culture. It is not
possible in this context to offer a history of Christian reflections on
gender. That would take us too far afield from the present study. We
may however quickly summarize some of the pertinent information.
The texts of Paul are notoriously ambivalent in this regard. He can
famously suppose that "in Christ there is neither male nor female"
(Galatians 3:28) and describe his own role in relation to his congregations as that of a mother who labors to bring birth and who suckles
his/her children in the faith.[10] Yet his texts also contain such gender dichotomizations as the one about hair length, to which we have
referred earlier, and the odd and much debated admonition for women
to keep silent in the assemblies of Corinth. The narratives concerning
Jesus, which were written after Paul, depict Jesus in ways that subvert
gender role expectations, most dramatically in the footwashing scene
in the Gospel of John.

Of far greater importance, however, is the way in which Christianity sought to instill "feminine" virtues in men like kindness,
meekness, humility, and gentleness, while instilling in women "masculine" virtues like courage, self-control, and wisdom. Early Christian
men were forbidden the manly pursuits of the military and the mag-
istracy as well as athletic competition. They were taught to forego
the practices of domination. Meanwhile women were encouraged to

have a certain independence of men by living together as widows and virgins in all-female communities even if these were their own households. This is not to say that early Christianity entirely escaped the gender system of the empire. There were inevitable compromises and attempts to consolidate Christian respectability within that system. But this meant that Roman gender identities were certainly rendered less stable as the empire became Christianized and that Greco-Roman gender suppositions could not be taken over wholesale into Christian discourse.

An interesting illustration of the resultant instability can be found in the writing of Clement of Alexandria. Of all Christian intellectuals of the early church, Clement is arguably the one who is most concerned about gender performance. Like a Roman doctor he dispenses advice about what makes for really manly comportment and appearance. Men must have beards and should not often bathe and should eschew overly comfortable sleeping arrangements.[11] This concern with masculine gender identity also leads Clement to worry about female gender performance. In this connection he also makes reference to the unnatural pairing of women in marriage, a custom that Bernadette Brooten shows to have been notable precisely in Clement's Alexandria.[12] At the same time Clement can insist that women are just as capable as men of philosophical understanding and virtue.[13] Like Musonius Rufus he supposes that gender should be no hindrance to virtue. Moreover he readily uses motherly images of God who as pedagogue is also our nurse who suckles us at the breast.[14]

In contrast to Clement's concern about gender performance there were many Christian males, probably including his successor, Origen, who had themselves castrated, perhaps in conformity with a literal interpretation of Matthew 19:12.[15] These Christian males would have appeared of somewhat indeterminate gender, at least by the standards of Tertullian and Clement. This practice, which may have been rather widespread in the third and into the fourth century, would run afoul of the imperial legislation of the later fourth century and of subsequent ecclesiastical legislation as well.

Now this suggests that when we encounter in Christian discourse the apparent echoing of Greco-Roman gender discourse that this will have more Roman than specifically Christian roots. If we leave aside the questionable edict of Constantius and focus attention on the decree of Theodosius, this may become more apparent. Theodosius was a great general from Spain, the son of another very famous general. When he became emperor he set about eliminating Arianism as well as all vestiges of pagan Roman cults. In addition he led expeditions to eliminate the threat of the Huns and the Vandals, thereby securing Roman rule throughout the empire. He was the last of the emperors to rule over a united empire. His position within the empire and his training and vocation as a military leader go some distance in suggesting how he could be considered an exemplar of a Roman masculinist ethos. Certainly within that ethos the demasculinizing, whether surgical or symbolic, of Roman males could be expected to produce a strong reaction.

Beyond this we have the imposition of a death penalty that is quite ferocious in its application. In the fourth century Christian bishops and theologians were still averse to the death penalty. Augustine wrote to Macdedonius, the Roman governor of Africa, explaining that it was the duty of Christian leaders to seek to forestall the imposition of the death penalty.[16] Thus the ferocity of the penalty envisioned by the decree of Theodosius owes far more to Roman than to Christian motivation. To this may be added the irony that a penalty, death by burning, that had so recently been the punishment for Christians is now imposed by a Christian emperor upon those whose sex-related practices he found abhorrent.

There is, however, no evidence that this emperor actually sought to carry out the death penalty that in this case and many others he so freely seemed to impose. The church historian Sozomen suggests that Theodosius decreed the death penalty in support of his various campaigns without the intention of actually carrying out the threat, intending simply to frighten his opponents.[17] In the absence of any record of executions under this statute, this must be regarded as a plausible understanding of his policy. Thus the threatening of the death penalty bespeaks a Roman tendency while the effective suspension of that penalty suggests that Roman policy has been mitigated by Christian considerations.[18]

Whatever may have been the original scope and motivation of the decree its inclusion in the code of his successor, Justinian, secures for it a certain permanence. When conditions changed it would be possible to cite this code as authoritative grounds for the burning of sodomites and catamites in the late medieval period and for other forms of the death penalty in the early modern period. It is this historical "fallout" from the decree of Theodosius that will produce the impression that a Christian emperor launched a sort of pogrom against practitioners of same-sex love.[19]

The statute of Theodosius with its combination of a horror of male gender deviance and its extreme interest in the death penalty clearly has roots more in Roman than in Christian perspectives. There is no attempt to relate the statute to any specifically Christian perspective. As we have seen, the appropriation of a homophobic hermeneutics of biblical texts was still in its infancy in the time of Theodosius. This development will come together with imperial legislation in the sixth century under the emperor Justinian, but with surprising effect.

## Justinian

After Theodosius, Justinian, who reigned from 527 to 565, may have been the most successful of the Roman Christian emperors. His empire, centered in Constantinople, was extended to recover Africa and Italy from the barbarians. He presided over the invention of what would be called Byzantine architecture and installed a Byzantine imperial absolutism that would be the standard for emperors to follow. But the accomplishment that earned him permanent fame was the fundamental reorganization of imperial law. This included the reorganization of the Theodosian compilation into a rational structure, the compilation of learned juridical opinion that interpreted the law, a manual for the training of persons in the law, and a compilation of new laws, many of them issued in his own reign. This enormous work would serve as the basis for law in all nations that were to be influenced by Christianity, including, of course, Europe. Thanks to this legal corpus the decrees that we have already considered were passed down to posterity with the effects that we have also noticed.

To this corpus Justinian adds two novella or new statutes that for the
first time indicate a specifically Christian foundation for homophobic
law. The first of these, issued in 538 (novella 77) appears as follows in
Bailey's version:

> Since certain men, seized by diabolical incitement, practice among
> themselves the most disgraceful lusts, and act contrary to nature;
> we enjoin them to take to heart the fear of God and the judgment
> to come, and to abstain from suchlike diabolical and unlawful
> lusts, so that they may not be visited by the just wrath of God on
> account of these impious acts, with the result that cities perish
> with their inhabitants. For we are taught by the Holy Scriptures
> that because of like impious conduct cities have indeed perished,
> together with the men in them. [Bailey notes that there follows a
> long section of forms of blasphemy, or taking God's name in vain.]
> For because of such crimes [unnatural lust or blasphemy?], there
> are famines, earthquakes, and pestilences; wherefore we admonish
> men to abstain from the aforesaid unlawful acts, that they may
> not lose their souls. But if after this our admonition, any are found
> persisting in such offenses, first they render themselves unworthy
> of the mercy of God, and then they are subjected to the punishment
> enjoined by the law.

The edict goes on to explain that the novella is necessary "so that
city and the state may not come to harm by reason of such wicked
deeds." Although there is ambiguity in this novella occasioned by
linking two quite different matters (unnatural lust and swearing by,
for example, God's whiskers), we do see the beginning of a linkage
between the destruction of cities and the practice of unnatural lust.
On the one hand this combination was already inscribed in Greek and
Hellenistic homophobia. The risk of depopulation occasioned by the
forsaking of "natural" intercourse goes back as far as Plato and was
certainly insisted upon by Philo. Of course for Christians this warning could not have anything like the same force as it did for Jewish
or pagan sensibilities since Christians extolled the virtues of permanent virginity for both men and women, certainly a far greater threat
to population than occasional or habitual practice of same-sex love.

This basic sentiment is, however, Christianized by reference to Scripture concerning the destruction of cities owing to divine judgment, a fairly clear reference to the story of the cities of the plain in Genesis. In the fourth century it had still been possible to think of the sin of Sodom and her sister cities in a largely generic fashion without an emphasis upon a particular category of sin. But the beginning of the appropriation of a homophobic interpretation of the story of Sodom made tentatively in the fourth century appears, now in the sixth, to be gaining some traction.

What this also provides is a rationale for imperial concern. For it is the vocation of the emperor, whether Christian or not, to provide for the welfare of the citizens of the empire. Clearly if certain acts are likely to carry as a consequence devastation like that of Sodom at the hand of a ferocious deity (by now somewhat reconstructed after the image of an absolute emperor), then it clearly behooves the emperor to safeguard his people from any such danger. This will later serve as a pretext for launching a crusade against practitioners of same-sex love in the late medieval and Renaissance periods.

However, contrary to that long-term consequence, this seems not to have been the intent of Justinian's novella. Rather it is an admonition and a call to the renunciation of such practices. Not without reason, Bailey protests against the view, common since Gibbon's history of the decline and fall of the Roman Empire, that Justinian may be regarded as having launched a merciless campaign against practitioners of same-sex love. On the contrary, not only is there a warning about potentially grave consequences and a call to desist from the offending behavior, but that behavior is itself placed on the same footing as simple profanity. To be sure, the penalties are serious and severe, as would be true of the violation of almost any imperial edict, but same-sex love is not yet singled out for special horror.

However, we should also remind ourselves that the connection between sexual transgression and national calamity is one that has been curiously revived in our own time with the suggestions made by the religious right that disasters like the events of September 11, 2001, or the hurricane that devastated New Orleans could be attributed to the existence of significant gay communities in New York as well as New

Orleans. In the time of Justinian, Bailey remarks, a series of catas-
trophes were fresh in the memory of the empire (77). A few years
before earthquakes and floods had devastated cities on both sides of the
Mediterranean, and the empire was always threatened by devastating
plagues.

Some such rationale seems even more obvious with respect to the
second of Justinian's novellas treating of male same-sex sexual practices, this time on March 15, 544. After a long preamble concerning
the importance of repentance, perhaps occasioned by the season of
Lent in which the novella is promulgated, Justinian informs us that
the sin of which he is writing is "the defilement of males [*de stupro
masculorum*] which some men sacrilegiously and impiously dare to
attempt, perpetrating vile acts with other men." He will then go on
to speak of the example of Sodom. As we have seen this story had
been connected with the question of penance before being attached by
Christians to a homophobic reading.

Justinian finds a way of bridging these two distinct readings of
the story: "For instructed by the Holy Scriptures, we know that God
brought a just judgment upon those who lived in Sodom, on account
of this very madness of intercourse, so that to this day that land
burns with inextinguishable fire." Here it has become self-evident that
Sodom is punished for same-sex sexual practices rather than Sodom
serving, as it had still in the fourth century, as a representative of all
sorts of public sin and injustice or as a generic call for repentance.
After five hundred years Philo's interpretation of this story is becoming a standard of imperial hermeneutics. Justinian immediately links
this example of divine anger as a reason for legislative remedy: "By this
God teaches us, in order that by means of legislation we may avert such
an untoward fate." Thus legislation against same-sex sexual practices
is connected quite explicitly with the need to protect the empire from
the wrath of God.

This is then connected by Justinian with the teaching of Paul, presumably in reference to Romans 1: "Again we know what the blessed
Apostle says about such things." Justinian does not inform the reader
about which specific texts he has in mind or how they are to be

connected to the theme of this novella, but it seems clear that some-thing like what we have found in the late fourth-century sermon of Chrysostom on Romans 1:26–27 lies behind this reference. Thus two elements of biblical authorization for homophobia come together here in Justinian.

This leads him also to refer to the laws of the Roman state, the very laws we have been considering. What is of greatest interest here is the way in which the homophobic hermeneutics that began to take hold in Christian discourse in the late fourth century now comes to be linked, or at least juxtaposed, to the imperial legislation that we have been considering. Thus biblical and legal authorization for public homophobia comes together for the first time. As we have seen this combination will last well into the twentieth century, as evidenced by the United States Supreme Court opinions that we considered in the first chapter.

Still lacking in this homophobic discourse, however, is the appro-priation of Leviticus. The time is not yet ripe for Christians to cite Mosaic Law in this respect. Moreover, this would scarcely serve Jus-tinian's purpose. For the novella aims strictly at a call to repentance motivated by a desire to avert disaster from the state. There is nothing here of the apparent severity of Theodosius. Instead, there is a call for the amendment of life: "Let those who have not taken part in such doings continue to refrain in the future. But as for those who have been consumed by this kind of disease, let them not only cease to sin in the future, but let them also do penance." Later he continues: "And we also, wisely and prudently having in reverence the sacred season, entreat God the merciful that those who have been contaminated by the filth of this impious conduct may strive for penitence." Indeed the whole tenor of the discourse from beginning to end is the call for repentance, in the assurance that where there is penitence, there will be found a merciful God.

The call is actually twofold. On the one hand, the "sinners" are summoned to repent so that God will forgive them (and the authorities will not be obliged to exercise the force of the law). On the other hand this will also have the result that God, who seems angry with the empire, will relax his anger and will bless the empire as this cause of anger is removed through penitence and through the diligence of the emperor, the magistrates, and the patriarch in reducing this cause of divine ire. It concludes: "If, with eyes as it were blinded, we overlook such impious and forbidden conduct, we may provoke the good God to anger and bring ruin upon all—a fate which would be but deserved."

Here one cannot help but be reminded of the biopolitics that Foucault attributes to the modern era.[20] Justinian refers to madness, disease, plague, and filth, all in describing what it is the duty of the state to redress through legislation and exhortation. What is most notably lacking in most modern biopolitics is the reference to the judgment of God. Another key difference is of course the much more sophisticated deployments of powers of control characteristic of modernity. In its place is offered the recourse of penance.[21] Indeed, Justinian's concern seems to be entirely with repentance in the holy season of Lent. The sword is sheathed. There is the strongly spoken desire not to make use of the power of the sword but instead to have recourse to the mechanisms of repentance and forgiveness. Thus, the ferocity of imperial law is ameliorated by the Christian proclamation of a good and merciful God. Hence the odd mutual transformation of Christianity and empire. Many centuries later it will become evident that at least in this connection the severity of Rome will triumph over the presumed mercy of the Christian God. But at this stage there is little evidence of the hysteria that will be invoked to justify a campaign to forcibly eradicate the plague of "homosexual vice."

It is most likely the question of a plague that opens up this theme for renewed consideration by Justinian, for in the year preceding this novella the capital and its environs had been decimated precisely by a plague. And the much more severe responses of Christian Europe to same-sex sexuality in the late Middle Ages and Renaissance may also owe to the sense of divine wrath occasioned by the appearance of the "Black Death" that wiped out large sectors of the European population. What will then come to expression is the combination of the severity of Theodosius and the rationale of Justinian in the authorization of campaigns of terror against male same-sex sexuality, now firmly associated with the sin of Sodom.

It is important, however, not to read these later developments back into the period we have been surveying. It is true that after its first half millennium Christianity was beginning to show signs of the social and legal homophobia that it had inherited from the cultures within which it had taken root. But even at this stage the signs of homophobia were relatively sparse. With Justinian we have seen the coming together of the results of an incipient homophobic hermeneutics with the responsibilities of the Roman State and its actual or potential power of the sword. But this only sketches the framework for what many centuries later would become authorization for official crusades against practitioners of same-sex love.

# – Conclusion –

# Grafting Homophobia

We began this study with a basic perplexity. On the one hand, Christianity has undoubtedly been a primary source of Western homophobia; on the other hand, the biblical sources to which Christianity appeals for its particular perspectives do not seem to warrant homophobic stances. But if homophobia does not come from the Bible, how does it come to be associated with Christianity? The short answer is that it comes not from the Bible but from philosophy; its native language is not Hebrew, but Greek; its home is not Jerusalem, but Athens (and Alexandria); its chief protagonist is not Paul but Plato.

To be sure this runs counter to the commonsense view of the matter, common to both homophobic and anti-homophobic scholars of the past. Yet the review of basic texts we have undertaken in this study does make it clear that Christianity comes to be a carrier of homophobia through accommodating itself to the "pagan" homophobic ethos that depends upon Plato for its rationale and its basic interpretive strategies.

Since Plato is often cited as a proponent of same-sex love in its Greek pederastic form, it has been important to show how the perspective of Plato changes from the apparent affirmation of same-sex love affairs, to the call for a sublimation of these in the direction of the contemplation of the beautiful, to the outright prohibition of same-sex love in the ideal state sketched out in the *Laws*. This very late text of Plato (which may well be earlier than the Holiness Code of Leviticus) lays out a detailed "homophobic project" by which Plato intends to demonstrate how to move society and opinion from the celebration of same-sex love toward its universal condemnation. Here all the most basic themes of homophobic discourse are proposed: the appeal to nature (including the appeal to animal behavior), the appeal to appropriate gender performance, the appeal to divine abhorrence, the linking to incest taboos, and so on. Moreover, Plato puts forward strategies for implementing

220

this project through the invention or reinterpretation of traditional stories (myths) and sayings. The aim or goal of this project is that those who continue to practice same-sex love will either keep silent for shame (and so not disturb the societal homophobic consensus) or kill themselves rather than to suffer the disgrace of public discovery. In short, Plato anticipates the most virulent forms of societal homophobia, forms that will not fully mature in the West until the late Middle Ages or even the modern period.

In this Plato may be said to be far ahead not only of his own time but of the work of his philosophical and social successors. In order to see how this homophobic project begins to take hold in the Hellenistic world, it was then important to look at several kinds of texts in which emergent homophobic discourse is deployed: literary dialogues on love, philosophical texts, and texts of Hellenistic Judaism that are deeply influenced by Plato. In all of these kinds of texts we find elaborations of Plato's project in overt dependence upon his views and even his very language. Yet still none of them go as far as Plato in developing and promoting the homophobic project to which he first gave expression.

Many of the Hellenistic texts to which we gave some attention were contemporary with Paul, and this enabled a rereading of Paul's supposed homophobic allusions in relation to the Hellenistic discourse of his culture. We saw not only that Paul's texts lend themselves to a nonhomophobic reading but that his basic perspectives seem to be at odds with the views of those who promote such perspectives.

The stage was thus set for exploring how Hellenistic (rather than biblical or Pauline) homophobia comes to be engrafted upon Christianity. Although there were a number of false starts in the second century (the concern with the corruption of youths, the concern with the cult of Antinous), the Christian apologists, whose goal was to assimilate Christianity to the best of Greek culture and philosophy, do make increasing use of the rhetoric of what is in accordance with or against nature. At first Paul's use of this terminology is simply cited in order to show that it is legitimate for Christians to use these philosophical resources, but in the fourth century it will come to be aimed at same-sex practices as "against nature," thus aligning Paul with Plato. Similarly, Philo's attempt to reinterpret the story of Sodom in ways that align it with Platonic and Hellenistic homophobia will, after the passage of several centuries, come to be adopted by Christian intellectuals as well. It is only in the sixth century, half a millennium after Paul, that the code of Justinian assimilates this homophonic hermeneutics into the tentative legal framework of the "Christian Empire" — and then primarily as a call to repentance!

What are the enabling conditions that make this grafting of homophobia onto Christianity possible?

Obviously the first is the attempt to make Christianity conform to the perspectives of prestigious public discourses. To the extent that Christianity seeks to demonstrate its compatibility with the most rigorous ethical formulations of paganism, it opens the door to the already existing homophobic ethos of the culture within which it finds itself. Under attack as subversive, irreligious, impious, and immoral, its intellectual defenders sought to demonstrate that Christian morals were not inferior to paganism's most exacting standards, just as it also sought to show that its views of God were not inferior to the best of Greek philosophy. In the course of this process, Christianity also came to adopt a fairly radical rejection of standard marriage and family values, adopting a stance that corresponded to the growing prestige in pagan thought of ascetic ideals. These of course also affected views of sexuality. While most of this suspicion was directed against what we would call heterosexuality and heterosexual marriage, same-sex love was also caught up in this general suspicion of the ways in which attachment to the things of the world distracted from the life of faith.

Christian apologetics was in fact remarkably successful. Not only did Christianity grow and even attract the loyalty of some of the best minds of the later empire, but it also came to install itself as the religious "glue" of the empire itself. Its imperial patrons increasingly insisted that Christianity speak with a single voice not only in matters of doctrine but also in other matters as well. Ultimately the Christian emperors began to install homophobia in both its pagan and its nascent Christian forms as the law of the empire.

Nevertheless, when viewed in hindsight, these moves seem remarkably tentative and fragmentary. Five hundred years after the emergence of Christianity, pagan homophobia has barely begun to be Christianized. In the last novella of Justinian we still find unmistakable echoes of Plato (in saying that even animals don't practice same-sex love). Yet we still do not find anything comparable to the radicality of Plato's homophobic project. Even the addition of the Roman predilection for the death penalty (there is not yet any interest in citing Leviticus in this regard) is mitigated by the call to repentance for the sake of the safety of the empire.

It is the very fragmentary and tentative character of Christian homophobia at this stage that will make it possible for there to be something like what Boswell termed a "gay renaissance" five hundred years later, as Europe emerged from the collapse of the empire and the resultant "dark" ages. Indeed, it will only be a millennium after Constantine that Christendom will really adopt a homophobic ethos as in some way essential to its self-understanding. When it does it will still be haunted by the ghost of Plato, adopting as its own the Platonic homophobic project now outfitted with a more fully developed Christian homophobic hermeneutics of biblical texts and with a thoroughgoing development of a theory of natural law. These developments have to do not with the origins but with the elaboration of homophobia.

Given the modern association of Christianity with homophobia it is still startling to see how slowly and hesitantly Christianity adopted Plato's homophobic project. It is our good fortune to be living in a time when Christianity and the post-Christian West may be beginning to awaken from its dogmatic slumber in this regard. However, even in this time of change there are many who still imagine that authentic Christianity must retain homophobia in order to be true to itself. I hope that this study will contribute to showing that there is no necessary or essential connection between Christianity and homophobia. The grafting of homophobia onto Christianity is indeed "against nature" and as such it may be undone without damage to the rootstock of faith.

Moreover, this unnatural joining of Christianity and homophobia must be undone if Christianity is not to continue to be guilty of the true crime of Sodom: the violation of the vulnerable. Too many lives have already been lost or incurably damaged by this unholy alliance. There was a time before homophobia insinuated itself into Christianity. It is long past time that we entered a new era, the era after homophobia.

# Notes

## Introduction

1. Eva Cantarella, *Bisexuality in the Ancient World,* trans. Cormac O. Cuilleanáin (New Haven: Yale University Press, 1992).

2. William Armstrong Percy III, *Pederasty and Pedagogy in Archaic Greece* (Champaign: University of Illinois Press, 1996).

3. Derrick Sherwin Bailey, *Homosexuality and the Western Christian Tradition* (London: Longmans, Green, 1955).

4. Mark Jordan, *The Invention of Sodomy in Christian Theology* (Chicago: University of Chicago Press, 1997).

5. See, for example, André Gide, *Saül* (written 1893, published 1903), in *My Theater,* trans. Jackson Matthews (New York: Knopf, 1951), and Tom Horner, *Jonathan Loved David* (Philadelphia: Westminster, 1978).

6. Theodore W. Jennings, Jr., *Jacob's Wound: Homoerotic Narrative in the Literature of Ancient Israel* (New York: Continuum, 2005).

7. Theodore W. Jennings, Jr., *The Man Jesus Loved: Homoerotic Narratives in the New Testament* (Cleveland: Pilgrim, 2003).

8. Ibid., 75–91. See also George Steiner, *No Passion Spent: Essays, 1978–1995* (New Haven: Yale University Press, 1996), in which the last two essays deal with parallels between Jesus and Socrates (361–414), and George Steiner, *Lessons of the Masters: The Charles Eliot Norton Lectures, 2001–2002* (Cambridge, Mass.: Harvard University Press, 2003).

9. Robin Scroggs, *The New Testament and Homosexuality: Contextual Background for Contemporary Debate* (Philadelphia: Fortress, 1983).

10. Bernadette Brooten, *Love between Women: Early Christian Responses to Female Homoeroticism* (Chicago: University of Chicago Press, 1996).

## 1. Affirmation

1. Alan Bloom, "The Ladder of Love," in *Plato's "Symposium,"* trans. Seth Bernadette (Chicago: University of Chicago Press, 1993), 57.

2. See, for example, Augustine, *City of God,* trans. Marcus Dods (New York: Random House, 1950), 14:15–18, and Hugh of Saint Victor, *On the Sacraments of the Christian Faith,* in *A Scholastic Miscellany: Anselm to Ockham,* ed. and trans. Eugene R. Fairweather (Philadelphia: Westminster, 1961), 318.

3. John Boswell cites texts from Basil and Chrysostom to demonstrate this point. See John Boswell, *Christianity, Social Tolerance, and Homosexuality* (Chicago: University of Chicago Press, 1980), 159–61.

4. Except where otherwise noted the translation for this and the following dialogues is from *Lysis, Phaedrus, and Symposium: Plato on Homosexuality*, trans. Benjamin Jowett, ed. Eugene O'Connor (New York: Prometheus Books, 1991). The Greek text referred to is the Loeb edition.

## 3. Rejection: The *Laws*

1. Plutarch, *Dialogue on Love*, 751f. See also the remarks in Percy, *Pederasty and Pedagogy*, 98, 112–16.

2. In early Christian literature we again encounter talk of the *koinonia* of males [*arrenou*], but this time in a positive sense as that which Christianity seeks to engender. See Acts of Thomas, sections 27 and 50. Whether we have here a Christian tradition that encourages same-sex love or instead the meaning of the terms has been drastically altered is something that would have to be considered in another place.

3. See Plutarch, *Life of Lycurgus* in *The Lives of the Noble Grecians and Romans*, trans. John Dryden, ed. Arthur Hugh Clough (New York: Random House, 1932).

4. Here and in the remainder of this discussion I follow the translation of A. E. Taylor in *Plato: Collected Dialogues*, ed. Edith Hamilton and Huntington Cairns (New York: Pantheon, 1961).

5. It is possible that Plato's language here has influenced the standard translation and interpretation of the prohibition in Leviticus. I have argued in *Jacob's Wound* that the prohibition actually has to do with the desire to be penetrated, to be the object of same-sex desire, something that standard translations, perhaps influenced by Plato, have obscured. The Platonic phrase in the *Laws* has, however, nothing in common with the Septuagint of Leviticus, which uses different words for male, female, and intercourse.

6. Plato does not use the term "abomination" (*bdelugma*), which may be imported here by the translator to make it conform to Leviticus, but rather "hated by God" (*theomisa*).

## 4. Other Greeks

1. Xenophon, *Conversations of Socrates*, ed. Robin Waterfield, trans. Hugh Tredennick and Robin Waterfield (New York: Penguin, 1990).

2. K. J. Dover, *Greek Homosexuality*, updated ed. (Cambridge: Harvard University Press, 1978, 1989).

## 5. Why Homophobia?

1. Eusebius of Caesarea, *Demonstratio Evangelica*, 2 vols., trans. W. J. Ferrar (London: SPCK, 1920).

2. Justin Martyr, *First Apology*, chaps. 49–50.

3. Herodotus, *The History*, trans. David Grene (Chicago: University of Chicago Press, 1987), 1.135.

4. *Stromata* 1.15, also 6.4.

## 6. The Arguments on Love

1. Plutarch, *Moralia*, in *Plutarch*, Loeb Classical Library 9, trans. Edwin L. Minar, F. H. Sandbach, and W. C. Helmbold (Cambridge, Mass.: Harvard University Press, 1961), 303–441.

2. Foucault points out that the relation between Ismenodora and the youth (Bacchon) is constructed on a pederastic model. Michel Foucault, *The Care of the Self: The History of Sexuality* (New York: Pantheon, 1986), 3:196–97. Almost the entirety of part 6 of this text ("Boys") is devoted to a reading of these dialogue texts.

3. *Achilles Tatius*, Loeb Classical Library, trans. S. Gaselee (Cambridge, Mass.: Harvard University Press, 1917).

4. The dating of this novel is unclear, although it certainly comes from some time in the early Christian era and probably follows the dialogue of Plutarch and precedes that of Pseudo-Lucian. The reference to crucifixion may suggest to some readers an acquaintance with Christianity's adoration of a crucified youth, but since crucifixion was an all too common form of torture and execution in the Roman Empire and certainly not reserved for Christians, it seems to me to be unlikely that there is a reference here to Christian discourse.

5. *Lucian*, Loeb Classical Library 8, trans. M. D. Macleod (Cambridge, Mass.: Harvard University Press, 1967).

6. We might also note a rather interesting discussion by Charicles of the proposition that if it's all right for males to have sex with one another, why not females? (28)

## 7. Stoic Homophobia

1. Musonius himself may be referring to this reputation when he suggests that youths "should not go near a philosopher, by which I mean those spoiled and effeminate [*malakoi*] fellows by whose presence the good name of philosophy is stained," in Cora E. Lutz, ed. and trans., "Musonius Rufus: 'The Roman Socrates,'" in *Yale Classical Studies* 10 (1947): 85. References to Musonius's text are page numbers from this edition.

2. For this information, see the very helpful introduction provided by Lutz to her translation of Musonius Rufus, 3–31.

3. For discussion of this, see Eva Cantarella, *Bisexuality in the Ancient World*, 136, and Susan Treggiari, *Roman Marriage: Iusti Coniuges from the Time of Cicero to the Time of Ulpian* (New York: Oxford University Press, 1991), 60–80.

4. Maximus of Tyre, *The Philosophical Orations*, ed. and trans. M. B. Trapp (Oxford: Clarendon Press, 1997).

5. In his notes Trapp cites not only the *Laws* of Plato but also Clement of Alexandria in *The Instructor* 20.9.4. This is thus a trope that descends from Plato through Hellenistic homophobic discourse to influence late second-century Christian discourse.

## 8. Hellenistic Judaism and the Hermeneutic of Homophobia

1. The views of Niels Peter Lemche to this effect have come in for considerable discussion. See "The Old Testament—A Hellenistic Book?" *Scandinavian Journal of the Old Testament* 7, no. 2 (1993): 163–93.

2. Werner Jaeger, *Paideia: The Ideals of Greek Culture* (New York: Oxford, 1944).

3. Werner Jaeger, *Early Christianity and Greek Paideia* (New York: Oxford, 1961).

4. See note to discourse 8.1.12 on p. 64.

5. Philo, *Special Laws* 3.30–51.

6. See Jennings, *Jacob's Wound*, 208–10.

7. The concern with transgendering that we encounter here is somewhat ironic since Israel's prophets make a good deal of God's own complicity in the transgendering of Israel, making of the male Israel into a virgin wife. The adulteries of this wanton feminized Israel are, to be sure, condemned but the goal appears not to be that Israel recover its "true" masculine identity but rather be taken back by God as his loving "wife." Thus God is in love with a feminized male. For more on this see my *Jacob's Wound*, part 3, "Transgendered Israel," 131–76.

8. See Bernard J. Bamberger in *Leviticus*, vol. 3 of *The Torah: A Modern Commentary* (New York: Union of American Hebrew Congregations, 1981).

9. J. A. Loader, *A Tale of Two Cities: Sodom and Gomorrah in the Old Testament, Early Jewish and Early Christian Traditions* (Kampen: J. H. Kok, 1990).

10. Gerhard von Rad, *Old Testament Theology*, trans. D. M. G. Stalker (New York: Harper, 1962), 1:216.

11. Jordan, *The Invention of Sodomy*.

12. See the introduction and translation of P. W. Van Der Horst in James H. Charlesworth, ed., *Old Testament Pseudepigrapha*, vol. 2 (New York: Doubleday, 1985), 565–82. Parenthetical references are to line numbers in this text.

13. For example by the translator of this text in his introduction, 572.

14. See my reflections on Joseph as a eunuch in *Jacob's Wound*, 187–93.

## Part 3: The Case of Paul

1. See Jennings, *The Man Jesus Loved*.

2. Theodore W. Jennings, Jr., *Jacob's Wound: Homoerotic Narrative in the Literature of Ancient Israel* (New York: Continuum, 2005).

## 9. In a Word

1. This term is used in the late first-century Epistle of Barnabas and by other Christian writers, as we shall see in the discussion of the beginnings of Christian homophobia. We shall also see that it is often misleadingly translated in the modern period to refer to pederasty in general or even to "homosexuality." This happens even in the case of anti-homophobic writers like David F. Greenberg, *The Construction of Homosexuality* (Chicago: University of Chicago Press, 1988), 218.

2. I am indebted to Bert Thompson for his research into the history of the translation of this term.

3. Recall the predominance of the discussion of masturbation in the first Vatican document discussed in chapter 1.

4. Cora E. Lutz, ed. and trans., "Musonius Rufus: 'The Roman Socrates,'" in *Yale Classical Studies* 10 (1947): 35.

5. This is the proposal of Robin Scroggs.

6. We must also be clear that a stigmatizing of prostitutes would be ruled out for followers of the Jesus tradition by the express words of Jesus (Matthew 21:31) and that a stigmatizing of the effeminate is similarly excluded by the gender subversion of Jesus in washing the feet of his disciples (John 13:1–17). To be sure, Paul may not have known these elements of the Jesus tradition, but there is no need to impute to Paul greater contradiction to this tradition than is clearly evident.

7. In "Homosexuals or Prostitutes" in *Vigiliae Christianae* 38 (1984): 125–53.

8. In Jennings, *Jacob's Wound*, 208–13. We should recall that this interpretation is verified by a reading of Philo's reading of Leviticus. In *Special Laws* 3.37–38 he depicts the "passive partner" of male same-sex relationships and then in 3.39 says, "the lover of such may be assured that he is subject to the same penalty." Thus Philo argues that it is the desire for female-type sex on the part of the male (who thereby becomes "man-woman") that is especially reprehensible but that the "active" partner must also be punished as a collaborator in this defacement of the male image.

9. It is therefore curious that Bernadette Brooten (*Love between Women*) supposes that it is by reference to this episode in 1 Corinthians 5 that it will be possible to strengthen her case for the interpretation of *arsenokoitai* as male-male sex of some kind and as deserving of death, as she has understood Romans 1:27 (289–92).

10. Curiously this would provide the only prohibition of rape or forcible seduction in the epistolary literature of the New Testament.

11. In this regard it is useful to refer to the discussion by Cantarella of the Roman laws that limited male same-sex activity (*Bisexuality in the Ancient World*, 104–19). As we shall see in a subsequent chapter, a review of the cases that she cites in favor of the view that consenting relations between Roman free males were prohibited shows instead that what was at stake was attempted rape or, at the least, the use of position and power to extract or attempt to extract sexual favors, that is, sexual harassment.

12. For a different assessment of the relevant literature see Dale Martin, *Sex and the Single Savior: Gender and Sexuality in Biblical Interpretation* (Louisville: Westminster John Knox, 2006), 37–50. Although I come to a different conclusion about the probable meaning of this term, this is consistent with Martin's larger point that even a historical-critical approach to the evidence will not deliver a single obvious and thus universally accepted conclusion.

13. William Petersen, "On the Study of 'Homosexuality' in Patristic Sources," *Studia Patristica* 20 (Peeters Press: Leuven, 1989), 284.

14. I will return to this case in the discussion of Christian reactions to this relationship and to the divinization of Hadrian's ill-fated beloved.

## 10. When in Rome

1. This is rather cheerfully accepted by Eva Cantarella in *Bisexuality in the Ancient World*, 191ff. However, Bernadette Brooten, in *Love between Women*, maintains that Paul is simply following the conventions of the Roman world in stigmatizing female homoeroticism. Since most of the documents cited by Brooten come from the period following Paul and those few (e.g., Ovid) that precede him provide debatable evidence (in my view), I am not persuaded that Paul had available to him a tradition of rejection of female same-sex eroticism. Brooten's evidence does, however, make clear how Christianity in the centuries following Paul could read his remarks in Romans 1:26 as reflective of their own cultural prejudices in this regard.

2. Bernadette Brooten argues that Paul is concerned with the same-sex behavior of females in verse 26 and of males in verse 27. I find that argument unconvincing. Notwithstanding the invaluable service of assembling considerable material on attitudes toward female same-sex eroticism, her interpretation of Romans depends upon several dubious exegetical steps. She accepts without argument the NRSV translation of *chreisin* as "intercourse" (and understands this as sexual intercourse) despite the fact that this meaning of the term is quite rare. Most often it means use or serviceableness, as it does in the only other biblical use of the term, in the LXX version of 1 Samuel 1:28. (Job 13:20 seems to be a special case but does not alter the point.) Brooten also attributes the description of male behavior (abandoning the use of...) to female behavior (changing the use of...) without attending to the important differences in these verb clauses. Finally, she follows the homophobic tradition of transferring verse 32 (the "death penalty") to verses 26–27 without even attempting to account for its context of verses 28–31. Such is the power of the tradition of homophobic interpretation of the text that its effects continue to be reproduced in the work of counter-homophobic interpretation.

3. Transferring verbs between verse 27 and 26 is a rather common practice of homophobic exegesis.

4. Among those who find a reference to female same-sex practice to be unlikely are Hans Asmussen, *Der Römerbrief* (Stuttgart: Evangelisches Verlagswerk, 1952), and André Viard, *Saint Paul, Épître aux Romains* (Paris: Gabalda, 1975). Many other commentators simply pass over the verse in silence.

5. It will be evident that I do not agree with the view of Dale Martin that the idea is that by marrying they will eliminate desire altogether. That seems to me to be a view that is more in keeping with a George Bernard Shaw at his most cynical. See Martin, *Sex and the Single Savior*, 65–76.

6. Brooten correctly recognizes that Paul cannot have nonprocreative sex in mind but does not seem to think that this would make it exceedingly unlikely that Paul could have been influenced by the sort of views that she cites from Pseudo-Phocylides, which is the only contemporary Hellenistic Jewish cognate to Paul's alleged condemnation of female same-sex eroticism. Apart from the uncertain attribution of this text to early first-century Judaism, the view of sexuality represented by the text (for example, compulsory marriage and procreation) makes it unusable as a parallel to Paul.

7. At the end of the fourth and beginning of the fifth century Jerome will use this description of divine work to great effect.

8. Later we will see that Augustine makes much of this distinction.

9. That Paul does not use any derivative of the term *koitas* here in a passage that so easily lends itself to an appropriation of the Levitical "males lying with males," especially when he has allegedly gone to the trouble of inventing such a term (*arsenokoitas*), is further evidence that the term *arsenokoitas* is drastically misunderstood. If anything, Paul may be regarded here as avoiding a term that might be understood in a Levitical framework. For his point is not that gentiles are at fault for not obeying Leviticus but that they are doing something that they know on their own terms to be inconsistent with the divine will for justice.

10. Thus I agree with Mark D. Smith and others against some of the formulations of Scroggs. See Mark D. Smith, "Ancient Bisexuality and the Interpretation of Romans 1:26–7," in *JAAR* 44, no. 2 (1996): 243–56. I do not agree, however, for obvious reasons, with his interpretation of Romans, which is based on the views of Cantarella and Brooten.

11. Not "instinctively" as the NRSV says. The sense is that they do this in accordance with their own customs.

12. This is a fairly common rhetorical practice in our own century. Thus to indict the whole program of National Socialism, or even of German society and culture generally, it was not uncommon to refer to the behavior of Hitler and his henchmen. Something similar was done in the case of communism: focus on the bad behavior of Stalin or Mao. In each of these cases the behavior of those at the top of their respective societies could be regarded either as indicative of the social reality as a whole or as corrupting all members of that society. The prophets make exactly the same sort of case with respect to Egypt or Babylon, Israel or Judah.

13. For more on this see my *Reading Derrida/Thinking Paul: On Justice* (Stanford, Calif.: Stanford University Press, 2005).

14. A very fine treatment of Paul's relation to the empire may be found in the work of Neil Elliott, *The Arrogance of Nations: Reading Romans in the Shadow of Empire* (Minneapolis: Fortress, 2008).

15. Suetonius, *The Twelve Caesars*, trans. Robert Graves, ed. Michael Grant (London: Penguin, 1957, 1979); Tacitus, *The Annals*, trans. A. J. Church and W. J. Brodribb (Chicago: Encyclopaedia Britannica, 1952); Dio Cassius, *Roman History*, Loeb Classical Library, trans. Earnest Cary (Cambridge, Mass.: Harvard University Press, 1924).

16. In Plutarch's *Dialogue on Love*, Pisias exclaims: "It is the very Laws of Nature that are transgressed when women take over the state" (755c).

17. Tacitus also reports a speech by Boadicea (14.35), but this speech does not refer to the sexual proclivities of the emperors, perhaps because Tacitus was writing at a time when the emperors (Trajan and Hadrian) were almost exclusively oriented to sexual relationships with young adult men.

18. A similar argument has been made by Neil Elliott in his *Liberating Paul: The Justice of God and the Politics of the Apostle* (Maryknoll, N.Y.: Orbis, 1994),

194–95. He aptly summarizes the material in Suetonius, but this can also be supplemented by other sources.

19. See Cantarella, *Bisexuality in the Ancient World*, where the appropriate ages for Greek males is addressed on page 40 and that of Romans on page 118.

20. Claudius's cruelty is documented not only in the histories (where it is often attributed to the influence of his wives) but also in Seneca's satirical *Apocolocyntosis*, trans. J. P. Sullivan (London: Penguin, 1986), where he is charged with murder of "30 senators, 221 Roman knights, and others 'to the number of the grains of sand and the specks of dust'" (chap. 14).

21. I am not arguing that either Paul or his readers would have precisely the same version of events to which we have access through historians of the period. Probably the rumors then circulating were even more lurid than the reports we have and would have concerned more than the few members of the imperial household whose exploits are recounted in these histories. But it seems likely that Paul and his readers would have known at least as much as we do since the historians regularly refer to "common knowledge" or widely circulated report. Nor do we have to determine whether the reports presented by the historians were factually accurate; it only matters that such things were widely believed to be true during the time in question.

22. Thus I agree with interpreters like Bernadette Brooten who see this text in relation to gender role issues even though I obviously do not agree with the supposition that this can be specified as female same-sex behavior.

## 11. The Corruption of Youths

1. In *The Apostolic Fathers: Greek Texts and English Translations of Their Writings*, 2nd ed., ed. J. B. Lightfoot, J. R. Harner, and Michael Holmes (Grand Rapids: Baker, 1992).

2. For a discussion of the relation between food and sex in the Hebrew Bible, see Ken Stone, *Practicing Safer Texts: Food, Sex and Bible in Queer Perspective* (New York: T&T Clark, 2005).

3. H. W. Hollander and M. D. E. Jonge, *The Testaments of the Twelve Patriarchs: A Commentary* (Leiden: Brill, 1985).

4. Theophilus of Antioch, *Ad Autolycum*, ed. and trans. Robert M. Grant (New York: Oxford, 1970). The older translation of the ANF uses the anachronistic "sodomy" to translate *arrenobasias*, which Robert Grant no less anachronistically but less misleadingly translates as "homosexual acts."

5. Cantarella, *Bisexuality in the Ancient World*, 104–10.

6. David M. Halperin rightly, in my view, takes Brooten to task for this in "The First Homosexuality?" in *How to Do the History of Homosexuality* (Chicago: University of Chicago Press, 2002), 72, referring to Brooten, *Love between Women*, 56.

7. Canon 71. For a discussion of the synod and of the stringent approach to lay sexuality and especially that of women, see S. Laeuchli, *Power and Sexuality: The Emergence of Canon Law at the Synod of Elvira* (Philadelphia: Temple

University Press, 1972). Boswell notes that the "youths" here were probably under fourteen and that nothing is said about other forms of same-sex sexual practices (*Christianity, Social Tolerance, and Homosexuality*, p. 179, note 35.)

8. Athanasius, *Contra Gentes and De Incarnatione*, ed. and trans. Robert W. Thomson (Oxford: Clarendon, 1971).

## 12. The Case of Antinous

1. See Theodore W. Jennings, Jr., *The Man Jesus Loved*, as well as Theodore W. Jennings, Jr., and Benny Tat-Siong Liew, "Mistaken Identities but Model Faith: Rereading the Centurion, the Chap, and the Christ in Matthew 8:5–13," in *Journal of Biblical Literature* 123, no. 3 (2004): 467–94.

2. It is interesting to speculate that some versions of the account of the voice from the heavens that affirms Jesus on the occasion of his baptism may have simply read "this is my beloved" without the addition of "son" (Mark 1:11 and parallels; also Mark 9:7 and parallels). However if any such variations did arise they have left no trace.

3. See the introduction to this text in *The Apostolic Fathers*, 530–31.

4. Cited in *Documents for the Study of the Gospels*, ed. David R. Cartlidge and David L. Dungan, revised and enlarged ed. (Minneapolis: Fortress, 1993).

## 13: Clement on Nature

1. Clement of Alexandria, *Christ the Educator*, trans. Simon P. Wood (New York: Fathers of the Church, 1954).

2. Brooten is thus quite correct to note that "in this focus on procreation, Clement differs from Paul" (*Love between Women*, 325) and to suggest that he is "close to Philo of Alexandria" (325, n. 91).

3. Aline Rouselle, in *Porneia: On Desire and the Body in Antiquity*, trans. Felicia Pheasant (New York: Oxford, 1988), notes: "The number of men who wanted to lead a life of continence was so great that research was devoted to them, books were written for them, and those who were unable to abstain completely from sexual activity had to be reassured. Self-imposed restraint in sexual relations had thus become quite a common feature of the society" (20). For further evidence of the popularity of these perspectives see further pp. 5–23 and 129–40. The definitive study of the views of emerging Christianity in this regard is Peter Brown, *The Body and Society: Men, Women, and Sexual Renunciation in Early Christianity* (New York: Columbia University Press, 1988).

4. Cantarella, *Bisexuality in the Ancient World*, 191, referring to, among others, Morton Scott Enslin, *The Ethics of Paul* (New York: Harper, 1930), 180.

5. For a contemporary reading of Paul to similar effect see Dale B. Martin, *Sex and the Single Savior*. As I have said in a previous note, I am myself rather dubious of this interpretation, preferring the somewhat more conventional view that Paul is to be understood as supposing that desire is not eliminated but rather given an outlet that makes it less distracting.

6. The controversial "Secret Gospel of Mark" contained in a letter supposedly written by Clement and discovered in the last century by Morton Smith also makes a connection between Carpocratian teaching and some same-sex practices. For a discussion of that text and its implications see my *The Man Jesus Loved*, 114–22.

## 14: The Emergence of Homophobic Hermeneutics

1. Tertullian, *Adversus Marcionem*, ed. and trans. Ernest Evans (New York: Oxford University Press, 1972). All references to Tertullian's other texts stem from the translations found in *The Ante-Nicene Fathers*, vols. 3 and 4.

2. Fragments of *Commentary on Proverbs*, *ANF*, 5:175.

3. In this discussion I will bracket the more popularly oriented literature of the early Christian apocalypses treated by Brooten, *Love between Women*, 304–14. First, it seems to me that the connection to Paul is tenuous indeed, depending on the conflation of 1:26 concerning women with 1:32 (death) and then conflating the latter ("worthy of death") with the tortures of hell, which is an apocalyptic notion very far removed from Pauline eschatology, or indeed that of patristic writers generally. In addition, the *Acts of Thomas* seems more likely to refer to incest, although in that text any heterosexual relation is typically regarded with loathing (thus more like Tatian than, for example, Clement).

4. Origen, *Commentary on the Epistle to the Romans*, 2 vols., trans. Thomas P. Scheck (Washington, D.C.: Catholic University of America Press, 2001, 2002).

5. I am thus not persuaded by Brooten's interpretation of this passage (*Love between Women*, 315–16). However, I do agree that Tertullian does evidence a certain distaste for *fricatrices* in other texts. Since this is linked to prostitutes it seems that this owes more to Platonic conflation, for example in the speech of Aristophanes in the *Symposium*, than to Paul, who makes no such connection.

6. Cf. *Against the Fundamental Epistle of the Manicheans*, where there are repeated references, all saying essentially the same thing: evil (or corruption) is not nature but against nature (chap. 35, par. 39; chap. 36, par. 41; chap. 40, par. 46; chap. 43, par. 49); and *On the Morals of the Manicheans*, where the references are similar to the other anti-Manichean document, simply saying that evil is not nature, but against nature (chap. 2, par. 3; chap. 8, par. 11).

7. Ambrosiaster (a name meaning Pseudo-Ambrose) in the commentary on Romans from the same period, makes a similar point: "Paul tells us that these things came about, that a woman should lust after another woman, because God was angry at the human race because of idolatry." Quoted in *Ancient Commentary on Scripture: New Testament*, ed. Gerald Bray (Downer's Grove, Ill.: Intervarsity Press, 1998), 6:46.

8. Chrysostom, *Against the Opponents of the Monastc Life*, 3. Greenberg's otherwise measured interpretation of the evidence concerning Christianity suffers from an understandable tendency to take the most extreme formulations (for example of Chrysostom) as typical of Christianity at this stage. It will take nearly a millennium for them to become so. See David F. Greenberg, *The Construction of Homosexuality* (Chicago: University of Chicago Press, 1988), 228–34.

## 15. Homophobic Christian Law

1. Derrick Sherwin Bailey, *Homosexuality and the Western Christian Tradition* (London: Longmans, Green, 1955).

2. It is unclear on what grounds Bailey speculates that this law may have had to do with male prostitutes.

3. Cantarella, *Bisexuality in the Ancient World*, notes (161) that the fourth-century Roman historian Aurelius Victor maintained that Constans was involved with youths. See Aurelius Victor, *Liber de Caesaribus* 41, 24. Cantarella notes that his father Constantine was also said, by another contemporary Roman historian, Ammianus Marcelinus, to have enjoyed the favors of male eunuchs. However she brackets this information out of her discussion of the edict of Constans and his brother Constantius.

4. Bailey, *Homosexuality and the Western Christian Tradition*, 71, and Cantarella, *Bisexuality in the Ancient World*, 176.

5. If this statute is to be read as a prohibition of same-sex marriage, then the evidence compiled by Boswell in *Same-sex Unions in Pre-Modern Europe* (New York: Vintage, 1994) would indicate that Christians found ways to transform the Neronic burlesque of marriage into a solemn liturgy of pledged faithfulness.

6. *Cod. Theod.* 9.7.6.

7. Boswell suggests that a longer version of this law makes clear that it is prostitutes that are targeted (124). If so it would seem to have had little lasting effect, since male prostitution was still legal into the sixth century.

8. For an extended commentary see Rouselle, *Porneia*, 5–23, and Craig A. Williams, *Roman Homosexuality: Ideologies of Masculinity in Classical Antiquity* (New York: Oxford University Press, 1999), especially 125–59.

9. Cantarella, *Bisexuality in the Ancient World*, 220.

10. For an extended treatment of this topic, see Beverly Gaventa, *Our Mother Saint Paul* (Louisville: Westminster John Knox, 2007).

11. Virtually the entirety of book 3 of the *Instructor* is taken up with discussions of the details of manly (and womanly) appearance and comportment. In book 2, chap. 12 he insists men should go barefoot.

12. Brooten, *Love between Women*, 322, 332–36. The reference to marriage of women is in *Instructor* 3.21. The wider context is a discussion of male appearance (shaving or not), which then digresses into a discussion of how male and female prostitutes display themselves. Thus while the Alexandrian custom of female marriage may indeed be in the background here, Clement seems concerned with how prostitutes flaunt the subversion of traditional gender roles.

13. *Strometeis* 4.8 (on philosophizing) and 9 (on virtue).

14. *Instructor* 1.6.

15. Peter Brown gives a more complete discussion of this phenomenon in his discussion of Origen in *The Body and Society*.

16. Augustine, Letter 153.

17. Sozomen, *History of the Church*, vii.12, referring to the campaign against heretics.

18. Cantarella, *Bisexuality in the Ancient World* (180), supposes that the harsh measures undertaken at Thessolonika by the military to put down an uprising occasioned by the arrest of an effeminate circus performer by a military commander suggests that Theodosius may have implemented the penalty. However, the story actually indicates the opposite. The emperor was excommunicated by Ambrose for the savagery of his response. In reply the emperor meekly submitted to nine months of public penance as the condition of being restored to the good graces of the bishop. If anything the story indicates that the ferocity of the Roman would be restrained by the piety of the Christian.

19. The same emperor insisted on restricting the rights of Jewish citizens of the empire, thereby setting an unwitting precedent for the ways in which the persecution of Jews and that of same-sex practitioners would come to be linked in the late medieval and Renaissance period, anticipating as well the linkage practiced in late modern Europe under the Nazi regime.

20. Michel Foucault, *Society Must Be Defended: Lectures at the Collège de France, 1975–76*, ed. Mauro Bertani and Alessandro Fontana, trans. David Macey (New York: Picador, 2003).

21. In this connection see Michel Foucault's *Security, Territory, Population: Lectures at the Collège de France, 1977–78*, ed. Michael Sellenart, trans. Graham Burchell (New York: Palgrave Macmillan, 2007), 115–254.

# Bibliography

## Ancient Sources

*Unless otherwise noted, classical sources are cited from the Loeb Classical Library edition, translations of patristic sources are from the Ante-Nicene Fathers or Nicene and Post-Nicene Fathers collections, and ancient texts are cited using standard textual divisions that are consistent across editions, rather than by using page numbers.*

*Ancient Commentary on Scripture: New Testament.* Vol. 6. Ed. Gerald Bray. Downers Grove, Ill.: Intervarsity Press, 1998.

*The Apostolic Fathers: Greek Texts and English Translations of Their Writings.* Ed. J. B. Lightfoot, J. R. Harner, and Michael Holmes. 2nd ed. Grand Rapids: Baker, 1992.

Athanasius. *Contra Gentes and De Incarnatione.* Ed. and trans. Robert W. Thomson. Oxford: Clarendon, 1971.

Augustine. *City of God.* Trans. Marcus Dods. New York: Random House, 1950.

Clement of Alexandria. *Christ the Educator.* Trans. Simon P. Wood. New York: Fathers of the Church, 1954.

Dio Cassius, *Roman History.* Loeb Classical Library. Trans. Earnest Cary. Cambridge, Mass.: Harvard University Press, 1924.

*Documents for the Study of the Gospels.* Ed. David R. Cartlidge and David L. Dungan. Rev. and enlarged ed. Minneapolis: Fortress, 1993.

Eusebius of Caesarea. *Demonstratio Evangelica.* 2 vols. Trans. W. J. Ferrar. London: SPCK, 1920.

Herodotus. *The History.* Trans. David Grene. Chicago: University of Chicago Press, 1987.

Hollander, H. W., and M. De Jonge. *The Testaments of the Twelve Patriarchs: A Commentary.* Leiden: Brill, 1985.

Hugh of Saint Victor. *On the Sacraments of the Christian Faith.* In *A Scholastic Miscellany: Anselm to Ockham.* Ed. and trans. Eugene R. Fairweather. Philadelphia: Westminster, 1961.

Origen. *Commentary on the Epistle to the Romans.* 2 vols. Trans. Thomas P. Scheck. Washington, D.C.: Catholic University of America Press, 2001, 2002.

Plato. *Laws.* 2 vols. Loeb Classical Library. Trans. R. G Bury. Cambridge, Mass.: Harvard University Press, 1961.

———. *Laws.* In *Plato: Collected Dialogues.* Ed. Edith Hamilton and Huntington Cairns. New York: Pantheon, 1961.

————. *Lysis, Phaedrus, and Symposium: Plato on Homosexuality.* Trans. Benjamin Jowett. Ed. Eugene O'Connor. New York: Prometheus Books, 1991.

Plutarch. *Life of Lycurgus.* In *The Lives of the Noble Grecians and Romans.* Trans. John Dryden. Ed. Arthur Hugh Clough. New York: Random House, 1932.

Pseudo-Phocylides. In James H. Charlesworth, ed., *Old Testament Pseudepigrapha.* Vol. 2. New York: Doubleday, 1985.

Seneca. *Apocolocyntosis.* Trans. J. P. Sullivan. London: Penguin, 1986.

Suetonius. *The Twelve Caesars.* Trans. Robert Graves. Ed. Michael Grant. London: Penguin, 1957, 1979.

Tacitus. *The Annals.* Trans. A. J. Church and W. J. Brodribb. Chicago: Encyclopaedia Britannica, 1952.

Tertullian. *Adversus Marcionem.* Ed. and trans. Ernest Evans. New York: Oxford University Press, 1972.

Theophilus of Antioch. *Ad Autolycum.* Ed. and trans. Robert M. Grant. New York: Oxford, 1970.

Xenophon. *Conversations of Socrates.* Ed. Robin Waterfield. Trans. Hugh Tredennick and Robin Waterfield. New York: Penguin, 1990.

## Contemporary Sources

Asmussen, Hans. *Der Römerbrief.* Stuttgart: Evangelisches Verlagswerk, 1952.

Bailey, D. S. *Homosexuality and the Western Christian Tradition.* London: Longmans, Green, 1955.

Bamberger, Bernard H. *Leviticus.* Vol. 3 of *The Torah: A Modern Commentary.* New York: Union of American Hebrew Congregations, 1981.

Bloom, Alan. "The Ladder of Love." In *Plato's "Symposium."* Trans. Seth Bernadette. Chicago: University of Chicago Press, 1993.

Boswell, John. *Christianity, Social Tolerance, and Homosexuality.* Chicago: University of Chicago Press, 1980.

————. *Same-Sex Unions in Pre-Modern Europe.* New York: Vintage, 1994.

Brooten, Bernadette. *Love between Women: Early Christian Responses to Female Homoeroticism.* Chicago: University of Chicago Press, 1996.

Brown, Peter. *The Body and Society: Men, Women, and Sexual Renunciation in Early Christianity.* New York: Columbia University Press, 1988.

Cantarella, Eva. *Bisexuality in the Ancient World.* Trans. Cormac O. Cuilleanáin. New Haven: Yale University Press, 1992.

Dover, K. J. *Greek Homosexuality.* Cambridge: Harvard University Press, 1978–1989.

Elliott, Neil. *The Arrogance of Nations: Reading Romans in the Shadow of Empire.* Minneapolis: Fortress, 2008.

————. *Liberating Paul: The Justice of God and the Politics of the Apostle.* Maryknoll, N.Y.: Orbis, 1994.

Foucault, Michel. *Security, Territory, Population: Lectures at the Collège de France, 1977–78.* Ed. Michael Sellenart. Trans. Graham Burchell. New York: Palgrave Macmillan, 2007.

———. *Society Must Be Defended: Lectures at the Collège de France, 1975–76.* Ed. Mauro Bertani and Alessandro Fontana. Trans. David Macey. New York: Picador, 2003.

Enslin, Morton Scott. *The Ethics of Paul.* New York: Harper, 1930.

Gaventa, Beverly. *Our Mother Saint Paul.* Louisville: Westminster John Knox, 2007.

Gide, André. *Saül.* Written 1893, published 1903. In *My Theater.* Trans. Jackson Matthews. New York: Knopf, 1951.

Greenberg, David F. *The Construction of Homosexuality.* Chicago: University of Chicago Press, 1988.

Halperin, David M. "The First Homosexuality?" In *How to Do the History of Homosexuality.* Chicago: University of Chicago Press, 2002.

Horner, Tom. *Jonathan Loved David.* Philadelphia: Westminster, 1978.

Jaeger, Werner. *Early Christianity and Greek Paideia.* New York: Oxford, 1961.

———. *Paideia: The Ideals of Greek Culture.* New York: Oxford, 1944.

Jennings, Jr., Theodore W. *Jacob's Wound: Homoerotic Narrative in the Literature of Ancient Israel.* New York: Continuum, 2005.

———. *The Man Jesus Loved: Homoerotic Narratives in the New Testament.* Cleveland: Pilgrim, 2003.

———. *Reading Derrida/Thinking Paul: On Justice.* Stanford: Stanford University Press, 2005.

———, and Benny Tat-Siong Liew, "Mistaken Identities but Model Faith: Rereading the Centurion, the Chap, and the Christ in Matthew 8:5–13." *Journal of Biblical Literature* 123, no. 3 (2004): 467–94.

Jordan, Mark. *The Invention of Sodomy in Christian Theology.* Chicago: University of Chicago Press, 1997.

Laeuchli, S. *Power and Sexuality: The Emergence of Canon Law at the Synod of Elvira.* Philadelphia: Temple University Press, 1972.

Lemche, Niels Peter. "The Old Testament: A Hellenistic Book?" *Scandinavian Journal of the Old Testament* 7, no. 2 (1993): 163–93.

Loader, J. A. *A Tale of Two Cities: Sodom and Gomorrah in the Old Testament, Early Jewish and Early Christian Traditions.* Kampen: J. H. Kok, 1990.

Martin, Dale. *Sex and the Single Savior: Gender and Sexuality in Biblical Interpretation.* Louisville: Westminster John Knox, 2006.

Percy III, William Armstrong. *Pederasty and Pedagogy in Archaic Greece.* Champaign: University of Illinois Press, 1996.

Petersen, William. "On the Study of 'Homosexuality' in Patristic Sources." *Studia Patristica.* Vol. 20. Leuven: Peeters Press, 1989.

von Rad, Gerhard. *Old Testament Theology.* Vol. 1. Trans. D. M. G. Stalker. New York: Harper, 1962.

Rouselle, Aline. *Porneia: On Desire and the Body in Antiquity.* Trans. Felicia Pheasant. New York: Oxford, 1988.

Scroggs, Robin. *The New Testament and Homosexuality: Contextual Background for Contemporary Debate.* Philadelphia: Fortress, 1983.

Smith, Mark D. "Ancient Bisexuality and the Interpretation of Romans 1:26–7." *JAAR* 44, no. 2 (1996): 243–56.

Steiner, George. *Lessons of the Masters: The Charles Eliot Norton Lectures, 2001–2002*. Cambridge, Mass.: Harvard University Press, 2003.

———. *No Passion Spent: Essays, 1978–1995*. New Haven: Yale University Press, 1996.

Stone, Ken. *Practicing Safer Texts: Food, Sex and Bible in Queer Perspective*. New York: T&T Clark, 2005.

Viard, André. *Saint Paul, Épître aux Romains*. Paris: Gabalda, 1975.

Williams, Craig A. *Roman Homosexuality: Ideologies of Masculinity in Classical Antiquity*. New York: Oxford University Press, 1999.

Wright, David F. "Homosexuals or Prostitutes." *Vigiliae Christianae* 38 (1984): 125–53.

# Index